Twayne's English Authors Series

EDITOR OF THIS VOLUME

George Economou

Long Island University

Cynewulf

TEAS 327

Folio 76a of *The Exeter Book* Lines 696a–731b of *Juliana*, containing Cynewulf's runic signature. (Reprinted from *The Exeter Book of Old English Poetry*, edited by R. W. Chambers, Max Förster and Robin Flower [London: P. Lund, Humphries & Co., 1933] by permission of the Dean and Chapter of Exeter Cathedral.)

CYNEWULF

By DANIEL G. CALDER

University of California, Los Angeles

TWAYNE PUBLISHERS
A DIVISION OF G. K. HALL & CO., BOSTON

Published in 1981 by Twayne Publishers,
A Division of G. K. Hall & Co.
All Rights Reserved

Printed on permanent/durable acid-free paper and bound
in the United States of America

First Printing

Library of Congress Cataloging in Publication Data

Calder, Daniel Gillmore.
Cynewulf.

(Twayne's English authors series ; TEAS 327)
Bibliography: p. 183–86
Includes index.
1. Cynewulf—Criticism and interpretation.
I. Title.   II. Series.
PR1664.C3   829'.4   81-2343
ISBN 0-8057-6814-9   AACR2

For
Joseph Turk
and
Sanford Kaufman

Contents

About the Author

Daniel G. Calder was born in Lubec, Maine, on February 10, 1939. He holds a B.A. from Bowdoin College (1960) and an M.A. from the University of Iowa (1962). From 1962 to 1964 he was an Instructor at Bowdoin College. In 1969 he received a Ph.D. from Indiana University. Since that time he has taught at the University of Washington and the University of California, Los Angeles. He is the editor of *Old English Poetry: Essays on Style* (1979) and the coeditor of *Sources and Analogues of Old English Poetry: The Major Latin Texts in Translation* (1976). He has also written essays on *Beowulf, The Phoenix, The Wanderer,* and *The Seafarer,* among other Old English poems. He is currently Professor of English at UCLA.

Preface

This book prefaces Cynewulfian studies, because they are yet in their infancy. We might suspect that Cynewulf, the only OE poet whose works we can identify, would have attracted great critical attention. In fact he has not. It is not that an insufficient number of items appear under his name in the standard bibliographies, but that these represent essentially nonliterary work. Historical and "biographical" studies comprise the bulk of what scholars have done with Cynewulf.

Two books, both written in the 1940s, make tentative stabs at criticism. Yet, despite their importance in establishing the canon, they have minimal value as pieces of literary criticism; while they differ greatly in focus and scope, they each hold to old-fashioned premises for literary analysis.

A new stage began about a decade ago, and since then a number of well-researched and perceptive essays has appeared. Some concentrate on historical, theological, and doctrinal matters; others have explored the standard literary concerns of imagery, structure, tone, and the relationship of these to Cynewulf's themes. But nearly all the recent criticism treats one poem at a time, and the effect gives us a fragmented idea of Cynewulf's whole work. In this study, I have tried to extract the best from these various pieces (including my own contributions) and to bind those insights together by relating all the poems to each other thematically and structurally. To do this I have had to go beyond mere summary of present scholarship, and I hope I have found some clues to Cynewulf's notions of structure and the characteristic mode of thought they reflect. Such understanding supports every interpretive act we make. I have wanted to bring the field into focus and to establish a base for more intense examination of the four poems. Cynewulf is not only "an" Anglo-Saxon poet; the accidents of history have also made him "the" Anglo-Saxon scop.

Many students and colleagues have aided in the writing of this critical study and I would like to express my appreciation to them all. In particular I am grateful to the members of my seminar on Cynewulf during the spring of 1978. I learned much from them, and I am sure that a great deal of what now seems to be mine originated with those students. I would like to thank Robert E. Bjork and Henry A. Kelly for reading the typescript and offering their most helpful comments. To Stanley B. Greenfield I owe a special debt of gratitude for his painstaking review of the first draft. Without his generous criticism this book would have been a poorer thing. For what now stands I take full responsibility; any errors, omissions, or blunders belong solely to me.

I would also like to thank the Research Committee of the Academic Senate at UCLA, which provided supporting funds for this project, and Jeanette Gilkison, who has served as typist *extraordinaire* on this, as well as on many another, undertaking.

Sections of this book have appeared in print before, though in each case I have expanded and completely reworked the earlier version for this endeavor. I would like to thank the editors of *English Studies*, *Medium Ævum*, and *Modern Language Quarterly* for granting me permission to use that material. The articles were originally published in the following order: "Strife, Revelation, and Conversion: The Thematic Structure of *Elene*," *English Studies* 53 (1972): 201–10; "The Art of Cynewulf's *Juliana*," *Modern Language Quarterly* 34 (1973): 355–71; "*The Fates of the Apostles*, the Latin Martyrologies and the Litany of the Saints," *Medium Ævum* 44 (1975): 219–24.

DANIEL G. CALDER

University of California
Los Angeles

CHAPTER 1

The Poet and the Canon

I Cynewulf and Old English Poetry

WHEN Cynewulf composed his four poems, presumably in the late eighth or early ninth century, he worked almost entirely within an old poetic tradition. His choice to write in the established forms of Anglo-Saxon poetry reveals that he did not envision himself as, for example, a Wordsworth casting off the shackles of an outworn mode. Instead he embraced the centuries-old habits of diction and style the Germanic invaders brought to England in the fifth century. Cynewulf is manifestly a literate poet, but the style he adopted was originally both oral and formulaic, and by his time it had crystallized into a stable, though expressive, manner.[1] Cynewulf inherited a poetry remarkable for its conservative and stylized qualities—ancient, abstract, ceremonial, elaborate, and somber.

Three items require brief elucidation: the structure of the individual line, the means of linking lines, and the usual subjects and themes. All had become highly conventional well before the eighth century. The individual line in Germanic poetry developed out of the normal stress patterns of the language. With heavy accents falling on root syllables, the Germanic tongues produced a poetic line that used alliteration to bind separate units together. A line from one of Cynewulf's own poems, *Christ II*, illustrates the principle: *Đa wæs wuldres weard wolcnum bifongen* ("Then was the Guardian of glory surrounded by clouds," line 527). Since rhyme was normally lacking (Cynewulf does, however, occasionally experiment with rhymes), the movement from line to line in Old English poetry proceeded in long, often uninterrupted, verse paragraphs. The division of lines into specific stanzas is very rare, though most scholars believe that the earliest Germanic poetry was so divided.[2] But early in the development of the English branch of the West Germanic family, the extended rhetorical section replaced the stanza. The poetry Cynewulf knew and imitated may be compared to a kind of alliterative blank verse.

Although Cynewulf continued the traditions of this ancient style, his choice of subject matter represents a significant departure from the topics usually treated in Germanic poetry. Apparently Cynewulf led what we might call the second revolution in the history of this otherwise unchanging verse. The typical subjects set to this alliterative meter were martial and heroic, the natural interests of a warrior society: the praise of kings and heroes, the celebrations of victory, the laments for the fallen and the dead. In the first revolution, initiated by the illiterate Caedmon in the late seventh century (657–680), this heroic verse was recast and made a vehicle for narrating the major events of the Old and New Testaments. While an aristocratic and heroic poetry was thus appropriated for religious use, it had not yet become the meditative, mannered poetry of the saints Cynewulf was to create. For his inspiration Cynewulf went directly to the secondary texts of Christian Latin literature, the saints' lives and the sermons which appeared long after the biblical narratives. And, like Caedmon, Cynewulf had followers who composed poems on similiar subjects in styles resembling the one he fashioned out of the old and hallowed practices of Germanic verse. It is to this singular poet and his poems we now turn.

II   The Discovery of Cynewulf's Identity

Whoever Cynewulf may have been, his existence remained unknown until the middle of the nineteenth century. Anglo-Saxon scholars from the Renaissance on had failed to notice the runic signatures which establish his authorship of four poems—*The Fates of the Apostles*, *Christ II*, *Juliana*, and *Elene*. For generations dedicated Saxonists knew just one important poet from this period in English literary history. Caedmon, the monk of Whitby whose miraculous poetic achievements Bede recorded in the *Ecclesiastical History*, was the presumed author of the biblical paraphrases found in the Junius manuscript. But, in fact, Caedmon's long works have not survived and each poem in the Junius manuscript has a different author. Caedmon can claim only his famous nine-line *Hymn* now. Bede does tell us he was a scop, as other texts report that Bede himself, Alfred, and Aldhelm were too. All their poems may have disappeared, but their reputations as poets have not.

Ironically, Cynewulf, who took such pains to be identified with his poetry, had no contemporary report on his endeavors. He composed his works, wove his name in runes at the end of each, and then vanished into that obscurity ignorance can often throw over both old poets and old documents. The resurgence of interest in Anglo-Saxon literature during the Renaissance developed for reasons of religious and political controversy, and attention paid to historical and homiletic prose far overshadowed that given to poetry for the first two centuries of reconstructive scholarship. The biases of a Protestant culture easily explain the disdain in which early scholars held hagiography, Cynewulf's main subject. Caedmon's paraphrases of the Old Testament suit a Protestant taste more than Cynewulf's "superstitious" legends of Catholic saints. However, the situation in Anglo-Saxon studies at the time researchers discovered Cynewulf's identity was complex. We must remember that *Beowulf* was not published in a modern edition until 1815; that Grimm's *Andreas und Elene* appeared in 1840; that *The Exeter Book* waited until 1842; and that Kemble's edition of the *Vercelli* poems took thirteen years to publish (1843–1856). Predictably, the revelation of Cynewulf's identity occurred at this time of concentrated editorial activity, and as such things often happen, two scholars made the discovery simultaneously and independently. Grimm could hardly have edited *Elene* without noticing the runes in lines 1257–69 (1257–70 in Grimm's lineation). He writes:

After the end of the saga of the cross and counter to the manner of epic recitation, the poet subjectively reflects in section 15 on his work, himself, and the end of all secular things. In the first portion the reflections are artificial and heavy (1237–76); later the narration becomes plain again. At line 1258 eight runes are inserted and woven into the poem which conceal for us the name of the poet and which put together clearly give CYNEVULF. That among the Anglo-Saxons letters were used for such playful purposes as early as the seventh and eighth centuries is evident in Aldhelm's Latin poems. The use of runic signs, which are now and then interspersed with the usual Latin script, is by itself remarkable and is evidence for the antiquity of the monument.[3]

Grimm's commentary shows no awareness of the importance of his discovery. He treats the unweaving of the runes as another editorial task solved. J. M. Kemble, on the other hand, displays more excitement in his finding of the runic signature. Writing also in 1840, Kemble's main concern is the whole topic of Anglo-Saxon runology, but he turns to the Cynewulfian examples as significant items of *runica manu-*

scripta. Kemble describes for us the process by which he deciphered the runes, and his account bears quoting in full because it accurately portrays the milieu in which Cynewulf's poems first came to the light of modern day. Kemble quotes *Elene* lines 1256b–71a and then comments:

> The extreme rudeness and abruptness of these lines and the apparent use-lessness of the Runes, led me to suspect that there was more in them than merely met the eye. And this I found to be the case: for on taking the Runes out of the context, using them as single letters and writing them in one word, they supplied me with the name CYNEWULF, undoubtedly no other than the author of the poem. It is now with the utmost interest that I read the follow-ing passage from the still more celebrated Codex Exoniensis . . . [Kemble quotes lines 795a–806a of *Christ II*]. Here then we have the same Runes, and that in a passage which bears a remarkable similarity in the thoughts and images to the one last cited: only the Rune, ᛗ. E, is wanting, from which we may conclude that at least one couplet is lost. . . . Not content with having once already given us this acrostic of his name, the poet repeats it at a later period in the Exeter book, and in a manner which renders it very difficult to translate the lines, so great is their obscurity . . . [Kemble quotes lines 697a–712a of *Juliana*]. It is evident here that the poet literally means to use the letters that make up his name, and that he does not introduce them as words, which he had done in the passages previously quoted.[4]

To Kemble belongs the greater credit, for he connected the runic sig-natures in *Elene*, *Christ*, and *Juliana* with one another and thus cre-ated a "new" poet with a corpus to rival Caedmon's. In fact, Kemble's conclusions extend further than simple observation. He writes:

> I cannot here bestow space upon a long argument to show who this Cyne-wulf was. I believe him to have been the Abbot of Peterborough of that name, who flourished in the beginning of the eleventh century, who was accounted in his own day a celebrated poet, both in Latin and Anglo-Saxon, whose works have long been reputed lost, but whose childish ingenuity has now enabled us with some probability to assign to him the authorship of the Vercelli and Exeter codices.[5]

So at the moment of his latter-day appearance, Cynewulf becomes the subject of two questions: who was he and what did he write? Kemble's hasty guesses set a pattern which grew to absurd proportions as the nineteenth century progressed, and which scholars have only recently pruned back to more sensible dimensions.

Because of severe damage to the relevant pages of *The Vercelli Book*, the runic conclusion to *The Fates of the Apostles* was not discovered until 1888 and not published until a year later. The lines in question are, as L. A. Muinzer describes them, so "incredibly mutilated and illegible,"[6] that none of the manuscript's early editors paid them any attention. In 1888 Arthur Napier managed to see "the familiar runes of a Cynewulf acrostic"[7] in the paleographical debris. Napier makes the obvious comment that the now retrieved ending to *The Fates* establishes this poem as a "genuine" *(echt)* poem by Cynewulf.[8]

Between 1840 and 1888 a new Anglo-Saxon poet emerged, the author of a poetic corpus nearly as extensive as that commonly ascribed to Caedmon, though he was interested in the postbiblical traditions of hagiography rather than the ancient Hebraic stories of the Heptateuch. During this period critics spent much labor in establishing Cynewulf's identity; even more ink was spilled in attempts to fix the canon of his poems. After more than a century the first question remains unanswered; the second now seems settled.

III *Cynewulf's Identity and Dates*

Kemble's identification of Cynewulf with Cenwulf or Kenulf, "abbot of Peterborough and bishop of Winchester (d. 1006), to whom Aelfric dedicated his life of St. Aethelwold,"[9] never gained acceptance. An early eleventh-century date for the poet cannot be defended, and the name Cenwulf in no way represents a variant spelling of Cynewulf. Two much more popular identifications rivaled each other up until the last generation of Cynewulfian scholars. The first made Cynewulf into a wandering minstrel.[10] Leo created this fanciful persona out of whole cloth, based on his belief that the "autobiographical" details in the runic epilogue to *Elene* should be taken literally. There Cynewulf says that he "received treasures in the mead hall, curved gold" (*þeah he in medohealle maðmas þege / æplede gold*, 1258a–59a), and that "horse" (the "E" rune) "measured the mile-paths" (*milpaðas mæt*, 1262a).[11] Adding this speculation to his conjecture that Cynewulf was the author of the Riddles, Leo claimed the *First Riddle* "could be interpreted as forming Cynewulf's name, and the last as meaning a wandering minstrel."[12] The question of identity inevitably becomes tied to the related controversy about Cynewulf's authentic works. But Leo's minstrel-Cynewulf, a wayward poet in youth and a devout Christian convert in old age, no longer deserves attention.

Although Kemble's abbot of Peterborough never won general scholarly approval, all subsequent commentary, with the major exception of the "wandering minstrel school," has agreed in seeing Cynewulf as an ecclesiastic. Whether monk, priest, or bishop, Cynewulf's extensive acquaintance with many different religious texts—the Bible, the liturgy, sermons, and a vast body of patristic writings—links him directly with the church. Cynewulf, bishop of Lindisfarne, has often been nominated as the most likely candidate. Unfortunately, Bishop Cynewulf died in 783 and this fact raises grave problems for the identification; linguistic evidence seems to prove that Cynewulf's signed poems come after that date. The last, and least acceptable, identification was made by Cook. He held that the poet was a certain priest, Cynulf, who signed his name after the bishop of Dunwich at the Council of Clovesho in 803.[13] Few, if any, scholars have adopted Cook's suggestion.

In its several forms the name Cynewulf appears frequently in Anglo-Saxon documents. But no reputable scholar now believes the author of the four signed poems can be connected to one of these historical personages. Strong Northumbrian partisanship once made the bishop of Lindisfarne an attractive candidate. Because eighth-century Northumbria represented the peak of European literate civilization in the early Middle Ages, scholars were naturally anxious to place Cynewulf under the protective halo of the Northumbrian renaissance. The preference for Northumbria must be understood within this context; Cynewulf's Northumbrian origins cannot be proved by the philological data. As with most Old English poetry, the Cynewulfian texts survive in West Saxon manuscripts. However, a number of Anglian (a term embracing both the kingdoms of Mercia and Northumbria) forms still remain, and philologists generally agree Cynewulf flourished north, not south, of the Thames. The rhymes in *Elene* offer conclusive evidence of Anglian origin. Gradon summarizes the linguistic situation this way:

These fall into three groups. Firstly, the rhymes *onwreah: fah* must be read as *onwrah: fah*. The form *onwrah* is more common in Anglian than in WS. Secondly, the forms *amæt: begeat* must be read as *amæt: begæt* or *amet: beget* if they are to rhyme. The former would be non-WS. . . . Thirdly, the false rhymes *riht: geþeaht* and *miht: þeaht* must be read as *ræht: geþæht* and *mæht: þæt* or *reht: geþeht* and *meht: þeht*.[14]

In 1933 Sisam reached this conclusion given the dialectal evidence: "It is, then, a fair deduction that Cynewulf wrote in the Anglian dialect—

in Northumbrian or in Mercian. A number of special reasons derived from the Cynewulf legend, and the literary prestige of Northumbria, have inclined most critics in that direction; but there is no ponderable evidence for the one kingdom or the other."[15] But Gradon's later investigations seem to have tipped the balance in favor of Mercia. She too sees the choice as between these two northern kingdoms, yet the runic signatures themselves make Northumbria an "exceedingly improbable" alternative.[16] Cynewulf spelled his name in two ways: "Cynewulf" in *Elene* and *Juliana* and "Cynwulf" in *Christ II* and *The Fates*. Early interpretations of this difference went as follows: "The name which our poet bore is found in three forms—*Cyniwulf, Cynewulf, Cynwulf (Cynulf)*. Of these the oldest is *Cyniwulf*, and the latest *Cynwulf*,—*Cynewulf* being intermediate in date between the two."[17]

Such "facts" easily established both Cynewulf's date and the chronology of his poems. *Juliana* and *Elene* must come after 750 (the approximate date of the change of i>e, when Cyniwulf would have been respelled Cynewulf), and *Christ II* and *The Fates* must have been composed late in the eighth century (because the loss of the medial vowel occurred about fifty years later).[18] However, Sisam demonstrated that the major text supposedly proving Cynewulf's Northumbrian identity is actually Mercian,[19] and these so-called "Northumbrian genealogies" must be dated around 812.[20] Finally, the evidence is this: Northumbrian spellings show no form with a medial *e;* only Mercian texts show the variation i/e. Therefore, Cynewulf must have been a Mercian. Further, the order of the apostles in *The Fates* corroborates the linguistic data supporting an early ninth-century date, since the slightly unusual listing in *The Fates* shows up in other texts only after that time.[21] All indications converge on the early ninth century as the most probable era for Cynewulf to have lived, though certainty in these matters is never possible. The latest history of Anglo-Saxon poetry straddles the fence on this issue; in his chronological table Derek Pearsall makes Cynewulf active during the fifty-year period on both sides of the century's turn, 775–825.[22] Precision of dating is not here a major concern. As with the problem of Cynewulf's identity, one must accept the large gaps in our knowledge. Our ignorance concerning the actual person in some ways facilitates critical examination of the poems he wrote. We need not be distracted by an imagined being hovering over his works and suggesting ways to read his poems; we are not hampered by an imperfect sense of his "personality." The search for Cynewulf's identity and his dates carries a final irony: he left his name in runes but it is unrecorded in other documents. Thus Cynewulf became a "fictional" character, existing only in the poems he created. Barring the discovery of wholly new evidence, the pursuit of Cynewulf's identity and the spinning out of a biography remain idle tasks. He emerges from the anonymity of Anglo-Saxon poetry long enough to sign his name and then disappears again into that great obscurity he shares with all the other scops who left no trace.

IV   The Canon

When Kemble and Grimm deciphered Cynewulf's name, the best scholarly opinion at the time firmly held that Caedmon composed all the poems in the Junius manuscript, a total of 5,019 lines. This represented a large corpus for an illiterate scop. Not surprisingly, scholars wished their new literate poet to have been equally prolific. What Caedmon did not write, so they reasoned, then Cynewulf did. *Beowulf* was usually excepted, though not even *Beowulf* entirely escaped a Cynewulfian attribution. The excesses of nineteenth-century scholars on the question of the Cynewulf canon do not require tracing in detail, but at no time did Cynewulf have more works credited him than in the first few years of his second existence. Finding runic signatures in both the *Vercelli* and the *Exeter Books*, Kemble, as we have seen, calmly assigned him the whole contents of each volume.

Kemble's grand notions did not convince many, and the dispute over the canon soon fell into several categories: we can take it as proved that Cynewulf wrote *Elene* and *Juliana*, but with many other poems there is no such certainty. The questions are: (1) did Cynewulf write the three sections of *Christ*, or only the second section where the runic signature appears? (2) was he the author of all the "Cynewulfian" poems, that is, *The Dream of the Rood*, *The Phoenix*, *Physiologus*, *Guthlac A* and *B* and *Andreas* (the question of *Andreas* also involves the relation between this poem and *The Fates*, which immediately follows it in the Vercelli manuscript)? (3) did he "sign" the *First Riddle* and thus proclaim his authorship of the Anglo-Saxon enigmas? (4) should *Beowulf* be ascribed to him as well?

Complicated proofs and disproofs for and against his authorship of one or another of these poems were proffered in numerous dissertations, German school programs, articles, notes, and books, based usually upon examinations of syntax, vocabulary, and meter. Many scholars held reasonable views on the canon, however, and it is instructive to listen to one example, especially since this opinion occurs in an article that laid to rest one of the principal fantasies in Cynewulfian scholarship. Reviewing Henry Morley's second volume on *English Writers*, Henry Bradley comments:

> In the chapter on Cynewulf, the author shows a good deal of whole-some caution in dealing with a subject that has been the theme of much controversy. His view is that the only works which can with confidence be ascribed to Cynewulf are those which are actually signed—the Elene, the Juliana, and the Crist. Prof. Morley does not seem to be acquainted with the dissertation of Ramhorst which to my mind appears to be conclusive in showing that the "Andreas" is the work of the same poet. I am myself inclined to think that some, at least, of the riddles are of Cynewulf's composition; but I fully agree with Prof. Morley in rejecting . . . the theory of Leo that the first riddle is a charade on the writer's name.[23]

Bradley's middle ground represents much sensible nineteenth-century criticism. He frees himself from the excesses of those who saw Cynewulf's pen in every Old English poem, though he cannot resist tacking on an extra poem or two to flesh out the corpus. But Bradley's chief contribution to Cynewulfian studies comes in his discussion of the *First Riddle*, and we should look more closely at this dispute over Cynewulf's authorship of the Riddles, taking it as symptomatic of the many arguments about the canon.

In 1857 Heinrich Leo proposed that the poem on folios 100b–101a (now known as *Wulf and Eadwacer*) was a riddle and that it too hid the name Cynewulf. Krapp and Dobbie note that Leo was not the first to think of this short fragment as a riddle; Thorpe printed the poem that way in the *editio princeps* of *The Exeter Book*.[24] Morley provides an excellent brief guide to Leo's fantastical hypothesis:

> Leo makes the riddle begin by saying
> "My limbs are related, as one gives them meaning
> They will disclose it, when the meanings join the throng
> [i.e., come together]."

Here the limbs are said to be the two related syllables of the name which is the subject of the riddle. Each syllable is then riddled by the use of its sound in different senses. The riddle proceeds with speech of the first syllable; the separation of the syllables is figured by placing each upon an island:—

"It is unlike with us.
A wolf is on one island, I on the other.
The island is wholly surrounded by fen;
Fierce men [that is *Cene*] are here on this island,
They will make it [the sense of the riddle] clear
    when the meanings join in one."

Here the rune "cen," a torch, is to be read as "cene," keen or fierce men, and we are to take "cene" as the rune hidden in the word "wælhreowe" which involves ideas of passion and slaughter. In the next section a new sense is given to the word cene; it is no longer keen, bold, fierce, but coen, for cwen, a queen or woman, who is in love with a man named Wulf. . . . it is guessed that Eadwacer, who belongs to both syllables, represents the particle *e* that joins the syllable cyn and wulf.[25]

This whimsical interpretation, together with forced readings of *Riddles* 90 and 95 (the Latin *Riddle* 90 twice uses the word *lupus*, "wolf"), served as the deciding evidence for Cynewulf's authorship of all the Riddles. Bradley demonstrated that the *First Riddle* was "not a riddle at all, but a fragment of a dramatic soliloquy, like 'Deor' and 'The banished Wife's Complaint,' to the latter of which it bears, both in motive and in treatment, a strong resemblance,"[26] and so destroyed the keystone of Leo's fragile edifice. Yet long-held and clever ideas die slowly. Most scholars, it is true, accepted Bradley's new hypothesis and gave over the identification of the Riddles with Cynewulf. Still in 1910, Frederick Tupper, one of the great students of riddles, insisted that the *First Riddle* contained not only a charade on Cynewulf's name, but an acrostic in runes as well. Leo's problem, Tupper maintains, was not his basic notion, but the flawed execution of his plan.[27] Tupper's own version surpasses even the most far-fetched aspects of Leo's interpretive gymnastics and it need not be outlined here. Its very existence marks the difficulty that a century of scholarship had in coming to a reasonable position on the canon.

   The situation remained more or less unchanged until Kenneth Sisam's influential lecture on Cynewulf before the British Academy in 1933. He states his conclusions so blandly that one can easily miss their importance: "On a strict reckoning," Sisam writes, "Cynewulf is still left—in *Juliana*, *Elene*, *Fates of the Apostles* and *The Ascension*—with roundly 2,600 lines of verse; while of the rest of English poetry written before Alfred's time, only nine lines by Caedmon and five lines by Bede can be attached to an author's name."[28]

Two long studies in the 1940s seem to have settled the problem of the canon. Working independently and using quite different methods of stylistic analysis, S. K. Das and Claes Schaar both reaffirm Sisam's position. Das employs metrical analyses; Schaar considers items of narrative structure and syntax. Both have been severely criticized on methodological grounds, though no one has seriously challenged their conclusion that the signed poems represent Cynewulf's only authentic extant works.[29] However, nostalgia for a past when Cynewulf could be thought of as an author with nearly Shakespearian breadth still lingers: John C. Pope ends a superb article on the manuscript of *Christ II* with this somewhat wistful comment: "Cynewulf's powers have been more sharply defined and his reputation somewhat lessened by the general agreement to credit him with no more than the four signed poems. It seems only fair to do what justice we can to these. . . ."[30]

V   *The Order of the Poems*

The order in which Cynewulf composed his four poems cannot be fixed. Scholars have offered all sorts of impressionistic and inaccurate justifications for each of the possible sequences. Cases made on the basis of the old Cyni>Cyne>Cyn spelling must be discarded at once. Impressions of the "goodness" or "ineptness" of one poem over another certainly do not provide adequate criteria for deciding anything. Two poems, *The Fates of the Apostles* and *Juliana*, usually receive bad notices and *Elene* and *Christ II* are, if begrudgingly, praised. Rosemary Woolf's opinions offer an example of a critic's speculation on an order for the poems derived from a personal sense of their value. Having concluded that *Juliana* "clearly comes at the end of a period" and "brings Old English poetry into a blind alley," she then cannot decide what that means regarding the order of Cynewulf's poems: "Whether the other 'signed' poems represent Cynewulf's efforts to retrace his steps, or whether *Juliana* was literally the end of his poetic career, remains in a sense an academic question. But all the other Cynewulfian poetry is but a temporary postponement of a natural conclusion reached in *Juliana*."[31] This reasoning is circular, as are all the arguments which rely on assessments of worth and skill in determining chronology. Woolf suggests the following arrangement: "It might therefore plausibly be maintained that the *Fates of the Apostles* with its Riddle-like signature was the first of the four Cynewulfian poems, that *Crist* Part II and the *Elene* represent the height of Cynewulf's poetic development, and that *Juliana* shows its decline."[32] Schaar takes a different stand: "It is probable that the Fates was written after the two longer poems [*Elene* and *Juliana*] and that the author, feeling a certain lack of inspiration, reverted to some ideas in these earlier poems and made use of them a second time. But he had no longer the power of reshaping his ideas and making something new out of them."[33] The only "fact" we have is Cynewulf's statement in *Elene* that he was an old man when he wrote that poem. Precisely what we ought to do with this information, however, is problematical. "Old" does not necessarily mean "at death's door," or "unable to write more poems."

The whole question must be left unresolved. Idle conjectures do nothing to bring clarity to a permanently teasing enigma. And the order of discussion in this present study is unrelated to any hypothetical order of composition. *The Fates* comes first for paradigmatic reasons only.

VI   *The Runic Signatures*

While no other Anglo-Saxon poet left his name inscribed in runes, the practice itself, using both runes and conventional Roman letters, was widespread. One of the oldest remnants of Germanic is an alliterative line scratched on the golden horn of Gallehus. Also written in runes, the letters transcribed read: *Ek HlewagastiR HoltijaR   Horna tawido* ("I, Hlewagast, Holt's son,   made [this] horn"). Hlewagast, Holt's son, wished to make the connection between the object he created and himself, the creator, in much the same way that Cynewulf desires his name and his poems be prayerfully associated. As Dolores Frese writes:

It is true that when Cynewulf came to construct his art of words, clerical copyists—especially those connected with the Alcuinian "diaspora"—had instituted something of a rage for the insertion of runic inscription into their manuscripts, and it was already a centuries-old custom in other arts to runically engrave the signature of the artificer upon the product of his art. Typically contained in a formula of donation, dedication, consecration or supplication, runic signatures were curiously applied to such movables as arms, jewels, coins, and drinking horns—as well as to more stationary objects like baptismal fonts, bell towers, and funerary monuments.[34]

In the Christian Latin tradition the numerous acrostics worked into poems spelling out the author's (and others') names occur frequently.

Otfrid's *Evangelienbuch*, a ninth-century work written perhaps only fifty years after Cynewulf's poems, has a preface in which the first letters of each line when strung together yield "Salomoni Episcopo Otfridus" (Otfrid, to Bishop Salomon). Tupper also demonstrates that extremely intricate combinations of runic charades and acrostics were widely used in later Old Icelandic poetry, and acrostics were a favorite device of Aldhelm, Tatwine, and Boniface.[35]

But Cynewulf's use of runic signatures differs markedly from other types of anagrams. First, he does not use the runic letters simply as letters to spell his name; second, he incorporates his name in such a way that the runes have a genuine poetic purpose. To the first problem: the Latin acrostics and the runic signatures are both alphabetic. But Cynewulf's usual habit is to employ the runes syllabically (except in *Juliana*, where he combines the runes into groups). Thus the "C" rune does not stand simply for *C*, but for its name, *cen*, "a torch." Shippey notes perceptively that Cynewulf's practice may have been dictated in part by an audience of mixed literacy; for if the runes represented only letters, then only literate readers could decipher them. But by using the names of the runes as sounds in the poem, Cynewulf's name could be *heard* as well as *seen*.[36]

The interpretation of the meanings Cynewulf intended is likewise problematic. Many attempts to decode the runes stick on the same puzzles. This book will offer no new solutions to these old cruces, but rather take the best from the several interpretations now current. Literary concerns do not depend on a precise explication of the runes. Cynewulf's intentions in general are clear, whatever the obscurities of some specific points.

VII   *The Background*

Assuming that Cynewulf did flourish during the fifty-year period divided at midpoint by the turn of the ninth century (775–825), and that he was a Mercian, then his active career came either at the end of or immediately following the reign of Offa, the greatest Mercian ruler (757–796). Offa rose to power after the decline of the Northumbrian dynasty, which had coincided on the scholarly side with the age of Bede. But even though Northumbria, mainly through Alcuin and his school at York, continued as the intellectual center of England through the late eighth century, the shift in dynastic power to the southern kingdom of Mercia had significant effects on the state of learning in

Cynewulf's native territory. When, for example, Charlemagne invited Alcuin, a Northumbrian, sometime in the early 780s to come and establish himself as resident scholar and court pedagogue, the emperor kept diplomatic channels open in political matters, not with Northumbrian chiefs, but with Offa, king of Mercia.[37] Offa's achievement was notable, and it was "not empty grandiloquence when Offa styled himself in so many words 'King of the English.'"[38]

Until recent times, Anglo-Saxon scholarship stressed Northumbrian cultural preeminence. While granting the political successes of Offa, historians slighted other Mercian contributions. Texts showing "Anglian" characteristics were ascribed promptly to Northumbria, and, as we have seen, Cynewulf himself was counted a Northumbrian for nearly a century. Frank M. Stenton, the founder of modern Anglo-Saxon history, offers this salutary corrective:

It is probable . . . that the Mercian contribution to English learning has been undervalued in the past. Cynewulf, the one Old English poet with whom a considerable body of verse is definitely associated, has recently been referred to this region with virtual certainty, and more than one important text which used to be assigned vaguely to Northumbria has now been traced with precision to Lichfield. It is gradually becoming less remarkable that King Alfred found at least four Mercian scholars to help him in his literary work.[39]

Cynewulf's life either coincided with or abutted a time of significant political and scholastic development in his homeland. And his acquaintance with theological materials demonstrates he drew upon the resources of a literate culture, however limited. If Mercian culture did not surpass Northumbrian and its school at York, nonetheless it is not to be scorned or disparaged on that account. Cynewulf's works themselves bear witness to a vital connection between the Anglo-Saxon present and the world of ancient Latin letters.

Late in the nineteenth century Cynewulf, the wandering minstrel, was replaced by a more accurate characterization—Cynewulf, the ecclesiastic. After early attempts to identify him with someone of major importance in the Anglo-Saxon church, preferably a bishop, most scholars now believe that the poet, still anonymous despite his runic signatures, was a monk. All the subjects for his poems are tied, as Sisam mentions, to the church calendar and its liturgical celebrations:[40] February 16 (*Juliana*), May 3 (*Elene*, the feast of the Invention of the Cross), the Ascension (*Christ II*) and November (*The Fates of the Apostles*). While his poems are independent of the liturgy, the choices themselves indicate an awareness of the feasts of the church year and the readings (the *Lectio Divina*) a monk would have experienced in the chapel, the refectory, and the cell.

It would be difficult to give a fair estimation of Cynewulf's "learning." The subjects of his poems were not hard to stumble upon. The life of Saint Juliana was widely available, the legend of the finding of the Cross was one of the most popular tales in the early Middle Ages, the material for *Christ II* comes mainly from a sermon by Gregory the Great with a generous admixture from the Bible, and the martyrological list in *The Fates of the Apostles*, whatever its idiosyncracies, was in widespread use. In short, Cynewulf chose no arcane subjects; he relied upon some of the most obvious sources available to him in his time.

But Cynewulf's acquaintance with Latin literature and the patristic tradition is not superficial. Although the nature of his subjects does not give him frequent opportunity to demonstrate great erudition—he must follow the received narrative outline and pointed interpretation would be inappropriate—nonetheless his poems reveal a mind trained in the history and mode of Christian thought. So much modern scholarship points out how deeply learned the Anglo-Saxon poets actually were, not only in the immense corpus of patristic writings, but also in the whole Latin grammatical and rhetorical traditions.[41] We have no reason to suppose, either from the historical situation or from the evidence of the poems themselves, that Cynewulf did not partake fully of the riches of his intellectual milieu.

The discussion of Cynewulf's relation to the techniques of exegesis raises subtle questions. Those habits of mind that had developed from a combination of rabbinic hermeneutics and neo-Platonic allegorizing had been codified by Augustine and passed on to Western Christendom; Gregory the Great represents no small link in the chain. Gregory's sermon, which is the source for *Christ II*, illustrates a specific kind of exegesis: Gregory takes a section of the Bible and threads his way through verse by verse, phrase by phrase, making connections, both obvious and startling, from one idea to another, and from one quotation to another. As we shall see, Cynewulf either did not understand or did not choose to imitate this particular cast of mind. His version of Gregory's sermon is much less "exegetical" as a result. However, an allegorical attitude does pervade Cynewulf's works. While we may not discover a strict adherence to an Augustinian four-level allegory, the sense that the surface narrative symbolizes another and larger truth is everywhere present. Several generations of Anglo-Saxon scholars missed this essential quality in Cynewulf and consequently depreciated his works by judging them on realistic grounds. Under the influence of the neo-Augustinian interpretations of medieval literature, the pendulum has now swung far in the opposite direction. Cynewulf's works have become, for some critics, conundrums which can only be understood by resorting to other texts—the Bible and the writings of the Fathers. The *via media* is not always a safe road, but in interpreting Cynewulf's poems it seems a suitable path. A major task for the critic is finding just where and how Cynewulf writes allegorically and where he does not. Cynewulf's attitude toward patristic exegesis and the body of Latin commentary seems more an acceptance of a perspective than a devotion to a rigid scheme, or the demonstration of great knowledge. Viewed in this way, background material can be illuminating, but its overuse can create severe critical distortion. The critical essays which follow do not try to prove Cynewulf a learned monk; rather the discussions aim at discovering what Cynewulf did with the materials he had at hand, that is, what makes him a scop, a shaper or poet in the basic sense of both words.

CHAPTER 2

The Fates of the Apostles

I *Sources*

CYNEWULF writes that he gathered his material for *The Fates of the Apostles* "far and wide" (*samnode wide*, 2b) "from holy books" (*þurg halige bec*, 63b). Since the turn of the twentieth century, however, scholars have searched for a single source which would contain the same information about the apostles as Cynewulf provides and in precisely the same order. No such source has come to light, though scholars have long known the general nonliterary tradition behind the poem.[1] Cynewulf's meditation on the deaths of the twelve apostles clearly derives from the ancient martyrologies. These were either historical or simply calendars, two branches of the tradition succinctly distinguished by René Aigrain:

A *martyrology* is not, as the etymology suggests, a discourse or a treatise concerning any particular martyr or martyrs in general . . . , nor a classification of martyrs or saints, whatever order may be adopted . . . , but a list of saints according to the dates on which they have customarily been celebrated in churches. . . . Another important distinction establishes itself following the presentation of the notices: while the mention of the saint in a calendar carries only, after the date, the name and a brief indication of place, many martyrologies append a résumé, more or less extensive, of the saint's history with the nature of his death, and the mention of the persecutors under which he has suffered.[2]

The Fates of the Apostles resembles the historical martyrologies rather than the purely calendrical versions.

Much of the investigation has focused on what appears to be Cynewulf's idiosyncratic order. As Kenneth Sisam notes, "The order of the Apostles is not likely to be random, because an ecclesiastic had constantly to repeat the names in prayers and litanies, and they are an integral part of the Canon of the Mass."[3] Unfortunately, all the early

Latin texts fail to yield an exact correspondence with the Old English work. The most recent editor of *The Fates*, Kenneth R. Brooks, suggests that the order "is closest to that of Jerome's *Notitia de Locis Apostolorum* [*Lists of Places Associated with the Apostles*]."[4] This text forms part of the introduction to the *Martyrologium Hieronymianum*, the earliest surviving text from the martyrological tradition. But it is not an authentic composition by Jerome.[5] Cynewulf's poem also corresponds in certain respects to the Pseudo-Isidore, *De Vita et Obitu utriusque Testamenti Sanctorum* (*The Life and Death of the Saints in Both Testaments*), but this piece depends almost entirely on another, the central analogue called the *Breviarium Apostolorum* (*The Breviary of the Apostles*).[6]

George Philip Krapp, the first editor of the complete text of *The Fates*, believes that "all the details in the poem may be derived, with one exception, from the martyrology of Bede and the *Breviarium Apostolorum*."[7] Bede's *Martyrology*, such as it is known today, is a composite text made up of additions from later martyrologies;[8] it could not have been the principal source, although Krapp contends that Cynewulf may have drawn on the "list or lists which Bede used in the preparation of his *Martyrologium*."[9] Krapp's "one exception" is Thomas's miraculous revival of Gad, an event recorded in the apocryphal *Acts of Thomas*. He maintains that Cynewulf here depended on his own store of knowledge rather than on any specific source.[10] In two other attempts to explain this discrepancy, George L. Hamilton and Ruth Perkins have posited different specific sources from the Irish-Latin tradition in which an account of Gad's resurrection would be found; Perkins examines the English breviaries of York, Sarum, and Hereford, while Hamilton turns to the Irish *Stowe Missal* and *The Book of Cerne*.[11] Sisam also shows that the order in Cynewulf is duplicated "in several late Old English litanies of varied provenance, e.g. The Paris Psalter . . . ; the *Liber Vitae of Newminster* . . . ; the Missal of Robert of Jumièges . . . all three South-Western books written about 1020."[12] These Litanies of the Saints may have been important for more than simply the listing order; they may also have supplied the inspiration for the ritual, consolatory, and eschatological tone of the poem.[13]

Cynewulf's *Fates*, then, has no single source.[14] It relies heavily on the martyrological tradition which spread rapidly throughout Western Christendom after the fifth century; it may depend as well on other liturgical and devotional texts and practices that invoked the twelve apostles in prayer. But whatever its antecedents, the poem is a special creation that only faintly reflects its various Latin analogues.

II   *Criticism*

For the most part critics have ignored or scorned *The Fates of the Apostles*. As Claes Schaar puts it, "the Fata Apostolorum would hardly have attracted attention if Cynewulf's acrostic had not been attached to it."[15] His statement is kinder than others which could be cited. Few scholars have heeded Krapp's statement written for the introduction to his edition of *The Vercelli Book*: "It may seem strange that Cynewulf should have taken the trouble to add his name to so slight a poem as the *Fates of the Apostles*, but on the other hand, it is not improbable that Cynewulf attached a higher value to the poem than the modern reader is inclined to do."[16]

The first attempt to rescue the poem from critical oblivion and assign it some aesthetic value is James L. Boren's rhetorical and structural analysis.[17] He constructs an elaborate scheme to explain the descriptive variations of each "fate," subdividing the whole account into a "*locative* element . . . , the definition of the place or locale in which the action takes place; the *instrumental* element . . . , the means by which an end is attained (in the case of the apostles, their persecutors . . .) . . . ; and the *nominative* element, which designates the subject of the individual narrative."[18] Although Cynewulf does vary the order of these three elements, the basic pattern exists in the *Breviarium Apostolorum*, and Boren's pattern could describe many different structures. Boren belabors the obvious, but his central point concerns the number of such patterns. He believes that Cynewulf repeated it twelve times—eleven in describing the apostles and a twelfth time in describing himself, so that the poet becomes "a participant in the tradition of Christ's followers."[19] Boren shares with later critics the desire to reduce the poem's structure to a numerical equivalent; however, his perception that Cynewulf here creates an analogy between himself as a poet and the apostles as evangelists and martyrs has proved seminal.

Constance B. Hieatt sees the flaw in Boren's critique; she remarks that a thirteenth example occurs in the invitation to "us" all to obey God and journey to heaven.[20] This "extra" piece of evidence does skew Boren's symmetrical pattern, and Hieatt erects another numerological grid for the poem. Her analysis is detailed, but she finds two patterns deriving from the structural divisions:

In a postulated prologue consisting of lines 1–15, two beguiling sums emerge. The epilogue has already been analyzed as two groups of 35 verses each, which means a total of 70 verses; similar division of the 15 lines of the prologue into verses gives 30; 70 plus 30 yields the satisfying round number 100. And, even more satisfactorily, the remaining lines 16–87—the central body of the poem—yield a total of exactly 144 verses (12 × 12).[21]

Her figures produce a mystical structure, a pattern of perfection, only if one agrees, *a priori*, with her sense of proper division.

Yet another formal and numerical analysis cuts the poem up in quite different ways: D. R. Howlett sees a structural diptych in the main body—the apostles who died in the West line up perfectly against those who died in the East. Further, Cynewulf binds his balanced lists together with repeated phrases, and he links them together again in reversed order.[22] A close examination of Howlett's lists shows some disturbing irregularities, though his notion that symmetry is a structural principle in *The Fates* remains unquestioned. Howlett believes Cynewulf composed the poem on the Golden Section:

In a work which conforms to the Golden Section the minor part relates to the major part as the major part relates to the whole: $m/M = M (m + M) = .618$. In a poem 122 lines long the minor part should occupy 46.6 lines and the major part 75.4 lines. Sections II and III, dealing with the martyrdoms of the twelve apostles, occupy 76 lines. Sections I, IV, and V–VIII, containing the prologue, epilogue, runic signature, and Cynewulf's requests for our prayers, occupy 46 lines.[23]

So Cynewulf imposed a great mathematical harmony on the whole.

Like many such hypotheses, proof is neither possible nor impossible. Both Hieatt and Howlett supply convincing evidence. But too many subjective assumptions must be fed into their numerical system to provide much confidence in the results. Who, for instance, decides where the prologue ends and the poem proper begins? In *The Fates of the Apostles* Cynewulf deliberately obscures this dividing line, for he comes to the deaths of Peter and Paul well within the compass of the first rhetorical section (lines 11b–15b within lines 1–15). Howlett and Hieatt each cut in different places, as they must do to produce their desired equations. Or another question, who can judge what is "major" and what is "minor"? Cynewulf does not designate any portion of *The Fates* as such, and imposing these criteria on the poem seems an arbitrary act at best.

Despite their differences, these three critics have performed a valuable service for the poem: they have raised the possibility that Cynewulf's briefest work may contain more than has met the eyes of three or four scholarly generations. The poem is indeed, as Hieatt notes, a "mannered, formal poem,"[24] and while we need not press for complete agreement regarding its structures— rhetorical, thematic, or mathematical—we do need detailed explications to give this nearly discarded poem its due.

The Fates of the Apostles is a paradigm of the Cynewulfian manner and variations on its structural patterns, extended to a greater or lesser degree, provide the skeletal outlines of all his poems. His ideas, both theological and aesthetic, emerge from meditations on conjunction and disjunction between forms, states, and beings. The basic rhetorical configurations of *The Fates* illustrate this well. Other critics' systems aside, the most obvious shift occurs at line 88: *Nu ic þonne bidde* ("Now then I pray"). With this phrase Cynewulf turns from the past narration of the apostles' deaths to present concerns for his own future state; or, he moves from his opening statement that he wrought this song (*Hwæt! Ic þysne sang siðgeomor fand*, 1, *my italics*) to an urgent request for prayers. These comprise the two large divisions and in each subsections are easily discerned. The poem contains a ritual series of verse paragraphs, held together in the first part either by simple repetition or by words which begin with the same sound (*Hwæt, Swylce, Hwæt, Huru, Swylce, Hyrde, Næron, Ðus*) and in the much briefer second series by words which emphasize present time and place (*Nu, Her, Sie, Ah*). But at the close of each section an unexpected switch occurs. For Cynewulf breaks the pattern in the former with a verb in the past indicative (*Næron*), in the latter with a verb in the present subjunctive (*Sie*). He then proceeds in the former with a term of logical demonstration (*Ðus*), and in the latter with one of admonition and exhortation (*Ah*). As this pattern indicates, Cynewulf explores the problems which arise from placing two things side by side. In this example the two items are the apostles and ordinary men, Cynewulf the poet included. This relation is analogical and explains the poem's basic theme: as the apostles gained heaven through their deeds, so let us pray that we may receive the same. But a sobering recognition of a great difference, of a chasm, undercuts the heartening aspects of the comparison. In purely grammatical terms, the difference can be seen in the shift from the certainty of a past indicative to the contingency of a present subjunctive, or in semantic terms, it is the difference between "thus" and "but."

Nonetheless, formal patterning does not exclude emotional effect, for this iterated series, itself only one of the poem's numerous repetitions, is a part of a consolatory litany as well as a prayer for salvation. These repetitions have troubled many unsympathetic critics, who dismiss the whole production as a mere versified catalog and so fail to see precisely what Cynewulf does in fashioning poetry out of lists and a comforting litany out of repeated formulas. In *The Fates* Cynewulf combines the biographical details in the historical martyrologies with the ritual catalogs comprising the Litanies of the Saints.[25] The incantatory quality of litany thoroughly permeates the poem; however *The Fates* departs from the strict martyrological tradition at the start:

> Hwæt! Ic þysne sang   siðgeomor fand
> on seocum sefan,   samnode wide
> hu þa æðelingas   ellen cyðdon,
> torhte ond tireadige.
>
> (1–4a)

Lo! I wrought this song travel-weary, sick at heart, gathered from far and wide how the nobles showed bravery, bright and glorious.

Cynewulf's narrative voice, *ic*, initiates a comparison between the poet and the subjects of his poem: whereas he is sick at heart and travel-weary, the "holy band" (*halgan heape*, 9a) of the twelve apostles is bright, glorious, and chosen by the Lord (*dryhtne gecorene*, 5b). Attention to the repetition of words and phrases reveals a chain of related perceptions. Cynewulf tells us that he wrought this song from stories about the apostles gathered from far and wide, and three times he repeats that the apostles' acts and praise, both individual and collective, have spread far and wide (*Lof wide sprang*, 6b and *Is se apostolhad / wide geweorðod ofer werþeoda!*, 14b–15b; *wide wearð wurd undyrne*, 42). The apostles disperse to declare the Lord's law and to make manifest His word before men (10a–11a) and in so doing "showed bravery" (*ellen cyðdon*, 3b). A vast distance separates the poet and the apostles, although structurally their tasks seem similar: the preaching of the Gospel, the creation of poetry. The reader's contemplation of that distance leads to a proliferation of ironic contrasts, all of which are subsumed into a sense of ultimate victory as each apostle receives his heavenly reward after the "success" of his mission. So, for example, Nero's persecution of Peter and Paul is, *sub specie aeternitatis*, a futile, as well as evil, act. Pursuing the metaphorical associations of "wide" one step further, Cynewulf calls Nero's treachery *nearwe searwe* (13b). Gordon accurately translates this phrase, "cruel cunning,"[26] yet he misses thereby the irony. Cynewulf's startling rhyme, one which occurs nowhere else in Old English poetry, requires a more precise rendering, for Nero's plotting is "narrow" before it is "cruel." Without comment Cynewulf then juxtaposes the lines quoted telling of Peter and Paul's apostlehood being "widely honored among the nations." Thus is the irony resolved. The apostles fulfill, as Robert C. Rice reminds us, Christ's paradoxical commandment spoken in Matthew 16:24–25: "Then said Jesus unto his disciples, If any man will come after me, let him deny himself, and take up his cross, and follow me. For whosoever will save his life shall lose it: and whosoever will lose his life for my sake shall find it."[27] Lot directs their dispersal (*Halgan heape hlyt wisode*, 9), and they each become "one sent forth." Isidore of Seville writes: *Apostoli missi interpretantur.*[28] Appropriately, the dominant image of Cynewulf's poem is the journey, and Cynewulf's description of himself in the first line as "weary of life," or better still "travel-weary," connects him directly to the poem's narrative. Cynewulf stresses the apostles' eager bravery to embark on their journeys to preach the Gospel and meet their fates. Their embrace of inevitable death stands in contrast to Cynewulf's fear of death and his journey to the unknown land (lines 109b–12b). The apostles avidly sought the journey (32a, 39b, 62a, 77a, 81a); they were neither negligent nor careless (*Næs his broðor læt, / siðes sæne*, 33b–34a). For Cynewulf they symbolize the assurance of the risky voyage overcome, a double voyage in fact, because it has taken them from Jerusalem to the corners of the earth, and from there to heaven. The verbs are those from the heroic vocabulary: *geneðde* (17b and 50b) and *gelædde* (43b), both meaning "risked." The apostles imitate Christ in the strict sense of the word. By seeking the lands to which lot directs them, they copy the ultimate model of grace, Christ's Incarnation. A description of the birth of Christ within the section on John makes this identification explicit:

> syððan wuldres cyning,
> engla ordfruma, *eorðan sohte*
> þurh fæmnan hrif, fæder manncynnes.
> (27b–29b; my italics)

when the King of glory, the Prince of angels, the Father of mankind, sought the earth through a woman's womb.

Then, too, theirs is an act of will freely chosen because they are Christ's chosen (5). As Christ's thanes, they reenact Christ's decision to suffer death on the Cross and thus "choose" eternal life (*ac him ece geceas, / langsumre life*, 19b–20a; and 38b–39b, 48b–49b, 61b–62b, 73b–74b, 79b–84b). With the apostles Cynewulf emphasizes choice and action, whether physical or spiritual.

As their individual fates lead all but Peter and Paul and Simon and Thaddeus (paired at beginning and end of the list) to separate deaths, so their martyrdoms bring them together into the eternal company of heaven. Fate directs each of them to his assigned province where the situation is reversed: the troop now is not the "holy band" of the apostlehood, but the bloodthirsty troops of hostile pagans. Andreas meets his end in Achaia surrounded by the noise of a troop (*heriges byrhtme*, 21b); Philip is hanged on the gallows by a warlike troop (*syðð̄an on galgan in Gearapolim / ahangen wæs hildecorð̄re*, 40a–41b); ironically, Thomas both awakens Gad before a multitude (*awehte for weorodum*, 55a) and then dies in turn before that same host (*wund for weorudum*, 61a); and James falls before the priests in Jerusalem (*fore sacerdum swilt þrowode*, 71). But the parting from the Lord's band is only the first division; the second is the parting of spirit from flesh, of soul from body (*ealdre gedælan, / feorh wið̄ flæsce*, 36b–37a; *þa gedæled wearð̄ / lif wið̄ lice*, 82b–83a). This sundering becomes the cause of the heavenly reunion, and it brings "unbroken glory" (*Tir unbrǣcne*, 86b). The pattern concludes with a long return to Cynewulf alone with the rest of humanity.

The assurances of eternal life which Christ's Resurrection promises are incorporated both structurally and metaphorically into the poem. Slight departures from the established scheme, in the descriptions of Christ's Incarnation (27b–29b) and Gad's resurrection (54a–59a), emerge so sharply from the careful ritual which controls the rest of the catalog that they define through structural means the theological truths upon which all Christians rest their hope. In each of these expanded sections Cynewulf may also have used the metaphorical interpretation of the names John and Thomas. The *Breviarium Apostolorum* etymologizes the Hebrew roots of all the apostles' names; John means "the grace of God," Thomas, called Didymus, comes to mean, "similar to Christ." Ginsberg argues persuasively that "the grace of God" assumes human form in John's section and an act "similar to Christ's," Gad's resurrection from the dead, occurs in Thomas's section.[29]

Physical resurrection has its analogues in the new life brought to the heathens through the word of the Gospel. The apostles are first and foremost teachers, messengers of God's word, who must declare and reveal God's law before men (*þær hie dryhtnes æ deman sceoldon, / reccan fore rincum*, 10a–11a). Thomas's words "enlightened the mind and encouraged the heart" (*mod onlihted, / hige onhyrded*, 52b–53a). Christian belief is likened to light that appears at the dawning of the day (*Dæges or onwoc, / leohtes geleafan*, 65b–66a); the land is purged through Matthew's glorious teaching (*land wæs gefælsod / þurh Matheus mære lare*, 66b–67b). These images cluster thickly in the two connected sections treating Thomas and Matthew, and here Cynewulf demonstrates his particular habit of exploring a brief train of associations for their ironic potential. Thomas enlightens the Indians' souls and wakes Gad before the multitude, only to die before that multitude, so he can himself receive the light of glory; Matthew wakes the dawn of faith's light for the Ethiopians (*Sigelware*, 64a, literally, "sun dwellers") through his teaching, but is then put to sleep by weapons (*wæpnum aswebban*, 69b).[30] Cynewulf does not prolong these connected ideas and images, although they fit easily into the poem's major themes.

The discontinuous examination of a metaphorical series stands out in high relief as one of Cynewulf's special characteristics, to which is related a corresponding attitude toward structure. The latter becomes more evident in his three long poems. The discontinuity, however, is neither abrupt nor absolute, for as with the images just discussed, Cynewulf usually makes a connection, implied or explicit, between the part and its immediate sequel or the part and the whole. In *The Fates*, however, the bond joining the poem proper with the so-called epilogue is hardly tenuous. The epilogue reflects the main narration just as its own two parts mirror each other. First, the "awkward double epilogue."[31] In lines 88–91 Cynewulf asks that any "man who may love the course of this song" (*beorn se ðe lufige / þysses giddes begang*) pray to the "holy band" to give him aid and comfort; again in lines 107–9 he requests the same, using almost identical formulas: "*Sie þæs gemyndig, mann se ðe lufige / þisses galdres begang, þæt he geoce me / ond frofre fricle* ("May the man who loves the course of this song be mindful of that, so that he help me and implore comfort for me"). Critical antipathy toward this obvious repetition has had many and powerful spokesmen. Kenneth Sisam gives a review of such opinions in "Cynewulf and His Poetry." He himself believes that "the ending is disproportionately long and repetitive," an example of "the structural looseness of Old English poems." Sisam mentions in passing that both Sievers and Skeat held the "second" closing to be "an alternative ending [which] has been preserved by accident."[32] Only Charles W. Kennedy would redeem the poem's two endings, but his rationale smacks of special pleading. Comparing the autobiographical sections in *Juliana* and *The Fates*, Kennedy concludes that Cynewulf repeated himself in the latter because the "first request for the prayers of readers is made before Cynewulf has disclosed his name." Inadequate as an explanation of the variation, Kennedy's point has some validity. He does conclude that "this repetition of the request for intercession . . . is in no structural sense inartistic. It is not a 'second' ending of the poem, but a resumptive device rhetorically not ineffective."[33]

As "resumptive devices" the poem's "endings" have their analogues in the Litanies of the Saints. Cynewulf's double plea for prayers expresses his notions of structural movement, a movement that is essentially ritualistic. Like that of the Litanies, the progression of *The Fates*, including the epilogue, depends upon a ritual formula that partakes of incantation, of prayer and of ceremony. And the epilogues themselves do not further mar an already tedious poem, but rather cap a litany that offers hope and consolation to a sinner. In other words, the double prayer finds both its formal and teleological analogue in the ritual suffrage of the litany: *ora pro nobis*. That Cynewulf places the petition at the end of the list of the apostles and their deaths should not cause surprise; contemporary litanies frequently reserved the intercessory plea till the end of a lengthy catalog.[34] And even the extension of the plea to the reader rather than to the apostles themselves, either singly or as a group, was in widespread and conventional use.[35]

But the double endings need to be understood in a much more specific way. Both Hieatt and Howlett note that the second is a mirror image of the first. Beyond the opening lines which repeat each other almost exactly, Cynewulf aligns many themes and images in what we may think of as parallel columns. In this way he contrasts the suffering sinner in a fleeting world with the joyful saints in eternity. Thus the second epilogue not only repeats the first, but also stands in stark contrast. This striking opposition has been present from the start. Following the request for prayers, Cynewulf dwells in each section on his lonely and approaching journey to the unknown land (*eardwic uncuð*,

93a; *Wic sindon uncuð*, 112b), but the first reference closed with a meditation on his corpse remaining behind "as a comfort to worms" (*wælreaf wunigean weormum to hroðre*, 95), whereas the second introduces the possibility of possessing and enjoying the divine spirit (*nempe he godcundes gastes bruce*, 114).

Next in each section comes an announcement or an exhortation in words, the first stated in the indicative, the second, in the imperative mood. The cryptic declaration that "a man who is wise in perception and who likes songs can discover who composed this fitt" (*Her mæg findan forepances gleaw, / se ðe hine lysteð leodgiddunga, / hwa þas fitte fegde*, 96a–98a) has its parallel in the exhortation that we send our prayers into the bright creation (*Ah utu we þe geornor to gode cleopigan, / sendan usse bene on þa beorhtan gesceaft*, 115a–16b). We may take Cynewulf's song as his prayer; our prayers come if we like his song; and both then become acts of spiritual creation analogous to the apostles' "making manifest" the word of God before men (10a–11a).

Cynewulf reveals who made this song through his runic signature, a passage which presents special problems. It is not the deliberate rearranging of the letters in his name ("FWULCYN") which causes the difficulty, but the passage's intensely riddling quality. R. K. Gordon's translation represents the best of the nineteenth- and early twentieth-century efforts to decode this short cryptogram:

Wealth (F) comes at the end; earls enjoy it on earth; they may not always remain together, dwelling in the world; *Our* (U) *Pleasure* (W) on earth shall pass away; the fleeting adornments of the flesh shall afterwards perish, even as *Water* (L) glides away. Then shall the *Bold Warrior* (C) and the *Wretched One* (Y) crave help in the anguish of the night; *Constraint* (N) lies upon them, the service of the king.[36]

This translation has the virtue of making some sense of the signature, but it takes unsupportable liberties with the use of rune names. R. W. V. Elliot reaches a different conclusion, and it is instructive to compare the two versions:

"Wealth" stands last; noble men enjoy it on earth, but they, dwellers in this world, cannot enjoy it for ever. Joy shall pass away; and then in the native land manly strength decays, the body's fleeting adornments, just as water glides away. While torch and bow continue to use their skill, constraint, the King's servitude, lies upon them in the anguish of the night.[37]

Objections have likewise been raised to Elliot's translation; his interpretation of "U" (Ur = Bison) as "manly strength" has met with vigorous criticism. Finally, R. I. Page's solution seems the most plausible,
but because he renders the passage as it is, we cannot always decipher
a clear meaning:

Last stands *feoh*, money, which men of rank enjoy on earth, though dwellers
in the world cannot have it for ever. *Wynn*, joy, must perish; *ur*, our joy in
our homeland. The brief trappings of the body must decay, gliding away like
lagu, water. While *cen*, torch, and *yr*, ? bow, carry out their office in the
closeness of the night, *nyd*, constraint, the king's service lies upon them.[38]

Clarity of detail aside, the general meaning comes through. Cynewulf
here composes a brief elegy within the Old English elegiac tradition.
The disclosure of his name has concomitant ironies; by concealing it in
this passage on mutability, he creates an emblem of the spirit
entrapped in the flesh, the name in the text. Only through cutting his
name from the context can we know who he is, and this intellectual
dissection symbolizes the coming split of spirit and body in his solitary
journey. The freeing of spirit from body is a central theme; this
emblematic "pun" has numerous siblings. Distorting the spelling of his
name, Cynewulf ties himself to all that has gone before and all that
will come after. Wealth does stand at the end, literally in his name as
well as at the "end" of the narration which closes with a reference to
"fleeting treasures" and the separation of soul and body (*þa gedæled
wearð / lif wið lice, ond þas lænan gestreon, / idle æhtwelan, ealle
forhogodan*, 82b–84b); and figuratively because all earthly wealth
comes to an end. By placing the "F" rune first, Cynewulf takes the
initial step on his journey, dissociating himself from material things. In
breaking his name, he begins the parting of soul from body. Then too
the spelling enacts poetically Christ's proclamation that the first will be
last and the last first. Wealth leads him to meditate on possessions,
dwellings, and the way such things perish with the passage of time.
The same interests reappear in the second epilogue, though reversed.
While the first examines earthly mutability, the second extols heavenly
permanence; the wealth which nobles enjoy (*brucaþ*, 99a) on earth
while they dwell in the world (*woruldwunigende*, 100a) is replaced by
the homeland given to those who possess (*bruce*, 114b) a divine spirit.
The constraint in the king's service from epilogue one is replaced by
the King of the angels who bestows eternal rewards on the pure in

epilogue two (*þær cyning engla clænum gildeð / lean unhwilen*, 119a–20a). Here the lexical and syntactical parallels are of special interest. This phrase must be read against its counterpart, *læne lices frætewa, efne swa lagu toglideð* ("the transitory ornaments of the body, even as water glides away," 102); these ornaments and wealth that *glide* away are reversed in heaven as Christ *gilds* (the word's associations with wealth are clearly intended) the pure with eternal reward; the eternal rewards *(lean)* supplant the fleeting *(læne)* ornaments of the body. Inverted word order, repetition, and variation first create a symmetrical analogy between the two sections and then reveal the awesome contrast that exists within this symmetry; the world of man and time remains absolutely distinct from God and eternity.

From the opening line of *The Fates* Cynewulf seems to establish an analogical relation between himself and the apostles, and we may extend this analogy to include their preaching and his art. He strikes a final note on this relation at the end of each epilogue. First he closes the runic portion by referring to the revelation of his identity: *Nu ðu cunnon miht / hwa on þam wordum wæs werum oncyðig* ("Now you may know who has been made known to men in these words," 105b–6b). Then he brings both the second epilogue and the poem to an end with a faint echo of these lines:

> Nu a his lof standeð,
> mycel ond mære,   ond his miht seomaþ,
> ece ond edgiong,   ofer ealle gesceaft.
> (120b–22b)

Now His praise/glory stands forever, great and glorious, and His might remains, eternal and ever-young, over all creation.

An overriding sense of the *word* provides the link between the two endings, between Cynewulf and the apostles, and between the poet and God. We can compare the passive revelation of the poet's name to men with the apostles' active declaration of the Lord's law, which made it manifest to men (10–11). And the apostles are "verbally" connected to God through the praise/glory they both receive: God's praise/glory, standing forever, is won by the apostles in their evangelical journeys as their "praise/glory sprang wide" (*Lof wide sprang*, 6b). Cynewulf's "words," his poem, are tied to mutability and take the form of prayer and injunction. What God always has and the apostles achieve, man only prays to be given. But Cynewulf's poem expresses the hope that all of us may enjoy or possess (*brucan*, again, 117b) a mansion, "a home on high" (*hames in hehðo*, 118a).

This complex of parallels and reversals in the double epilogue forms a microstructure reflecting the poem's whole movement. Returning to the beginning, we recall that the apostles' dispersal to their allotted destinies follows Cynewulf's brief reference to himself as poet. The apostles are at the start of their journey. In the opening of the epilogue Cynewulf again points to himself as the poem's author and then turns to the question of his own journey, fearful and already "travel-weary." The fates of the apostles are told in the first division; Cynewulf awaits his with trepidation. But the whole poem has been a "course" (*begang*, 89a, 108a), a word we could translate as "journey" and not be untrue either to its literal meaning or to its associations with related images in context. Neither should its second meaning "service" or "religious worship" be ignored; the journey the poem symbolizes is analogous to the apostles' journeys and both are acts of devotion, or service, or worship in the search for eternal life. However, the paradox remains that the apostles' dispersal leads to reunion, while Cynewulf's human solitude and mortality make him subject to division and dissolution. He must make his journey alone (92b–93b, 110a). That Cynewulf breaks his name in this poem perhaps illustrates his spiritual anguish in emblematic form.

Each of Cynewulf's four narrative poems is constructed in much the same way. *The Fates of the Apostles*, shortest of all by far, affords a glimpse at that paradigm. The basic unit of Cynewulf's thought and his conception of structure find their origin in the pun and their full realization in manifold analogies. Criticism could begin either with the word or with the meaning and structure. Such collocations as the rhyming pun in *nearwe searwe*, or the alliterative rhyme heavy with import in *leofe on life. Lof wide sprang* (They were "beloved in life. Their fame sprang wide," 6) must be intentional. At the root of the pun is the idea of the hidden analogy and from this Cynewulf fashions the string of precise analogies we have traced in the rhetorical and metaphorical structures. Dolores W. Frese writes perceptively that some detail in *The Fates* often "distinguishes, as it associates."[39] We could take this concept one step further and say that all the various strategies and structures in *The Fates of the Apostles* work similarly. Cynewulf creates analogies between the human and the divine only to reverse them in order to point to the ironic distance which separates these realms. As a perusal of the possible analogues for *The Fates* indicates, these structures are Cynewulf's additions, buttressed by the inherent ironic stance the style of Anglo-Saxon poetry contains.[40]

Because recent criticism of *The Fates* has tried to overturn several generations of neglect and aversion, it proffers corrective analyses usually accompanied by a disclaimer that the poem is not, of course, great art. This does not seem much to the point. That it is a considered piece of poetry, intricately and carefully wrought and rich in expressive irony, cannot be doubted. The ideas may be entirely conventional Christian topics, though Cynewulf combines them in a matrix that is his own. For those who can readily distinguish between the subject of a poem and its craft, *The Fates of the Apostles* will suffice.

CHAPTER 3

Christ II

I Sources

UNLIKE *The Fates of the Apostles,* Cynewulf's sources for *Christ II* are known. F. Dietrich discovered the principal source in 1853 when he proved that a portion of a Gregorian homily gave Cynewulf his main text.[1] The homily, *No. 29* of Gregory's *Forty Homilies on the Gospels,* contains a complicated exegesis, verse by verse, of the Gospel reading for Ascension Day, Mark 16:14–20; but Cynewulf uses only the last three sections of Gregory's work as a model for his poem.

While Gregory treats only a specific biblical passage, Cynewulf draws on several portions of Scripture to complete his narrative, mainly Psalm 23, Matthew 28:16–20, Luke 24:36–53, and Acts 1:1–14.[2] And he seems acquainted with the rich iconographic tradition which had grown up around this central event in Christ's life.[3] In addition, a hymn ascribed to Bede called *On the Lord's Ascension* appears to be a source. The great editor of the *Christ* trilogy, A. S. Cook, suggested this possibility at the turn of the century;[4] later scholars have corroborated Cook's view and used Bede's Ascension hymn to sketch in the subjects Cynewulf must be describing in some of the manuscript lacunae.[5] Brief sections of the poem also derive from other biblical and patristic texts; these will be dealt with in due course.

II The Unity of the Christ Poems

Christ II forms the second panel in a triptych describing Christ's Advent, Ascension, and Second Coming. The debate concerning the interrelations among these three panels has been long and inconclusive. Obviously the three poems or parts of a single poem were meant somehow to go together. The scribe or his patron has juxtaposed them in *The Exeter Book* in such a manner that the problem cannot be disregarded. Historically the argument follows several tortuous paths, and these may best be explored by consulting Cook's edition. As he remarks, "The unity of the *Christ* was apparently never suspected until Dietrich undertook his investigation."[6] Dietrich proposed a unity based on theme: the three poems represent the "threefold coming of Christ," His first coming at the Advent, His "coming" into glory at the Ascension, and His Second Coming at the Last Judgment. Even Cook, who strongly maintains that *Christ* is a unified poem, castigates Dietrich for this overelaborate and strained notion.[7] During the last half of the nineteenth century many scholars took up various positions regarding the "whole" text. The 1,664 lines were divided and redivided, sometimes into two poems, sometimes into three. Cynewulf's runic signature was assigned to the end of the second part (where all now agree it belongs), as well as to the beginning of the third. Given the ease with which this signature could be relocated by the stroke of an editorial pen, it is not difficult to see how questions of authorship and unity became inordinately complex.

Several indisputable pieces of evidence have emerged from these often confused deliberations. Speaking of the paleographic data, Krapp and Dobbie assert that the "major divisions of the manuscript clearly indicate three distinct structural units."[8] The careful studies of Cynewulf's style by Claes Schaar and S. K. Das also require our viewing *Christ II* as a discrete poetic unit. Yet these facts do not mean that someone—anthologizer, scribe, or perhaps even Cynewulf himself—intended that the three parts of *Christ* be viewed as one. Kenneth Mildenberger's unconvincing attempt to demonstrate the importance of an iconographic tradition in eighth-century Northumbria which associated Advent, Ascension, and Last Judgment has not been generally credited.[9] Two recent efforts make much more radical, and more persuasive, claims for the unity of the whole. Both rely on liturgical parallels to reinforce their positions.

Colin Chase returns, though in a quite different way, to Dietrich's idea of the three-fold coming of Christ. Chase finds himself in agreement with George A. Smithson, who held that the connection among the poems corresponded to St. Bernard's portrayal of Christ's advent *ad homines, in homines, contra homines* ("to men, into men, against men").[10] He supplies liturgical examples illustrating the presence of this triple paradigm in sources contemporary with Cynewulf.[11] Chase does not choose among the alternatives available. Although he raises the possibility that Cynewulf may have "composed *Christ II* in order to join together two poems already in existence according to [a] liturgical theme," he leaves an answer unspecified, concluding only that "an alert Christian reading the first three poems in the Exeter Book in the early eleventh century would have recognized their unity."[12]

Dolores Frese goes beyond the somewhat tentative decision Chase reaches and proposes "that the signature section of *Christ II* has in fact been consciously and deliberately artificed to establish that poem as a poetic fixture of unity between pre-existing texts, yoking the precedent Advent focus of *Christ I* and the subsequent apocalyptic focus of *Christ III*."[13] For this "centrist" position of *Christ II*, Frese ventures that "we can plausibly infer a compelling unitive liturgical rationale for a three part *Christ* poem that surprisingly ignores such signal Christian events as the Crucifixion and Resurrection, to place the Ascension of Christ at the exact poetic midpoint between His first and His second Coming."[14] Frese and Chase each depend heavily on the references to Christ's birth at the beginning of *Christ II* and the allusions to the Last Judgment at the end to tighten the joints between this poem and its neighboring panels in the triptych. But Gregory makes the same references in his homily. While it is true that Cynewulf expands Gregory's details to a degree, the fact itself cannot be passed lightly by. Without doubt a logical and liturgical relation exists among the Advent, the Ascension, and the Second Coming. Whether this relation secures the desired unity is still arguable; whether it is organic or only formal and architectural must remain undecided. We can defend no more than a broad thematic unity among the three panels, and Cynewulf may have had nothing to do with the setting of his poem in the second spot. His poem has its own separate plan and themes, which must now be examined in detail.

III *Criticism*

Explicitly theological literature usually exhibits a profound conventionality in theme, but an analysis of an individual poem's unique structures must also be part of any valid criticism. Cynewulf certainly never deviates from orthodox Christianity, yet this does not mean that his orthodoxy dictates his poetic forms. Those who would hold a contrary position do so by supporting a dominant assumption in the criticism of medieval literature: that the thought is separate from the mode of thinking, that the idea exists apart from its specific context. Perhaps criticism should begin with a different assumption: that there is more

than one way to think a Christian thought. The unlocking of Cynewulf's distinctive modes of thought stands as one of the most important
contributions literary analysis can make.

We have already seen in *The Fates of the Apostles* that Cynewulf
customarily perceives serial analogies among the holy persons, acts,
and images of his sources, and then, including himself among the comparisons, attains an ironic perspective on the distance between the
human and the divine. This same disposition recurs in *Christ II*,
though the particular strategies here are more complex and the patterns more intricate. When compared with that part of Gregory's homily he uses in *Christ II*, Cynewulf's characteristic structuring becomes
apparent at the outset. Cynewulf begins working at section 9 of the
Gregorian text, though we do not know whether this is choice or accident. Had he read the whole homily or did he only know these last
three portions through hearing them delivered during the liturgy of
the Ascensiontide?[15]

However that question may be resolved, Gregory's homily itself
breaks neatly in two: the first section explicates the Gospel reading for
Ascension Day (Mark 16:14–20) and the second turns to the narrative
recorded in Acts 1:1–14. Gregory's method changes also from section
to section: in the second half he no longer takes up biblical verses singly, but ranges over a series of associated questions, probing their
typological significances with reference to the Ascension. He signals his
intent to employ a different exegetical mode in this second part: *Sed
quia, auctore Deo, breviter lectionem Evangelicam exponendo tran-
scurrimus, restat ut aliquid de ipsa tantae solemnitatis consideratione
dicamus*[16] ("But now that, with God's help, we have gone through and
briefly commented upon the Gospel reading, it remains that we say
something in consideration of such a great solemnity"). Once Gregory
feels compelled to speak generally about this great "solemnity," he
proceeds to explain the importance of the Ascension in a series of logical and quasi-logical interpretations, and he begins with the formal
declaration: "This is the first question we must ask" (*Hoc autem nobis
quaerendum est*).[17] Gregory goes on to inquire why angels in white
appeared at the Ascension when they did not at the Incarnation. Many
critics have been troubled by Cynewulf's handling of this "question."
Stanley B. Greenfield offers a possible defense: "Gregory proceeds to
answer this question directly, in terms of the humbling of Divinity on
the former occasion and the exaltation of humanity on the latter; but

Cynewulf, addressing his poem to an 'illustrious man,' asks him to meditate on this question, and never does give an explicit answer, though he hints at it in lines 550–554 and 755."[18]

In fact, Cynewulf does not pose his version of the problem in the form of a question; he tells the "famous" or "illustrious" man (*mon se mæra*, 441a) to seek "how it happened" (*hu þæt geeode*, 443a) that no angels in white appeared at Christ's birth. Then, in a nearly tangential continuation of this thought, he adds:

> Hwæþre in bocum ne cwið
> þæt hy in hwitum þær   hræglum oðywden
> in þa æþelan tid,   swa hie eft dydon
> ða se brega mæra   to Bethania,
> þeoden þrymfæst,   his þegna gedryht
> gelaðade, leof weorud.
>
> (453b–58a)

Nevertheless it does not say in books that they appeared in white garments at that glorious time, as they did afterwards, when the Glorious Prince, the famous Lord, summoned his band of retainers, his beloved company to Bethany.

Cynewulf's departure from Gregory's clear logic requires scrutiny. First, Cynewulf alters Gregory's rhetorical "we" to the individual "thou," the famous man; second, he shifts the Latin passive periphrastic construction with its force of necessity ("must") to the Old English imperative ("seek ... so that you may know the truth," *sec ... þæt þu soð wite*, 441b–42b). What Gregory confidently discovers in open, logical analysis, Cynewulf evokes in a personal meditation.

For Cynewulf, Gregory's is an intermediary text. Cynewulf not only has to study the Bible, as Gregory did, but also ponder Gregory's interpretation of that sacred book. Perhaps the "famous man" Cynewulf addresses is Gregory himself. Of course this cannot be proved, though it deserves some consideration. The "question" in the opening lines belongs to Gregory; Cynewulf already knows the answer—it is there in Gregory's homily. What interests him is Gregory's process of finding that answer, the way he creates it out of his own wisdom. Cynewulf's meditation on Gregory's text brings the process of creation—both Gregory's and his own—into present focus. When Cynewulf instructs the illustrious man to seek the truth "through the wisdom of his heart" (*þurh sefan snyttro*, 442a), he imaginatively recreates Gregory's act of composition in his own mind. In a sense, Cynewulf's poem, or at least the opening portion, is a commentary on Gregory resembling Gregory's commentary on the Bible. Gregory treats the Bible as a work which can be dissected and recombined in many ways to reveal hidden associations delineating the truth. Cynewulf likewise takes liberties with Gregory's text; he does not have to versify Gregory point by point to cover the logic of his argument. Cynewulf turns away from Gregory's systematic reasoning to produce a poetic vision of the three occasions in which the eternal intersects with time—the Incarnation, the Ascension, and the Last Judgment.

We need not accept this highly speculative identification of *mon se mæra*[19] with Gregory to see that Cynewulf does incorporate Gregory's paradoxical answer to the question into his Old English poem. For Gregory, divinity humbled at the Incarnation becomes humanity exalted at the Ascension; for Cynewulf, this paradox becomes another of his involved and ironic contrasts between earth and heaven. Cynewulf departs abruptly from Gregory in order to make his parallels and contrasts the more explicit. Gregory's concerns are wholly abstract; he writes about the Nativity and the Ascension, humiliation and exaltation. Cynewulf first establishes a sense of the concrete before he constructs his larger patterns. Turning to the Gospel accounts of the Ascension, he takes from Luke (24:50) the detail that the Ascension occurred in Bethany (456a); then Cynewulf juxtaposes Bethany to Bethlehem (449a). The alliterative correspondence between the two cities in the Holy Land no doubt attracted Cynewulf's attention, but it is the contrast between the "bairn" *(beorn)*[20] who comes down to Bethlehem and "the famous prince" (*se brega mæra*, 456a) who ascends in Bethany[21] which deserves special notice.

Cynewulf delays any mention of the actual Ascension until line 464 (*ærþon up stige ancenned sunu*, "before the only-begotten Son ascended"). The "famous prince" leads his "band of thanes" (*þegna gedryht*, 457b) to Bethany, but the central event waits for an interposed description of Christ, the disciples' teacher. They do not "scorn His words" (*Hy þæs lareowes / on þam wildæge word ne gehyrwdon*, 458b–59b), and He gives them "many signs" revealed through "parables" before He returns to Heaven (*þær him tacna fela tires brytta / onwrah, wuldres helm, wordgerynum*, 462a–63b). The inspiration for this section comes also from Luke, for nowhere in Gregory do corresponding ideas occur.

And beginning at Moses and all the prophets, he expounded to them in all the scriptures the things that were concerning him. . . . And he said to them: These are the words which I spoke to you while I was yet with you, that all things must needs be fulfilled which are written in the law of Moses and in the prophets and in the psalms, concerning me. Then he opened their understanding, that they might understand the scriptures. (24:27, 44–45)

Cynewulf stresses from the start the importance of the word, Christ's words, the necessity of obeying these words, and of interpreting these parables, these "word-runes," through reflection or "spirit-runes" (*gæstgerynum*, 440b). Although he does not state it openly, his basic premise rests on Augustine's elucidation of Paul's distinction between the letter and the spirit.[22] All the personages in *Christ II*, present either as actors or as allusions, are keepers of Christ's word. This list includes Gregory as well, if the identification of *mon se mæra* be accepted; it most assuredly embraces the poet who inherits the twin tasks of keeping the word and recreating the events in Christ's life and the parables He spoke. The final effect represents the antitheses to the calm assurance of Gregory's logic: where Gregory answers his question by precise deduction, Cynewulf replaces the notion of question and answer, concentrating instead on the mystery which contains truth. This mystery can only be penetrated by profound meditation on all the correspondences the "books" and the "words" provide. Less important for Cynewulf is the color of the heraldic messengers' clothing than the fact that they speak, that they announce Christ's birth, "the true joy," through speech to the waiting shepherds (*Bodan wæron gearwe / þa þurh hleoporcwide hyrdum cyðdon, / sægdon soðne gefean*, 449b–51a). The Incarnation itself fulfills the prophets' "words" (*Hæfde þa gefylled, swa ær biforan sungon, / witgena word*, 468a–69a). Christ instructs the apostles at the Ascension to go forth and preach the word, "the bright faith," to men (*Farað nu geond ealne yrmenne grund, / geond widwegas, weoredum cyðað, / bodiað ond bremað beorhtne geleafan*, 481a–83b). Angelic messengers, prophets, the Word Himself, the apostles, and Gregory form a line of keepers of the word, to which Cynewulf appends his own being and talent at the poem's conclusion. However, Cynewulf's poetic associations are not Gregory's enigmatic connections between diverse biblical passages; Cynewulf's analogies define the ultimate truth and power of the Eternal Word in contrast to the limitation of the human poet.

Christ's charge to the apostles at His Ascension (476a–90b) to go into the world and preach the Gospel derives from several biblical accounts, though most directly from Mark, which also contains Christ's promise to remain "with you always, even to the end of the world" (28:20).[23] A reminiscence of Psalm 23, an exact source of a later section, may also be interwoven through Christ's speech, for Cynewulf does not simply paraphrase two verses from Matthew but adds other details that expand his whole conception. The apostles receive not only grace, but power as well (478a, 488a, 490a). Cynewulf could have found the idea of the fulness of power related to the act of ascending into or being in a holy place in Psalm 23: "The earth is the Lord's, and the fullness thereof. . . . Who shall ascend into the hill of the Lord? or who shall stand in his holy place?" (1, 3). In this light, Christ's promise to "hold peace with you in steadfast strength in every place" (*eow friðe healde / strengðu stapolfæstre on stowa gehware,* 489b–90b) heightens the biblical echoes behind His speech. Cynewulf's poem transcends mere versification of a composite Gospel account. Grace is also related to fullness of power; it is a gift (*þurh gife mine,* 480a) that brings peace and comfort through such fulness (*þurh meahta sped,* 488a). Psalm 23 is a "warrior-enthronement hymn," as Brown reminds us,[24] and Christ, the warrior about to ascend into glory, commands His disciples to become warriors of His word, a collocation not present in the Gospel versions. They must baptize the heathen and destroy their idols (*hergas breotaþ,* 485b). Some have found here a hidden reference to the conversion of the English, but Christ's speech before His Ascension is self-contained. It illustrates a series of mysterious opposites which paradoxically unite in Christ, and in the disciples who imitate Him: power and grace, the making known of the new religion (*weoredum cyðað,* 482b) and the putting out of the old (*feondscype dwæscað,* 486b), destruction and peace (*hergas breotaþ,* 485b; *sibbe sawað,* 487a), time and eternity and their correlatives in space—the spot where the disciples now stand with Christ and the "every place" where Christ will be mystically present with them as they carry out their mission.

The first description of the Ascension (491a–532b) demonstrates Cynewulf's scheme and technique so precisely it deserves full quotation:

Ða wearð semninga   sweg on lyfte
hlud gehyred.   Heofonengla þreat,
weorud wlitescyne,   wuldres aras,
cwomun on corðre.   Cyning ure gewat
þurh þæs temples hrof   þær hy to segun,
þa þe leofes þa gen   last weardedun
on þam þingstede,   þegnas gecorene.
Gesegon hi on heahþu   hlaford stigan,
godbearn of grundum.   Him wæs geomor sefa
hat æt heortan,   hyge murnende,
þæs þe hi swa leofne   leng ne mostun
geseon under swegle.   Song ahofun
aras ufancunde,   æþeling heredun,
lofedun liffruman,   leohte gefegun
þe of þæs hælendes   heafelan lixte.
Gesegon hy ælbeorhte   englas twegen
fægre ymb þæt frumbearn   frætwum blican,
cyninga wuldor.   Cleopedon of heahþu
wordum wrætlicum   ofer wera mengu
beorhtan reorde: "Hwæt bidað ge,
Galilesce   guman on hwearfte?
Nu ge sweotule geseoð   soðne dryhten
on swegl faran;   sigores agend
wile up heonan   eard gestigan,
æþelinga ord,   mid þas engla gedryht,
ealra folca fruma,   fæder eþelstoll.
We mid þyslice   þreate willað
ofer heofona gehlidu   hlaford fergan
to þære beorhtan byrg   mid þas bliðan gedryht,
ealra sigebearna   þæt seleste
ond æþeleste,   þe ge her on stariað
ond in frofre geseoð   frætwum blican.
Wile eft swa þeah   eorðan mægðe
sylfa gesecan   side herge,
ond þonne gedeman   dæda gehwylce
þara ðe gefremedon   folc under roderum."
    Ða wæs wuldres weard   wolcnum bifongen,
heahengla cyning,   ofer hrofas upp,
haligra helm.   Hyht wæs geniwad,
blis in burgum,   þurh þæs beornes cyme.
Gesæt sigehremig   on þa swiþran hand
ece eadfruma   agnum fæder.

(491a–532b)

Then suddenly a loud sound in the sky was heard. The company of heavenly angels, the glorious band, messengers of glory, came in a host. Our King passed through the roof of the temple where they looked on, those who still watched over the footprints of the Loved One in the meeting-place, the chosen thanes. They saw the Lord arise to the heights, the Son of God from the earth. Their hearts were sad, hot at heart, sorrowing spirits, because they could no longer see the Loved One under the heaven. The heavenly messengers raised a song, praised the Prince, glorified the Author of Life, rejoiced in the light which shone from the Savior's head. They saw two radiant angels shine in ornaments nobly about the First-born, the Glory of Kings. They called from on high with wondrous words over the host of men with clear voices: "What are you waiting for in a circle, men of Galilee? Now you clearly see the true Lord pass to heaven; the Lord of Victory will rise up hence to His dwelling, the Chief of Princes, with these hosts of angels, the Ruler of all Peoples, to the royal seat of His Father. With such a band we will carry our Lord, the best and the noblest of all sons of Victory, over the vaults of heaven to the bright city with these glad hosts, He whom you gaze on here and see joyfully shine in ornaments. Nonetheless, He will again Himself seek the peoples of the earth with a mighty host and then judge every deed which men have done under the skies."

Then was the Guardian of Glory surrounded by clouds, the King of Archangels, up above the heights, the Protector of Saints. Joy was renewed, bliss in the cities through the Prince's coming. The Eternal Giver of Joy sat in triumph on the right hand of His own Father.

This long passage closely resembles the "double epilogue" in *The Fates of the Apostles;* as in that poem Cynewulf uses repetitive structures at a crucial point. He signals his intent by obvious verbal echoes, in this instance two repetitions, making a double contrast and reversal. The whole is a narrative envelope pattern, beginning and ending with a description of Christ's Ascension. Formulaic phrases call immediate attention to themselves: *Ða wearð semninga sweg on lyfte* and *Ða wæs wuldres weard wolcnum bifongen.* The first section narrates the Ascension entirely from the perspective of the apostles looking up as Christ ascends through the temple roof;[25] the second outlines a heavenly perspective as archangels welcome Christ back into paradise. An appropriate emotional shift corresponds to this change in visual perspective—the apostles' sadness, the angels' joy. The apostles' grief, however, remains implied in the opening lines and waits full development until the next lines which open yet another diptych—*Gesegon hi on heahþu hlaford stigan* (498) and *Gesegon hy ælbeorhte englas twegen* (506). The entire section contains a series of envelope patterns, both rhetorical and formulaic. Cynewulf connects this second reflecting pair to the larger encompassing envelope by having the first *Gesegon hi* refer back to the Ascension seen from an earthly perspective and the second *Gesegon hy* look forward to Christ's return to His Father's kingdom. Cynewulf shows concern for the apostles' humanity. Although before He ascended Christ had commanded them to "Rejoice in spirit" (*"Gefeoð ge on ferððe!"* 476a), they succumb to predictable human emotions once He has departed. (Because it goes directly counter to the report in Luke that the apostles "returned to Jerusalem with great joy" 24:52, this scene in the poem is all the more realistic psychologically.) The mourning apostles are likewise contrasted with the radiant angels, shining in ornaments, who share the light of Christ's halo. The angels become Christ's new and happy band (*bliðan gedryht*), the band which the apostles formed while Christ lived on earth. Again at the end of the first portion, angels *raise* a song of praise to Christ (*Song ahofun*), whereas in the second, angels *call down* to the apostles standing amazed in Bethany (*Cleopedon of heahþu*). Each section concludes with a description of Christ's radiance, although in the second instance the angels make a proleptic reference to Christ's Second Coming on Judgment Day. A two-fold effect results from these repetitive and reflecting formal patterns imposed on the Ascension narrative: first, they provide another example of the serial reversals which structure Cynewulf's perception of the Christian faith; second, they imitate in poetic form the main paradox of the Ascension, that time and eternity intersect at this moment. For Cynewulf describes the Ascension as taking place now in each of the four panels and yet in each he also sees it as being complete. Thus he freezes the movement implied in the Ascension by the formal repetition of the frames depicting that movement. Cynewulf's structures express the combination of change and stasis inherent in the idea of the Ascension; the temporal movement becomes eternally fixed in this ritual reconstruction.

Following the Lord's Ascension, Cynewulf continues his narrative in two directions: he traces the disciples' return to Jerusalem and he sketches Christ's welcome into heaven. Images depicting the two destinations clearly indicate that Cynewulf interprets them allegorically. He refers to both places as "the bright city" (*beorhtan byrg*, 519a and *torhtan byrig*, 542a); the earthly Jerusalem is further characterized as "the holy city" and "the Prince's city" (*halgan burg*, 534b; *þæs þeodnes burg*, 553a). Both heaven and Jerusalem stand in opposition to hell, shortly tagged "the city of fiends" (*feonda byrig*, 569a). But the curious aspect of this section is not such expected polarities; rather it is the continued emphasis on the disciples' sorrow at Christ's departure:

> Þær wæs wopes hring,
> torne bitolden;   wæs seo treowlufu
> hat æt heortan,   hreðer innan weoll,
> beorn breostsefa.
>
> (537b–40a)

There was a cry of lamentation; their true love, hot at heart, was grievously overwhelmed; hearts welled within, breasts burned.

As mentioned, the stress on the disciples' sadness in spirit (*geomor-mode*, 535a) contradicts the only biblical statement that they had "great joy." The passage patently copies the conventional lament for the departed (fallen) hero in Germanic verse; however, Cynewulf's use of these stock devices does not strike the discord in this Christian poem that many have charged. While Cynewulf achieves some realism in the process, his main reason for the disciples' emotional state is simple contrast. Cynewulf imagines the two scenes which come after the Ascension in the boldest possible scheme: the disciples return to the earthly Jerusalem desolate at the loss of their leader; Christ returns triumphant into the heavenly Jerusalem accompanied by a new band of angels.[26] To effect this scheme Cynewulf merges two divergent sources, a composite retelling of the Gospel story and a direct borrowing from Bede's Ascension hymn. That he has put them together in precisely this way demonstrates his persistent concern with the gulf between earth and heaven and all the multiple differences deriving from this contrast. Cynewulf's mode of thought bears no resemblance to Gregory's; at this juncture, Cynewulf does not even use his Gregorian homily for a source. He manufactures a source for his own purposes by conflating the Bible with a liturgical text.

The heavenly rejoicing continues in the next passages; the members of the troop Christ leads out of hell are "glad at heart" (*glædmode*, 576) and the covenant which Christ's return to the celestial Jerusalem, itself the "joy of joys" (*dreama dream*, 580a), establishes between angels and men is "the joy of all light" (*ealles leohtes gefea*, 585b).

The passage as a whole represents a chronological displacement, because Cynewulf has already presented Christ's enthronement at the right hand of His Father. He retraces his steps at this point, not so much treading the same ground, but opening new paths for which a different source provides the opportunity. Cynewulf's basic inspiration for the long speech of the angelic herald (556b–86b) is verses 19–25 of Bede's Ascension hymn, though the sources of this hymn also figure prominently in the poem. They are, as Pope lists them, "the apocryphal accounts of the harrowing of hell, the corresponding inferences about the host of the redeemed that Christ led to heaven at his ascension, and the twenty-fourth (twenty-third in the Vulgate) psalm."[27] A missing leaf in *The Exeter Book* cuts out the middle of the herald's speech, but Pope's reconstruction from the sources is indisputable. What remains is a "single coherent speech by the herald angel in reply to the watchers within the gates,"[28] who are puzzled by the throng approaching heaven and the herald's claim that the leader of the band is the King of glory. Presuming that Christ has never left heaven, the guard within demands a more specific identification before he will permit the troop to enter. In the speech preserved, we have the herald angel's reply and his documentation of Christ's credentials as this "King of glory" (*wuldres cyning*, 565b) who harrowed hell. Pope's general outline of the missing lines based on Bede seems accurate, and certainly a synopsis of the herald's speech would tally with Bede's Latin verses. Yet certain differences in imagery and emphasis once again demonstrate Cynewulf's special perceptions. Bede's hymn, narrative combined with dialogue, is essentially devoid of images. Beyond typing Satan as "the world's black prince" (*atrum ... mundi ... principem*) and Christ as "the King of virtue and grace" (*Rex ... virtutis atque gratiae*), Bede's poem dramatizes the event in compressed form.

Cynewulf's additions to Bede's liturgical piece are numerous and complex. Cynewulf chooses the fundamental image of Christ the King, acting by His own and singular might (*anes meahtum*, 567b, *þurh his sylfes sygor*, 581a), robbing hell of the treasure it wrongfully possessed (*Hafað nu se halga helle bireafod / ealles þæs gafoles þe hi geardagum / in þæt orlege unrhyte swealg*, 558a–60b). The image of wealth and its various associations appears consistently in all Cynewulf's poems; its use in this context may not be as abruptly intrusive as it first seems. At the opening of the poem Cynewulf has connected Christ the teacher, the giver of the Word, with treasure (*Hy þæs lareowes / on þam wildæge word ne gehyrwdon, / hyra sincgiefan,*

458b–60a). By this appositional variation Cynewulf equates the Word with treasure; both are and are given by Christ. The irony that portrays Christ as hell's thief is both conventional and explicit. But in Cynewulf's version of His Ascension into heaven with a double host (*corðre ne lytle*, 578b)—the band of welcoming angels and the group He has released from hell—we perceive a more deliberate extension of this ironic frame. The host Christ leads is an "army" (*se þisne here lædeð*, 574b) and they approach a spiritual throne (*gæsta giefstol*, 572a) with the troop He redeemed in battle. And as a last result of His subjugation of Satan, the covenant of peace is restored—not, of course, between Satan and God, but between man and God (*Wær is ætsomne / godes ond monna*, 583b–84a). Peace is also reestablished between angels and men (*Sib sceal gemæne / englum ond ældum*, 581b–82a). From all this the disciples present at the historical Ascension are now conspicuously absent; Cynewulf leaves them waiting for "the Prince's promises" (*þeodnes gehata*, 541b), the coming of the Holy Ghost, in Jerusalem. His interest now lies in those events surrounding the Ascension that are beyond its earthly manifestations—the Harrowing of Hell and the entry into heaven;[29] from these descend the moral commandments which affect all living Christian men. The apostles, as representatives of humanity, now disappear from the poem and their place is taken by a meditation on mankind as an idea. That they have symbolized man is clear and helps account for their unusual reactions to Christ's leavetaking. The final irony in the imagery here is that Christ the robber now has "gifts" to give, to present to His Father and to bestow on man below. Besides the appellation "treasure giver," Christ has been previously called the "Joy-Giver of nobles" (*eorla eadgiefan*, 546a) and "Giver of Life to men" (*folca feorhgiefan*, 556a). Now He becomes the giver of salvation for those who choose it (*hals eft forgeaf*, 587b).

Cynewulf does not restrict the importance of the gift theme and its relation to allotment and choice solely to the famous passage on "the gifts of men" (654a–85b). In the opening reference to the Incarnation Christ is said to have "chosen" the protection of Mary (*siþþan he Marian, mægða weolman, mærre meowlan, / mundheals geceas*, 445a–46b), an accurate theological metaphor for the Savior's birth. And later the disciples are called, in a formula similar to that which occurs in *The Fates of the Apostles*, Christ's "chosen thanes" (*þegnas gecorene*, 497b). These early examples reveal Christ as the active force, the chooser; but these initial choices of the Divine Being also fix the need for man to choose as He did. At the Ascension itself exists the most propitious time for exercising such choice. For behind the Ascension, the return to heaven, lies the expectation of the second return to earth at Judgment Day. Cynewulf even makes the Ascension, the return to heaven (*hydercyme*, 587a), the agent of salvation. Displacing the usual prominence of Christ's sufferings on the Cross, His death and resurrection (mentioned only once in lines 465a–70a), Cynewulf turns the Ascension into the culmination of Christ's salvific mission, the final moment in the drama of the Passion which began on Palm Sunday.

The complex rhetorical and structural interlace so evident in the main section treating the Ascension, the reflecting panels, and the chronological distortion of movement alternating with stasis now yields to transparent moral statement. The completion of Christ's redemptive act in the Ascension recalls for Cynewulf (as it did at the beginning) the Incarnation, that "hither-coming" which is the inverse image of the Ascension. Having both "freed and protected" (*gefreode ond gefreo*þade, 588a) man through His sacrifice, Christ offers man the choice. The passage outlining this choice in a series of antithetical rhyming half lines has received much attention:

> þæt nu monna gehwylc
> cwic þendan her wunað,   geceosan mot
> swa helle hienþu   swa heofones mærþu,
> swa þæt leohte leoht   swa ða laþan niht,
> swa þrymmes þræce   swa þystra wræce,
> swa mid dryhten dream   swa mid deoflum hream,
> swa wite mid wraþum   swa wuldor mid arum,
> swa lif swa deað,   swa him leofre bið
> to gefremmanne,   þenden flæsc ond gæst
> wuniað in worulde.
>
> (589b–98a)

so that now every man while he dwells here alive may choose either the infamy of hell or the glory of heaven, either the light of light or hateful night, either the fulness of majesty or the doom of darkness, either the joy of the Lord or the noise of devils, either torment among foes or glory among the messengers, either life or death, as he prefers to do, while body and soul dwell in the world.

Peter Clemoes comments that here Cynewulf "uses rhythm to create outward pattern. . . . The rhymed pairs of half-lines form the referen-

tial pattern hell/heaven, heaven/hell, heaven/hell, heaven/hell, hell/
heaven, clinched by the concluding, summarizing single half-line *swa
lif swa* deað."[30] Coming in the midst of *Christ II*, the passage strikes
a clarion note that prepares for Cynewulf's closing apocalyptic ruminations. The section also stands out in sharp relief against the rest of
the poem; yet it does not signal a shift in strategy, but represents an
intense distillation of all the patterns throughout. All the antithetical
configurations which precede it find their realization here. The structural principle of conjunction and disjunction now reaches a purity
matched only by the rhyming epilogue of *Elene*. The "thanks without
end" (*þonc butan ende*, 599b) Cynewulf demands be given to the
Trinity are precisely for this choice, that unclouded sense of either/or
which can only obtain in a world where clarity (and freedom and protection) reestablish the covenant of peace. Christ's Ascension, then, and
the process of salvation which it completes, has its formal analogue in
the utter lucidity of this rhetorical device. Cynewulf would not, of
course, phrase the problem in these terms, nor would he perceive any
essential distinction between the theology "behind" his poem and the
style which expresses those notions. However, from a strictly rhetorical
point of view, Christ's Ascension is a climax and a clarification; it pur-
ifies the embodied world, whether that be the world of men or the
world of words.

In the next section (600a–617a) Cynewulf composes a bridge
between the narrative of the Ascension, the highly symbolic passage
just discussed, and his return to a dependence on Gregory's homily. His
themes connect several recurring topics. He expands the enjoinder to
give thanks to God by enumerating the many benefits God has
bestowed on mankind "through the mystery of His manifold powers"
(*þurh monigfealdra mægna geryno*, 603). Chase sees here a division
into "the gifts of both nature and of grace,"[31] the wealth, good weather,
and protection under the sky (*welan ofer widlond, ond weder liþe /
under swegles hleo*, 605a–6a). Cynewulf does focus on all the graces
God has made available, but other items are also important: the significance of mystery and the fulness of power (*æhta sped*, 604b) with
reference to God and man. These have their source once again in
Psalm 23, a crucial document for all Ascensiontide motifs.

The rhyming series of antithetical choices opened by reminding us
that man's salvation arrived with the Incarnation; this related passage
ends with another, though complementary, assertion:

> þæs we ealles sculon
> secgan þonc ond lof   þeodne ussum,
> ond huru þære hælo   þe he us to hyhte forgeaf,
> ða he þa yrmþðu   eft oncyrde
> æt his upstige   þe we ær drugon.

(611b–15b)

For this we all should render thanks and praise to our Prince, and indeed for that salvation which He gave us as a hope, when He again brought an end to the miseries which we suffered before, at His Ascension.

Man's sufferings are substituted for Christ's, the present celebration of our bounty and of the Ascension as a salvific event must contrast with our former woes. Cynewulf understands Christ's mission to redeem mankind as having two temporal poles—the Incarnation and the Ascension. Cynewulf's habitual patterning concentrates his thoughts on those aspects of Christ's life which offer the greatest possibility for dialectical structure; by so doing he strongly underscores the absolute nature of man's options, as they have been effected in the Incarnation and the Ascension, both identified as deliverances. In purely human terms, we perforce see the analogy between Christ's entrance into and exit from the world and our own similar journeys.

With line 618b Cynewulf returns to his Gregorian text, although his additions continue to mark off his poem from Gregory's sermon distinctively. Gregory identifies the Ascension as "the very day that the certificate of our damnation was destroyed, the sentence of our corruption commuted" (*quia deletum est hodierna die chirographum damnationis nostrae, mutata est sententia corruptionis nostrae*).[32] Gregory draws obviously from the Roman legal tradition for his metaphors to describe the theological implications of Christ's ascent; so, too, does Cynewulf, to a point. He writes that the *cwide*, the speech or judgment or decree, was again reversed (618b). But *cwide* in Anglo-Saxon lacks the overtones of a legal document written *in one's own handwriting* that *chirographum* has in Latin (see also Colossians 2:14). And given this semantic difference, Cynewulf does not try to extend the legal metaphor further. Instead he reverts to the images of his own poem and composes another antithetical series. In *Christ II* the *cwide* is a song which has been sung; its reversal now brings peace for souls. Before it had caused sorrow for men (*Cwide eft onhwearf / saulum*

to sibbe, se þe ær sungen wæs / þurh yrne hyge ældum to sorge,
618b–20b). This parallel continues on in the verse from Genesis which
Gregory cites: *quia pulvis es et in pulverem reverteris* ("because you
are dust and to dust you will return," 3:19). Cynewulf's version ampli-
fies the brief biblical comment on mortality and includes a capsule
history of the fall and the last judgment:

> "Ic þec ofer eorðan geworhte,   on þære þu scealt yrmþum lifgan,
> wunian in gewinne   ond wræce dreogan,
> feondum to hroþor   fusleoð galan,
> ond to þære ilcan scealt   eft geweorþan,
> wyrmum aweallen,   þonan wites fyr
> of þære eorðan scealt   eft gesecan."
>
> (621a–26b)

"I made thee from earth, you shall live on it in sufferings, dwell in strife and
endure misery, sing a song of death as a delight for the fiends, and to the
same earth you shall again turn, swarming with worms; thence the fire of
torment you shall again seek from the earth."

The "song" which carried the original message of damnation produces a "death song" sung for the fiends. By contrast we can recall the
words of the wise men singing prophecies of the coming Savior. The
Cynewulfian passage also picks up the idea of turning and movement
which is explicit in the biblical verse, and which Gregory chooses to
ignore: the *cwide* is "turned round," man will "turn to" earth and then
"seek" the fire of torment. In the poem as a whole, and in the next
section, Cynewulf contemplates the concept of movement itself, for his
poem has as its principal action a great and decisive movement—the
Ascension. These interconnected ideas and motifs play no part in the
exegetical wit of Gregory's homily.

For Cynewulf the proleptic vision of judgment raises the memory
of redemption. At this point he inserts a short introduction to his own
reworking of Gregory's explication of the bird figure from Job. Cynewulf reminds us that the Incarnation and the Ascension represent two
aspects of the same movement; the coming down and the rising up
form the completed arc which constitutes salvation. As we have seen,
he rarely conceives of the Ascension without associating Christ's birth
and Second Coming with it. And it is the polarity of this progression

that Cynewulf here stresses; in the Incarnation Christ made our miseries easier to endure (627a–29a); in His Ascension He gave help to us in our wretchedness (629b–32b).

The sequence of interpretations of Job 28:7 is complicated and perhaps unrecoverable; but, in one way or another, both Gregory and Cynewulf take the text to be a reference to salvation. The Vulgate reads *Semitam ignoravit avis*, usually translated from the Hebrew as "the bird does not know the path." Gregory may be misinterpreting the biblical phrase, for he renders the sentence: "It [i.e., Judea, the Jews] does not know the path of the bird." Gregory goes on to interpret the bird as the Lord, the path as His Ascension, and, metaphorically, the "lightening" of our flesh which occurred at that time *(Pro hac ipsa namque carnis nostrae sublevatione per figuram beatus Job Dominum avem vocat).*[33] Cynewulf may have recognized Gregory's presumed error, for he does not follow his teacher closely. While he keeps the allusion to the ignorant Jews (637a–38b), he "simplifies" the subtle theological pun Gregory provides. Furthermore, Cynewulf does not incorporate the quotation from Job specifically into *Christ II;* he only refers to Job as having composed a "song" in which Christ is surnamed a "bird" (633a–38b). The Jews were unable to comprehend the bird's meaning and thus they become the bird's foes, from whose "dark wit" and "hearts of stone" Christ must fly:

> Wæs þæs fugles flyht   feondum on eorþan
> dyrne ond degol,   þam þe deorc gewit
> hæfdon on hreþre,   heortan stænne.
>   (639a–41b)

The concept closely resembles the situation of the Jews in *Elene,* who refuse to accept Christ's divinity.

Once more Cynewulf creates a double perspective as he makes the bird's flight both up to heaven and down to earth, representing both Ascension and Incarnation. Cynewulf brings his sense of structural contrast to bear on a text which Gregory has possibly confused. Throughout the poem he repeats the associations and contrasts of movement implicit in the Incarnation and Ascension. Working this antithesis into the rhetoric and diction, he gives us another example of his classic compositional method. Failure to note both this set of mind and habit of structuring has led critics to serious misinterpretations. By treating the section which includes the famous "gifts of men" passage out of context, critics have frequently distorted its meaning. We must quote the complete division to see Cynewulf's technique properly and to understand what he intends:

> Noldan hi þa torhtan   tacen oncnawan
> þe him beforan fremede   freobearn godes,
> monig mislicu,   geond middangeard.
> Swa se fæla fugel   flyges cunnode;
> hwilum engla eard   up gesohte,
> modig meahtum strang,   þone maran ham,
> hwilum he to eorþan   eft gestylde,
> þurh gæstes giefe   grundsceat sohte,
> wende to worulde.   Bi þon se witga song:
> "He wæs upp hafen   engla fæðmum
> in his þa miclan   meahta spede,
> heah ond halig,   ofer heofona þrym."
>   Ne meahtan þa þæs fugles   flyht gecnawan
> þe þæs upstiges   ondsæc fremedon,
> ond þæt ne gelyfdon,   þætte liffruma
> in monnes hiw   ofer mægna þrym,
> halig from hrusan,   ahafen wurde.
> Ða us geweorðade   se þas world gescop,
> godes gæstsunu,   ond us giefe sealde,
> uppe mid englum   ece staþelas,
> ond eac monigfealde   modes snyttru
> seow ond sette   geond sefan monna.
> Sumum wordlaþe   wise sendeð
> on his modes gemynd   þurh his muþes gæst,
> æðele ondgiet.   Se mæg eal fela
> singan ond secgan   þam bið snyttru cræft
> bifolen on ferðe.   Sum mæg fingrum wel
> hlude fore hæleþum   hearpan stirgan,
> gleobeam gretan.   Sum mæg godcunde
> reccan rhyte æ.   Sum mæg ryne tungla
> secgan, side gesceaft.   Sum mæg searolice
> wordcwide writan.   Sumum wiges sped
> giefeð æt guþe,   þonne gargetrum
> ofer scildhreadan   sceotend sendað,
> flacor flangeweorc.   Sum mæg fromlice
> ofer sealtne sæ   sundwudu drifan,
> hreran holmþræce.   Sum mæg heanne beam
> stælgne gestigan.   Sum mæg styled sweord,
> wæpen gewyrcan.   Sum con wonga bigong,

wegas widgielle.   Swa se waldend us,
godbearn on grundum,   his giefe bryttað.
Nyle he ængum anum   ealle gesyllan
gæstes snyttru,   þy læs him gielp sceþþe
þurh his anes cræft   ofer oþre forð.

(642a–85b)

They did not want to recognize the bright tokens which the noble Son of God
wrought before them, many and various, throughout the world. So the
beloved bird tried flight; sometimes the home of the angels he sought up
above, undaunted, strong in might, the glorious home; sometimes he again
sank to the earth, by the grace of the spirit, sought the face of the earth,
turned to the world. Of that the prophet sang, "He was caught up into the
bosoms of the angels in His great fulness of power, high and holy above the
glory of the heavens." Nor could they know the flight of the bird, those who
denied the Ascension, and did not believe that the Author of Life had been
raised up in the form of a man above the glory of hosts, holy from the earth.
Then the One who created the world, God's spiritual Son, honored us and
gave us gifts, on high with the angels, eternal dwellings, and also manifold
wisdoms of mind He sowed and planted throughout the breasts of men. To
one wise eloquence He sends into the thought of his mind by the spirit of his
mouth, noble understanding. He can very many things sing and say; to him
is the excellence of wisdom entrusted to his spirit. One may play the harp
well with his fingers, loudly before heroes, sweep the strings. One may make
known the divine, right law. One may reveal the secrets of the stars, the vast
creation. One may skillfully write in word-speech. To one victory of war is
given in battle, when a shower of darts a bowman sends over his shield, flying
arrows. One may drive the ship bravely over the salt sea, stir the raging water.
One may climb the steep, high tree. One may a tempered sword, a weapon
make. One knows the sweep of plains, the far-reaching paths. Thus the Lord,
the Son of God on earth, grants us His gifts. He will not give all spiritual
wisdom to anyone, lest pride harm him, raised by his own power above
others.

Again each part of this double panel begins with the familiar repetition: *Noldan hi þa torhtan tacen oncnawan* and *Ne meahtan þa
þæs fugles flyht gecnawan.* Christ's many miracles recall the *tacna
fela* He revealed before the disciples in *wordgerynum* before His
Ascension; they also parallel the bird's flight, which here stands for the
Ascension, above the glory of the hosts. But Cynewulf is more concerned with the paradox of Christ's dual nature; and he concentrates
in the first section on the bird's flight up and down, and in the second
section on both earth and heaven (*in monnes hiw, halig from hrusan*

versus *ofer mægna þrym* and *ahafan wurde*). Verbal parallels are important too: *hwilum* introduces each of the bird's antithetical flights, and *sumum* introduces each of the gifts—spiritual and intellectual versus physical—in the long list of men's talents. In the first section Cynewulf twice underscores Christ's fulness of strength (*modig meahtum strang* and *in his þa miclan meahta spede*), but in the contrasting second section, the "gifts of men" are definitely individual and limited. By means of these rhetorical parallels, the spiritual gifts are made to correspond to Christ's Ascension, and the physical gifts to Christ's descent into the world at His Incarnation. Each passage ends with a similar note: Christ in His Ascension manifests His fulness of power (651a–54b), but to no man is given all the spirit's powers, lest he become proud in his own strength and injure himself trying to *rise* above others (683a–85b).

Cook finds the immediate source for this thought in another homily by Gregory and he quotes the relevant phrase: *Non enim uni dantur omnia, ne in superbiam elatus cadat* ("For all things are not given to one man, lest he, puffed up in pride, should fall").[34] The tradition of the "gifts of men" is an ancient classical and Christian one; several biblical verses form the background for this topos in Anglo-Saxon and other medieval literatures.[35] Gregory relies mainly on I Corinthians 12:8–10:

For to one is given by the Spirit the word of wisdom; to another the word of knowledge by the same Spirit; to another faith by the same spirit; to another the gifts of healing by the same Spirit; to another the working of miracles; to another prophecy; to another discerning of spirits; to another divers kinds of tongues; to another the interpretation of tongues.

Gregory also quotes Psalm 67:19 in this context, and Ephesians 4:8, which paraphrases this psalm, must also be cited: "Wherefore he saith, When he ascended upon high, he led captivity captive, and gave gifts to men." The association of the Ascension with the giving of gifts to men stems from these biblical references, but Cynewulf's elaboration of the topos depends more on the later tradition than on either the Bible or Gregory's sermon. Cross notes a sermon by the ninth-century Haymo of Auxerre that separates each of man's talents into two categories, the spiritual and the physical.[36] While there is thus precedent for a division of gifts, Cynewulf's own listing must be interpreted in context. Earlier critics of Old English literature liked to comment on the splendid picture of Anglo-Saxon life Cynewulf here paints; later critics, chafing at this literalism, believed that the list demands a figurative explanation. The portrait of Anglo-Saxon life is, of course, realistic and interesting; the question remains whether it has a metaphorical reality beyond its surface import. The most extensive claim for a figurative reading comes from Oliver Grosz: he quotes only a part of the whole series, the gifts of making war, and states that they have "a spiritual meaning . . . equivalent to the warfaring Christian." He goes on to say that "the figurative sense of this warrior becomes clear later when Cynewulf elaborates, by an extended metaphor, how the Christian must defend himself against the temptations of the devil" (766-71).[37]

To arrive at this explanation is to ignore the basic structure and presentation of the complete division. The first series of gifts does indeed pertain to the spirit, the mind, and their capacity to penetrate mystery, to speak, to create, and to interpret. They are greater powers than the purely physical occupations, different both in kind and degree. In the use of these powers man approaches the power expressed in the act of the Ascension. But the physical gifts do not require a metaphorical interpretation to make them acceptable. Grosz's error is twofold: first, he "edits" the catalog of manual gifts to encompass only those associated with warfaring (as this is the single category which lends itself easily to figurative analysis); second, he takes the list out of context. Man's physical endowments, which correspond in the rhetorical structure to Christ's *descent* to earth, are various, limited, and of the earth. This is likewise true of the spiritual gifts to a certain extent, but being of the mind and spirit they more nearly approximate a divine power. The individual physical talents are explicitly contrasted with Christ's fulness of powers, which is all strength united into one majority. Unity and division, boundlessness and limitation, the universal and the individual, and the way these relate to both Christ's dual nature and man's spiritual potential are the topics which emerge from a critical examination of this sequence. Grosz's error stems from a misperception about "discontinuous form."[38] Perceiving quite correctly that all themes and images in *Christ II* are not developed logically and continuously, Grosz insists that a figurative unity must be superimposed in order to justify the defects of this discontinuity. In fact, the opposite is true: the discontinuous forms require a more intense analysis of each section, from which a final conception of structure and movement emerges. The long set piece on Job's bird and the "gifts of men" provides just such an example.

Cynewulf demonstrates his awareness of the figural or allegorical mode in the verse paragraph which follows (686a–711b). But first he draws a summarizing conclusion to the "gifts of men." He does so by making precisely the same distinctions he has delineated throughout; now the entire catalog of gifts becomes terrestial awards, as he describes God honoring the earth's offspring with liberal gifts (*geofum unhneawum,* / *cyning alwihta, cræftum weorðaþ* / *eorþan tuddor,* 686b–88a) and then heaven's "blessed" with glory (*swylce eadgum blæd* / *seleð on swegle,* 688b–89a). All this quite transforms Gregory's simple "so he gave gifts to men" *(Dedit ergo dona hominibus).*[39]

Gregory's homily does imply that the gifts of men are a glorification, for his next sentence, a quotation from Habacuc, begins with "Habacuc *also* says about the glory of His Ascension" *(De hac Ascensionis ejus gloria etiam Habacuc ait).*[40] Cynewulf has already anticipated the idea of glory in the preceding section. But of greater interest are the allegorical identifications each makes of Habacuc's sun and moon. The Latin text, as Gregory presents it, reads: *Elevatus est sol, et luna stetit in ordine suo* ("the sun was raised up, and the moon stood in its course"). Cynewulf's reference to Habacuc fuses the two verbs in Gregory's quotation; he says that both "holy gems were raised up" (*þæt ahæfen wæren halge gimmas,* 692). This technique of careful distinction, redefinition, and merging occurs frequently in *Christ II* and is the source of much adverse criticism. The gifts of men are divided into spiritual and physical; then they merge to represent the earthly as opposed to the heavenly rewards (although the spiritual talents have always been analogous to heavenly gifts). Gregory assigns the sun and the moon different actions, but Cynewulf fuses their symbolic significance: both come to stand for God Himself (695b) and, by extension, the glory of Christ's Ascension through the verbal action *(ahæfen wurde).* Just prior to this portion Cynewulf also adds a detail not found in Gregory, namely, that God "raises" eternal peace between angels and men (*sibbe ræreþ* / *ece to ealdre engla ond monna,* 689b–90b).

Once he has blended the two symbols of sun and moon into one figure, Cynewulf then returns to Gregory's explicit distinction; God becomes the "true brightness of the sun" (*se soðfæsta sunnan leoma,* 696) and the moon shines over the earth like the church (698a–701b). But a further and similar confusion ensues. Gregory writes that *before (quousque)* the Lord's Ascension the church feared the world's adversities; *after (at postquam)* the Ascension, however, the church was strengthened and preached openly.[41] Again Cynewulf seems to have fused these two ideas; his is obviously a meditative and not a logical

habit of mind. He dwells on the *adversa* that the church suffers and
mixes points of temporal reference until a purely logical restatement
becomes impossible: both the persecution of God's faithful by heathen
shepherds and the glory of His servants in the church take place after
the Ascension. All Gregory's essential points are present—the persecution and the eventual glory stemming from Christ's Ascension. However, Cynewulf may have been puzzled by Gregory's assertion that the
church suffered trials and tribulations before the Ascension (the church
had hardly come into being by that time) and so muddied his explanation accordingly. Or, he may be examining post-Ascension history
from another perspective. The history of God's church requires a grasp
of the idea that as time progresses in history, the eternal is paradoxically always present in it. Perhaps Cynewulf here "spiritualizes"
Gregory's purely historical account of the Ascension and its importance
for the church. Cynewulf may be suggesting that after the Ascension
the church came into existence and has (demonstrably) suffered the
ravages of heathens, yet nevertheless God's glory has prevailed through
the spiritual grace following this central event.[42] What does come
through is another example of Cynewulf's mode of thought. He does
not make the same sharp and rational distinctions as Gregory; on the
contrary, he perceives both similarities and dissimilarities in the various
figural equations Gregory discusses. There is a tendency for Cynewulf's images and symbols to fuse, and then to reform in new ways
which demand a corresponding transformation of our critical perspectives. This merging and reshaping is a poetic practice which develops
from his ingrained analogical way of thinking.

Behind the intricate pattern of descent and ascent in *Christ II*, a
pattern implicit but undeveloped in Gregory's homily, stands the text
from Solomon which both authors treat in varying detail, though
Cynewulf's additions are the more numerous and more in keeping
with the general pattern: "Behold, He comes leaping upon the moun-
tains and springing across the hills" (Canticle of Canticles 2:8). As
Gregory explains, these "leaps" accomplished man's redemption.
Cynewulf incorporates the idea of the redemption into his version of
the biblical passage; he is already in the process of explaining and
imagining while offering the text to be commented upon:

> "Cuð þæt geweorðeð,   þætte cyning engla,
> meotud meahtum swið,   munt gestylleð,
> gehleapeð hea dune,   hyllas ond cnollas

> bewri∂ mid his wuldre,   woruld alyse∂,
> ealle eor∂buend,   þurh þone æþelan styll."
>   (715a–19b)

"It will be made known that the King of Angels, the Lord strong in might, shall go up the mountain, leap upon the high dunes, He will garb the hills and the peaks with His glory and will redeem the world, all earth-dwellers by that noble leap."

Christ is again the "Lord strong in powers" and the "noble leap" is an archetypal symbol of the entire redemptive act which is then broken down into its component "leaps," the individual actions that together comprise the whole. Cynewulf has six leaps instead of Gregory's five— he adds a relatively long allusion to the descent into hell—but this minor factual alteration should not obscure Cynewulf's quite different descriptive and symbolic processes. In this well-known portion Cyne- wulf characteristically again fuses distinct ideas: first he divides Christ's noble and redemptive leap into six separate leaps, and then he makes the sixth the Ascension, a part as well as an analogue of the overriding symbol. Cynewulf, in fact, makes little of Gregory's terse distinction between the various leaps. Each is part of the whole: the Ascension holds the highest rank and also symbolizes that whole.

Cynewulf works into his version a sense of correspondence and con- trast; Gregory lists the events in a deliberately plain narrative mode: "He came from heaven into the womb; from the womb He came into the manger . . ." *(De coelo venit in uterum, de utero venit in praesepe . . .)*.[43] Gregory's repetition of *venit* is nearly matched by Cynewulf's thrice repeated *astag* (720b, 727b, 737b); he uses this verb to depict Christ's action in the Incarnation, the Crucifixion, and the Ascension. The word itself in Old English means both ascend and descend. Semantically, then, these actions are equivalent: descent at the Incar- nation is the *same* leap as the rising at the Ascension. Cynewulf exploits a fortunate paradox in the language to contain and express a paradox- ical idea.

He especially emphasizes Christ's dual nature. Twice Cynewulf calls him a "child" *(bearn,* 724a; *cild,* 725a), juxtaposing this appellation directly with the "glory of all glories" *(ealra þrymma þrym,* 726a). Certain purely theological issues also concern Cynewulf. Christ's "rush" when He "arose" on the Cross *(rodorcyninges ræs, þa he on rode astag,* 727), becomes an action of the Trinity, the Father and the

Comforting Spirit (*fæder, frofre gæst*, 728a). In addition we find Cynewulf's oft-repeated pun on *rodor* and *rode*, heaven and cross.[44] The swaddling clothes binding the Christ child (*claþum bewunden*, 725b) counterbalance the many kinds of fetters with which Christ binds the devil in His Harrowing of Hell (732b, 733b, 735, 736a). But the joy befitting the redemption Cynewulf reserves for the sixth leap— the Ascension—and so equates this leap with the encompassing symbol of the one noble and redeeming leap. Christ's leap in the Ascension becomes a "sport," a "joyous play" (*hyhtplega*, 737a; *plega*, 743b). The angelic spectators (*engla þreat*, 738b) at Christ's game are "happy with laughter" (*hleahtre bliþe*, 739b), "overcome with joys" (*wynnum geworden*, 740a), for the Ascension finally is an "eternal delight" (*ece gefea*, 743a). The athleticism inherent in Solomon's phrase Cynewulf develops on both a literal and a metaphorical level. Cynewulf perceives more complex patterns than Gregory, who outlines a basic scheme and passes on. For the Old English poet, Solomon belongs to the class of prophets, of "men wise in songs" (*giedda gearosnottor*, 713a) and in "spirit-runes" (*gæstgerynum*, 713b); he is like all keepers of the word. Cynewulf's extensive schematic and metaphorical alterations indicate a totally different sensibility. Where Gregory perceives a simple rational scheme in Solomon's words, Cynewulf discovers analogies that generate a series of interrelations, both poetical and complete.

The "gifts of men" and "Christ's leaps" sections Cynewulf treats as formal structures set off from their immediate contexts; each contains an appropriate figural interpretation, and a moral exposition follows. A recent essay on *Christ II* is aptly subtitled "Man's Imitation of the Ascension"; indeed, in the lines following "Christ's leaps," Cynewulf expressly calls on man to imitate Christ: as He "sprang in leaps" (*hlypum stylde*, 745b), so all "men should spring in leaps in the thoughts of their hearts, from strength to strength" (*Swa we men sculon / heortan gehygdum hlypum styllan / of mægne in mægen*, 746b–48a). Gregory proffers the general suggestion that we should follow Christ in our hearts, but Cynewulf pursues the figure even one step further: not only through thoughts, but also through good works may we *ascend* to the highest roof (*þæt we to þam hyhstan hrofe gestigan / halgum weorcum*, 749a–50a); then he returns to the necessity of a faith in salvation so that the Christ child (a term reintroducing the Christ of the Incarnation) may *ascend* on high with our bodies (*þæt þæt hælobearn heonan up stige / mid usse lichoman*, 754a–55a). Man's imitation of Christ's Ascension is manifold and embraces

all the activities—physical and spiritual, external and internal—which
he can perform. Cynewulf's dictum that man model his life on Christ's
must not be restricted solely to figural interpretations of texts. Grosz
writes: "the inability or unwillingness to understand figurative meanings of signs becomes associated with the state of the damned."[45]
Cynewulf insists only that man think and act rightly, according to the
truth, as Gregory has it, though Cynewulf does not choose to translate
this particular term. And the truth revealed in words exists on a con-
tinuum of meaning, extending from literal to figurative. Grosz's error
is symptomatic of those who seek with too much speed and too little
scope for a meaning, and so slight the process of thought which creates
that meaning.

The conclusions to both Gregory's homily and Cynewulf's poem are
explicitly moral and apocalyptic; but they are so in different ways.
Gregory admonishes us to "flee from earthly desires" *(Desideria ter-
rena fugiamus)* because the peace of Christ's Ascension will turn to the
terror of judgment, His gentleness to severity *(qui placidus ascendit
terribilis redebit, et quidquid nobis cum mansuetudine praecepit hoc
a nobis cum districtione exiget).*[46] Gregory places all responsibility on
the individual Christian. Cynewulf, while he certainly does not deny
a burden for each man, sketches the scene otherwise. He too warns
that we must "despise vain desires and the wounds of sin" *(Forþon we
a sculon idle lustas, / synwunde forseon,* 756a–57a), but Cynewulf
dramatizes the psychological and moral struggle as a battle between
attacking demons and a protecting God. The background of this alteration is clear; it derives from the Antonian tradition of the eremetical
saint beset by fiends in the desert. The motif is common in Old English
and Anglo-Latin literature, the most pertinent examples being Felix of
Crowland's *Vita Sancti Guthlacii* and the poem, *Guthlac A.*[47] Of
interest for *Christ II*, however, are the metaphors which reemerge in
this section. Cynewulf turns repeatedly to the comforting image that
God shields the good Christian who keeps watch against the devil's
arrows (761a, 767, 771–72a, 775a, 781b). These incremental repetitions
begin to resemble a refrain and a prayer, an urgent request from an
anxious sinner. Gregory's majestical exhortation is replaced by a much
more tremulous voice, and this in turn prepares for the runic signature
and epilogue shortly to follow. As Christ chose the protection of Mary
to come into the world *(mundheals geceas,* 446b), so the sinner can
choose the protection of God to take him safely out of this perilous
world (771b–78b). And the covenant of peace which Christ's Ascension

reestablishes between angels and men (583b–85b, 689b–90b) comes to
man's aid in this battle, for God sends His messengers *(aras)* from on
high to shield us against the fiend's grievous arrow flights (759b-62a).
These *aras* bring a protection greater than the simple military image
implies; throughout the poem the *aras* have been heralds of the Word,
proclaimers of the fact of salvation. Their presence as shields against
the demons' arrows directs us to all the words found in books, where
Cynewulf believes the ultimate safeguard lies.

Cynewulf opens the final section on the vision of the Last Judgment
with just such a reminder of the protection books offer. Recapitulating
in theme and structure the movement of the whole poem, this last seg-
ment begins with another description of the Incarnation:

> Us secgað bec
> hu æt ærestan   eadmod astag
> in middangeard   mægna goldhord,
> in fæmnan fæðm   freobearn godes,
> halig of heahþu.
> (785b-89a)

Books tell us how at the beginning the Goldhoard of Hosts, God's glorious
Son, holy from on high, humbly came down into the world, into the Virgin's
womb.

It ends with a final reference to the Ascension:

> Utan us to þære hyðe   hyht staþelian,
> ða us gerymde   rodera waldend,
> halge on heahþu,   þa he heofonum astag.
> (864a-66b)

Let us fix our hope to that port, which the Ruler of the skies prepared for us,
holy on high, when He ascended into heaven.

The two passages obviously echo each other and together they form an
envelope pattern: Incarnation and Ascension enclose the Last Judgment. With such a structuring of history and theology Cynewulf
implies a faith in the efficacy of salvation that overshadows his fear of
damnation. Our shield is the book with its account of Christ's redeem-

ing power. But Cynewulf subtly, yet openly, points out that man must win the redemption through his own choice, just as Christ "chose" the "protection" of Mary. In a rhyming antithesis which summons the reader back to the *swa lif swa deað* section following the Harrowing of Hell (591a–98a), Cynewulf presents the common case: *Is þam dome neah / þæt we gelice sceolon leanum hleotan, / swa we wide-feorh weorcum hlodun* ("The Judgment is near when we will obtain rewards according to the works we have laid up for a long time," 782b–84b): *leanum hleotan / weorcum hlodun,* "rewards allotted / works laid up."

Cynewulf's own trepidation in envisioning the fire of judgment comes precisely because he believes he has not chosen the protection of the word nor held in reckoning what his Savior bade him in books (*þe ic ne heold teala þæt me hælend min / on bocum bibead,* 792a–93a). His runic signature in *Christ II* thus becomes a self-imposed penance, a function none of the other signatures serves. Because of his dereliction, Cynewulf feels he "must" look on terror, on the punishment of sin (*Ic þæs brogan sceal / geseon synwræce,* 793b–94a). He projects his name into his imaginative vision of judgment to experience that apocalypse forcefully so he can atone for his sins. The judgment in *Christ II* starts with an indirect report of God's words: "Then *CEN* will quake, will hear the King pronounce" (*þonne · ᚳ · cwacað, gehyreð cyning mæðlan,* 797). For not having obeyed God's previous "words," Cynewulf now does penance by encasing his name in God's angry words spoken at the day of reckoning. This is a striking participation in the terror of judgment on Cynewulf's part. When broken into runes, his name itself automatically evokes associations with the end of the world in a Christian context: need, joy, floods, wealth:

> þonne · ᚳ · cwacað,   gehyreð cyning mæðlan,
> rodera rhytend,   sprecan reþe word
> þam þe him ær in worulde   wace hyrdon,
> þendan · ᚹ · ond ᚢ·   yþast meahtan
> frofre findan.   þær sceal forht monig
> on þam wongstede   werig bidan
> hwæt him æfter dædum   deman wille
> wraþra wita.   Biþ se · ᚦ · scæcen
> eorþan frætwa.   · ᚾ · wæs longe
> · ᛁ · flodum bilocen,   lifwynna dæl,
> · ᚠ · on foldan.   þonne frætwe sculon
> byrnan on bæle;   blac rasetteð

recen reada leg,   reþe scriþeð
geond woruld wide.   Wongas hreosað,
burgstede berstað.   Brond bið on tyhte,
æleð ealdgestreon   unmurnlice,
gæsta gifrast,   þæt geo guman heoldan,
þenden him on eorþan   onmedla wæs.

(797a–814b)

Then *cen* will tremble, will hear the king pronounce, the ruler of the heavens speak angry words to those who had been feeble in obeying him in this world, while *yr* and *nyd* could find solace most easily. In that place many a one, terrified, shall await wearily what harsh penalties he will adjudge him in consequence of his deeds. The joy *(wynn)* of earthly treasures will have passed away. Our *(ur)* portion of life's delights will long have been encompassed by the water's floods *(lagu)*, our wealth *(feoh)* in the world.[48]

Dolores Frese finds that Cynewulf departs from his usual pattern in this runic signature. She holds, quite rightly, that the signatures in *The Fates of the Apostles, Juliana,* and *Elene* "seem to provide a kind of glossary of major ideas and images in each work and appear to be elaborate verbal networks that link by name the fact of the poet to the fact of the preceding poem."[49] But she remarks that "nowhere do the ideas and images that vivify this signature section invoke the prior poetry that deals with the central Ascension event of *Christ II*."[50] Since Frese restricts herself to corresponding images (and ideas contained in those images), she misses the interesting ways Cynewulf has joined his signature to the poem which precedes it. He matches the vision of the Ascension with its complex perspectives and chronological shifts against the vision of judgment with its simple pronouncement and temporal finality; he replaces the watchers at the Ascension, earthly and heavenly, who continually "stare" at the miraculous event, with himself who "must look" on the terror of judgment by being *in* the vision itself; and he reminds sinners that the laughter and joy of the hosts suitable for the Ascension become God's anger (790b, 798b, 804a) and man's terror at the judgment (793b, 801b). Cynewulf's technique in *Christ II* does not exactly resemble his handling of the signatures in his other poems; in this work, he joins signature to poem through a series of structural contrasts, not through imagistic echoes.

Cynewulf moves on from his self-imposed penitential vision with a renewed commitment to take up his task as a keeper of the word:

Forþon ic leofra gehwone læran wille / þæt he ne agæle gæstes þearfe ("Therefore I want to teach every loved one that he not neglect the needs of the spirit," 815a–16b). He turns from his entirely personal dread of judgment to a concern for the common doom. This two-fold interest leads to a second portrait of judgment, reminiscent of the double epilogue in *The Fates*. The verbal echoes are by no means as exact as in that poem, but the structural pattern is the same: each section has a preparatory allusion to the judgment and then the full horror erupts when God meets the assembled (*on gemot læded,* 795b; *on gemot cymeð,* 832b) who must receive their awards before his countenance (*fore onsyne eces deman,* 796 and 836). An angry fire-bath burns the world and fitting sentences are meted out. In these looser double panels Cynewulf does not employ the device of ironic contrast within parallel passages; that contrast only exists while time and eternity are discrete modes. With the coming of judgment, God brings such a distinction to a close and the irony that attaches to it disappears in the apocalyptic conclusion. Man's only hope, as Cynewulf twice states with a reference back to the poem's first line, is to "earnestly ponder" (*georne biþencan,* 821b, 849b) both the "spirit's beauty" (*gæstes wlite,* 848a) and God's mercy proclaimed by the angel's words (822a–23b).

A conventional image in Gregory's homily becomes an intricate and extended simile at the very end of *Christ II*. Gregory says simply "now fasten the anchor of your hope in the eternal homeland" (*jam tamen spei vestrae anchoram in aeternam patriam figite*).[51] Cynewulf transforms this metaphorical injunction into a sixteen-line epic simile, comparing man's life to a windy and difficult sea journey with heaven as its port. But the kennings for the ships man can use on this voyage, the "seahorses" and "wavemares" (*sundhengestas,* 862b; *yðmearas,* 863a) have yet another figural meaning. They are the gifts of grace Christ has given mankind (866) through His Ascension (865a–66b); they are manifold, secure, but they must be realized (*þæt we oncnawan magun,* 861a). This phrase directly recalls the reiterated lines describing the Jews who would not so recognize Christ as the bird and what His ascent and descent meant as redemptive figures. Cynewulf begins and ends his poem with an enjoinder to penetrate the mystery and acknowledge the signs. *Christ II* is another parable or "word-rune" requiring such understanding.

Cynewulf's other poems have much sharper structural outlines than *Christ II*. *The Fates of the Apostles* divides neatly into narrative and rhetorical frames. In his two hagiographical poems, *Juliana* and *Elene*,

Cynewulf also imposes tight schematic patterns on the narratives. But *Christ II* lacks this clarity of structure, perhaps because the movement of homiletic discourse does not lend itself to the set and dramatic oppositions of hagiography. However, the underlying structural principles in *Christ II* recur in the architecture of his other poems. Here various facets of ideas replace narrative characters, and Cynewulf juxtaposes them, probing their interrelations in a manner similar to the "panel" construction of all his works. The sense of merging, splitting, remerging, shift in direction, and return in *Christ II* is a formal embodiment of the metaphysical and theological truths inherent in the Incarnation, the Ascension, and the Last Judgment; for these are the three great events where time and eternity merge, where movement and stasis join. The diverse segments of *Christ II* imitate in their structure the ideas they express.

CHAPTER 4

Juliana

I *Source*

MEDIEVAL Christians found the legend of Saint Juliana particularly appealing. Early versions of her martyrdom exist in Greek and Latin; vernacular redactions appear in later Latin, Middle English, Middle High German, Old French, and Middle Irish.[1] Cynewulf's Anglo-Saxon poem is, however, the earliest example in a medieval European language. Juliana's death occurred on February 16 at Nicomedia sometime between 305 and 311 A.D. She was beheaded by the Prefect Eleusius during Diocletian's persecution of Christians and the events of her life were probably recorded in the reign of Constantine. This most ancient narrative has not survived, although many relatively early Latin manuscripts do contain a life of Juliana. The great editor of saints' lives, Jean Bolland, printed an edition made from a collation of eleven such manuscripts, which he called *Acta auctore anonymo (The Acts [of Saint Juliana] by an anonymous author).*[2] If not the source, this text is commonly considered the closest surviving analogue to Cynewulf's poem. Rosemary Woolf holds that "none of the surviving texts represents that followed by Cynewulf,"[3] but Bolland's composite version must still be used (if carefully) for any comparative purposes.

Bede's *Martyrology,* or at least the one ascribed to Bede, contains an epitome of Juliana's life, which parallels the events chronicled in both the *Acta* and Cynewulf's poem; and S. T. R. O. d'Ardenne believes that "Bede had access to a detailed LATIN version of the life of St. Juliana, one MS. of which was probably the principal source used by Cynewulf."[4] There are crucial differences between the *Acta* printed by Bolland and Cynewulf's work. In discussing these variations, critics must be extremely cautious regarding any "originality" these differences may imply. What appears to be a striking change on Cynewulf's part may only be an existing variant in the actual source, though it could well be Cynewulf's addition, too. Until the exact source is identified, the question will remain in doubt.

II *Criticism*

Juliana shares with *The Fates of the Apostles* the distinction of being judged one of Cynewulf's least successful poems. As Stanley Greenfield writes in his influential history of Old English literature, "Cynewulf's treatment of his material [in *Juliana*] deserves respect, if not admiration."[5] Woolf, the poem's most recent editor, finds the story itself "an uncomfortable mixture of the didactic and the spectacular";[6] and she holds a severe opinion of Cynewulf's poem: "competent in itself, though lacking the poetic mastery of the *Elene* or *Christ*, *Juliana* brings Old English poetry into a blind alley."[7] *The Fates of the Apostles* and *Juliana* are saints' lives in the most general sense; but *The Fates* belongs to the subcategory of the historical martyrology, while *Juliana* is a "passion"—a story retelling a saint's martyrdom.[8] Woolf notes concerning *The Fates:* "With such limited compass the brief characterisation of the apostles as heroic and loyal thegns and their persecutors as devil-inspired heathens seems exceptionally mechanical."[9] But *Juliana* is a long narrative poem (731 extant lines) and this extended compass gives both the author of the Latin life and Cynewulf ample opportunity to create "characters" in a series of dramatic actions. Consequently, the whole history of criticism of medieval hagiography has imposed the formulations and expectations of a mimetic literature that puts a high value on verisimilitude. Modern critics have frequently rejected as absurd, even revolting, the extremes of medieval saints' lives. The comments of William Strunk, an earlier editor, epitomize these mimetic criteria: "Nowhere in the *Juliana* is there any real evidence that the author knew more of the acts and speech of men and women than what he had read in books. Little worse could be said of any poem introducing human figures."[10]

There have been attempts to rehabilitate the genre of the saint's life, and Woolf herself has written intelligently on some of the larger changes in perspective required to comprehend and appreciate this now discarded religious and literary genre:

The saint's life is a highly conventional form, and it must never be measured by the criteria which would be relevant to a modern biography. We should no more look to it for historical or psychological truth than we would to a medieval romance. In origins it is part panegyric, part epic, part romance, part sermon and historical fact dissolves within the conventions of these forms.

Woolf continues with examples illustrating the oft-mentioned distinction in styles which Bede clearly makes between the methods of history and hagiography.[11]

Yet even a dedicated Bollandist, Hippolyte Delehaye, finds it necessary to apologize for hagiography. The crudities of hagiography are the inevitable results of a homiletic literature intended for the highly uneducated.[12] More sophisticated theoretical attempts to explore the rationale of hagiography have appeared very recently, one of the most significant being James W. Earl's exploration of the relation between a figural mode of thought and an "iconographic style" in the genre: Earl expands the accepted notion that all saints have the same existence and reality, each individual saint being simply a figure of "saintliness." An anonymous monk of Whitby expresses this idea succinctly in his *Life of Gregory the Great:* "So let no one be disturbed even if these miracles were performed by any other of the saints, since the holy Apostle, through the mystery of the limbs of a single body, which he compares to the living experience of the saints, concludes that we are all 'members of one another.' "[13] Such is the communion of saints.

Earl argues that the saint's life is "an attempt to draw *moralia* [the third of the four levels in biblical exegesis] into the typological structures of sacred history," resulting in a "tendency toward generalization and deindividualization in hagiographic narrative."[14] A moralizing direction thus leads logically to a particular stylistic realization, which Earl labels "iconographic," i.e., like an icon: it is frontal, lacking in shadows, conventional, unrealistic; it reaches toward heaven by renouncing worldly realism; it is concerned with the communion of saints rather than the unique and the individual.[15] The various defences made of hagiography stand up well as explanations for the genre. But the criticism of specific Old English poems most frequently turns to generic arguments for support. Consequently, what begins as an attempt to rescue *Juliana* from critical oblivion ends as a defense of hagiography and yet another apology for the individual work. Joseph Wittig, for example, gives us a detailed "figural" interpretation of *Juliana;* however, he still finds it necessary to add a disclaimer: "But in the last analysis, acknowledging that *Juliana* is consistently shaped by figural and rhetorical design will not promote the poem to the ranks

of the greatest Old English poetry. . . . One can only urge that its matter, which may not interest us, and its form, which may not meet our
expectations, need not obscure the care, learning and imagination with
which Cynewulf composed it."[16]

It is worth considering why the question of merit, with its concomitant (and usually severe) judgments, looms so large in the discussion
of Anglo-Saxon religious poetry. Wittig's statement reveals a basic dis-
trust of the poem he has been treating; his is an admission that, in the
case of *Juliana*, he finds what lurks behind the poem (the structure of
figural narrative) more interesting than the work itself. At this point it
might do well to invoke John M. Ellis's warning against the eager
imposition of value judgments on literary works: "An analytic investigation of structural properties is to be preferred to general evaluative
judgments of the simple form, X is a great work; such judgments function only as crude incitements to action, and are the starting points for
precise analysis rather than the end point to which analysis must
lead."[17] Although with *Juliana* the problem is the overly negative, not
the overly positive, general judgment, the concern over its worth must
be replaced by an analysis of what it is. A familiarity with generic
perspectives on saints' lives can be extremely useful in reading *Juliana;*
certainly if earlier critics had been so informed they might have transcended their late nineteenth-century novelistic criteria. But an understanding of the genre cannot be automatically transferred to an understanding of the poem: while all saints may belong to one mystical
communion, their "lives" can represent many variations within this literary genre.

Recent criticism of *Juliana* has begun to strike a balance in com-
prehending the poem as a saint's life and as a specific text. Alvin Lee
writes persuasively:

Juliana is a conventional and very abstract poem—in its use of the images
and concepts of the dryht; in its focusing of the whole mythological sequence
of Satan's war against Christ on its protagonist; in its use of solar imagery; in
its stylized, hieratic presentation of human figures; and in its dependence on
a schematic pattern carefully worked out rather than on any realism in the
depiction of the conflict.[18]

In *Juliana* the action "is not character-revealing but theme-revealing,"
as Pamela Gradon says with reference to other medieval literature.[19]
Cynewulf has conceived a poem in which the plot may more appro-

priately be compared to a graph than to an "imitation of an action," and Juliana and her several antagonists, both natural and supernatural, become figures in a religious and poetic calculus, ciphers in a set of coordinates that reveal Christian truths.

The singularity of *Juliana* is implicit in much of the criticism that compares this Old English poem with its Latin prose source. Cynewulf's changes are clear and at least the most obvious have often been noted.[20] Most significant is the "polarization" of character and attitude in the Old English version.[21] From the beginning Cynewulf presents his Juliana as a nearly hysterical (though such a weighted psychological phrase is probably not warranted) and unswerving Christian; moreover, the sweet reasonableness of Eleusius, her fiancé, has vanished, leaving as the saint's adversary only an equally passionate devotee of Satan. Critics have frequently noted that the Latin seems more believable: in this version Juliana first asks Eleusius to become a prefect and when he has accomplished this, she changes her conditions and insists he convert to Christianity. The Latin Juliana has also frequently been charged with duplicity, a charge that could never be leveled at her Old English counterpart, whose adamant refusal on the grounds that she wishes to maintain her virginity for God's sake never wavers. R. Barton Palmer summarizes the changes thus: "the general effect of [Cynewulf's] handling of the *vita* is the thorough elimination of the delicately pointed psychology of his source."[22] This metamorphosis of Juliana and Eleusius from their Latin "characters" skews the story in which they participate. A double perspective results, with important ramifications for the narrative structure. The reader perceives two states simultaneously—the actuality of Juliana's sainthood and the process by which she achieves it. In the Latin source the case is far simpler; there the reader sees only Juliana's growth in grace—a growth which the writer presents more humanistically. Permeating the Old English *Juliana* is a vague determinism which, if typological identifications are not considered, could raise difficult theological problems. But Wittig is undoubtedly correct that the double perspective stems from Juliana's dual identity: she is both herself acting out her martyrdom and a figure of *ecclesia*, the church already established and engaged in the unending temporal war with the devil.[23] This perspective is a logical consequence of the view that all saints participate in one eternal communion, for they thus acquire both a temporal and eternal existence. And the church, as Wittig notes, is often defined as "the collective assembly of martyr-witnesses."[24]

This sharp change in perspective which Cynewulf introduces into *Juliana* alters the motivations of the characters and their very mode of being. For as personages who already perceive their ends, Juliana, Affricanus, Eleusius, the emperor, and the devil perform roles that require only the fulfillment of a known teleology—the triumph of Christian right over Satanic wrong. And the narrative pattern in *Juliana* accordingly is ritualistic, not merely sequential or synoptic.

The action of the poem is not an attempt to record accurately the significant deeds committed by historical persons, but a fixed ceremony and public ritual involving figures reenacting the cosmic struggle between Christ and Satan. From Cynewulf's point of view the events chronicled can only gain in effect from being both iterative and ineluctable. Each successive torture Juliana endures glorifies the truth for which she suffers, assures her beatific recompense, and symbolizes the trials of the church in a hostile world.

Cynewulf's purely rhetorical amplifications show a similar concern: they are used to simplify (from one point of view), elevate, and formalize a narrative that moves in the direction of the abstract; for as repetitious as the Old English *Juliana* may seem, it is actually less so than the Latin prose version. Several unnecessary and "unseemly" pieces of action have been omitted (e.g., Juliana's torture in molten bronze and her dragging the devil through the open forum so she may throw him into a dung pit). The quality of the dialogue exchanged between Juliana and her several tormentors has also been drastically transformed. T. A. Shippey characterizes the Latin dialogue aptly when he praises the early Middle English *Seinte Iuliene* for "picking up a colloquial sensationalism genuinely present in the Latin." Surely he errs, however, in his assessment of Cynewulf's rhetorical talents: "It hardly needs to be said that any such effects are right outside the range of Cynewulf or any Old English poet.... It makes one wonder whether Cynewulf was capable of realising the full stylistic force of his original, or whether he merely realised that he could never reproduce it."[25] The set speeches which comprise the Old English colloquy are more like a series of declamations from a cosmic stage than a conversation. And it is a mistake to see this as a failure on Cynewulf's part. Cynewulf is about other things. He invariably cuts down the crisp and short Latin exchanges to the barest bone, but only so that he can flesh out a formal *amplificatio* to suit his own entirely different needs. One example will illustrate the remarkable differences in rhetorical tone between the Latin and the Old English. At one point the Latin reads:

"Filia mea dulcissima Iuliana, lux oculorum meorum, quare non vis accipere Praefectum sponsum tuum? En vero volo illi complere nuptias vestras" ("My sweetest daughter, Juliana, light of my eyes, why don't you want to take the Prefect as your husband? I wish to make your marriage to this man final").[26] Here is the corresponding Old English version:

> "Ðu eart dohtor min   seo dyreste
> ond seo sweteste   in sefan minum,
> ange for eorþan,   minra eagna leoht,
> Iuliana!   Þu on geaþe hafast,
> þurh þin orlegu,   unbiþyrfe
> ofer witena dom   wisan gefongen;
> wiðsæcest þu to swiþe   sylfre rædes
> þinum brydguman,   se is betra þonne þu,
> æþelra for eorþan,   æhtspedigra
> feohgestreona;   he is to freonde god.
> Forþon is þæs wyrþe,   þæt þu þæs weres frige,
> ece eadlufan,   an ne forlæte."
>
> (93a–104b)

"Juliana, you are my daughter, the dearest and the sweetest in my breast, my one and only in the world, the light of my eyes. In folly have you taken a vain course through your hostility against the judgment of wise men. You oppose your bridegroom too strongly according to your own counsel; he is better than you, nobler in the world, wealthier in treasures. He is good to have as a friend. Therefore it is proper that you do not lose the undying affection, the love of this man."

Affricanus's speech contains most of the images and themes that form the threads of this poem's highly schematic weave. Cynewulf, dilating upon the curt and strictly informational Latin sentence, lists the motifs which become central to his interpretation of the narrative as a whole: love and affection, wisdom and judgment, vanity, wealth and treasures, position and protection. Two contexts determine the reader's attitude: the immediate dramatic circumstances and the overriding Christian context that provides the poem's ideological base. As in all his other works, Cynewulf's perspective remains uncompromisingly ironic throughout—in marked contrast to the Latin *Acta*. When Juliana's father warns her not to reject "undying affection," the proper Christian response can only be ironic, religious laughter.[27] Any reader

sufficiently attuned to the purposes of Cynewulf's expansive rendering
should realize at once that Juliana's alleged "folly" *(geaþ)* should be
attributed instead to her father; that the "hostility" *(orlege)* is not hers
in the present but will be her bridegroom's in the future (which makes
doubly ironic her father's claim that "he is good to have as a friend");
that Juliana, and no other character, possesses the "judgment of wise
men" *(witena dom);* that Eleusius's earthly rank is illusory; that his
"treasures" *(feohgestreon)* mean nothing compared to the riches of
heaven; and that this father's counsel ultimately offends against the
very bonds of filial affection which should reflect divine love on earth.
To be sure, this series of ironic motifs does not fulfill the modern critic's
notion of a complex and subtle irony that turns on ambiguity. Yet the
ironic note sounded here resonates throughout *Juliana;* the clarity of
the irony matches the clarity of the Christian paradoxes on which it
depends, and these paradoxes in turn give the entire poem its crystal-
line effect. Cynewulf actually exploits a double irony: exultation in
Juliana's triumph through torment and just rejoicing at the devil's
defeat and return to torment—an irony that elicits a sympathetic
response only from those who cleave to Cynewulf's definite and trans-
lucent ideology.[28]

Inherent in the legend itself is a basic pattern, but this pattern
remains essentially unrealized in the sometimes cluttered and thematically unfocused account of the Latin *Acta.* The anonymous author
rests content with reporting the sequence of events, their causes and
effects, and does not abstract any scheme from the linear narrative.
Cynewulf, however, perceives in this Latin story a clear structure and
he turns the realistic Latin version into a sharply etched ritual drama.
The characters, visible and invisible, perform the requisite parts: there
are three fathers who reflect varieties of love (God, Affricanus, and
Satan), three emperors who embody quantities and qualities of power
and judgment (God, Maximianus, and Satan), three tormentors who
show varying degrees of mercy or its absence (Eleusius, the devil, and
Juliana), and two bridegrooms who would take their brides in different
ways (Christ and Eleusius). These characters and their actions illustrate
the nature of power and love, judgment and mercy, torment and
reward in a fallen, though redeemable, world.

Enhanced by the heroic conventions of Old English poetry, Cynewulf creates an incantatory effect at the start. As an invocation to a
ritual drama rather than an historical and realistic narrative, the opening lines delineate the ethical qualities of the whole milieu in which

Juliana's spiritual battle and eventual triumph will occur. The Latin presents a bare factual statement: *Denique temporibus Maximiani Imperatoris, persecutoris Christiane religionis, erat quidam Senator in civitate Nicomedia, nomine Eleusius, amicus Imperatoris* ("In the days of the Emperor Maximianus, a persecutor of the Christian religion, there was a certain senator in the city of Nicomedia by the name of Eleusius, a friend of the Emperor").[29] Cynewulf's opening displays a compelling rhetorical power that defines the thematic constituents of his vision:

> Hwæt! We ðæt hyrdon   hæleð eahtian,
> deman dædhwate,   þætte in dagum gelamp
> Maximianes,   se geond middangeard,
> arleas cyning,   eahtnysse ahof,
> cwealde Cristne men,   circan fylde,
> geat on græswong   Godhergendra,
> hæþen hildfruma,   haligra blod,
> ryhtfremmendra.   Wæs his rice brad,
> wid ond weorðlic   ofer werþeode,
> lytesna ofer ealne   yrmenne grund.
> Foron æfter burgum,   swa he biboden hæfde,
> þegnas þryðfulle;   oft hi þræce rærdon,
> dædum gedwolene,   þa þe Dryhtnes æ
> feodon þurh firencræft;   feondscype rærdon,
> hofon hæþengield,   halge cwelmdon,
> breotun boccræftge,   bærndon gecorene,
> gæston Godes cempan   gare ond lige.
>   Sum wæs æhtwelig   æþeles cynnes,
> rice gerefa;   rondburgum weold,
> eard weardade   oftast symle
> in þære ceastre   Commedia,
> heold hordgestreon.   Oft he hæþengield,
> ofer word Godes,   weoh gesohte
> neode geneahhe.   Wæs him noma cenned
> Heliseus,   hæfde ealdordom
> micelne ond mærne.

(1a–26a)

Lo! We have heard heroes praise, brave men proclaim, what happened in the days of Maximianus, who throughout the world, the cruel king, raised up persecution, killed Christian men, destroyed churches; the heathen leader shed the blood of the praisers-of-God, of the saints and the doers-of-right on the grassy plain. His kingdom was broad, wide and exalted among the nations, nearly covering the whole wide world. Powerful thanes travelled through the cities, as he had commanded. Often they raised violence, perverse in deeds, those who in their wickedness hated the Lord's law. They raised enmity, set up idols, killed saints, destroyed scholars, burned the chosen ones, persecuted God's warriors with spear and fire. One was a rich man from a noble family, a powerful reeve. He ruled cities, kept his home most often in the city of Nicomedia, possessed a store of treasures. Again and again in his zeal he sought heathen gods and idols against God's word. His name was Heliseus; he held a great, famous dominion.

Besides the easily recognized emphasis on wickedness and opposition to God's true law, the general slaughter that foreshadows Juliana's specific torment, this passage dwells on one major theme: the imperium with its ironic contrast (here implicit) between the worldly emperor whose kingdom was broad, *"wid and weoðlic ofer werþeode,"* and the ultimate power of the Christian God who will eventually reveal the glory of His Imperium through Juliana's ritual suffering. This theme has a biblical parallel in Ephesians 6:10–19, especially verse 12: "For we wrestle not against flesh and blood, but against principalities, against powers, against the rulers of the darkness of this world, against spiritual wickedness in high places."[30] These motifs are not even suggested in the Latin life. Additions to the Latin are numerous; in line 15, for example, Cynewulf relates that Maximianus's thanes "raised up idols" *(hofon hæþengield)*—hardly a surprising act, but still one not mentioned in the Latin. His choice of word—*hæþengield*—cannot be fortuitious, for Cynewulf immediately develops his own idea that Satan's idols are connected with treasure:[31]

> Hire wæs Godes egsa
> mara in gemyndum   þonne eall þæt maþþumgesteald
> þe in þæs æþelinges   æhtum wunade.
> Þa wæs se weliga   þære wifgifta,
> goldspedig guma,   georn on mode,
> þæt him mon fromlicast   fæmnan gegyrede,
> bryd to bolde.   Heo þæs beornes lufan
> fæste wiðhogde,   þeah þe feohgestreon
> under hordlocan,   hyrsta unrim,
> æhte ofer eorþan.

(35b–44a)

For her was the fear of God greater in mind than all that treasure that dwelt in the nobleman's possessions. Then was the rich man, the gold-wealthy man, eager in his heart for the marriage, that someone should prepare the maiden at once, the bride for his house. She firmly opposed that man's love, although he had treasure in his chest, countless ornaments on earth.

Such concerns are neither arcane nor trivial; they stand at the very center of the Christian drama and reenact, as Lee suggests, the eternal war between the *dryht* of heaven and the *dryht* of hell. The narrative proceeds from this situation heavy with the moral ironies provided by these images in the context of the Juliana legend. Examples multiply: in the Latin, Eleusius is simply one partner of an arranged marriage (*Hic desponsauerat quamdam puellam nobili genere ortam, nomine Iulianam*, "he was betrothed to a girl from a noble family named Juliana"); in Cynewulf's poem Eleusius's sexual eagerness contrasts with Juliana's insistence on her virginity (*Ða his mod ongon / fæmnan lufian, [hyne fyrwet bræc]*, "his mind began to love the maiden [desire tormented him]," 26a–27b). Given this disposition of the characters, there is no room for the diplomatic parries which surround the negotiations concerning the marriage in the *Acta*. One need not presume a lost source for this important alteration from the Latin, or try to explain it as a change designed to please a certain audience, perhaps a group of women in a convent.[32] The answer may be both more obvious and more weighty: in a Christian poem clearly structured on the ironic implications of extreme contrasts, the love of a wicked earthly bridegroom must be countered by a heroine's chaste love for Christ. For as Eleusius *heold hordgestreon* ("held a treasure hoard," 22a), so Juliana desired that her virginity be "*held* pure for Christ's love" (*fore Cristes lufan clæne geheolde*, 31). This initial section extends the concatenation of these motifs with several examples (27, 31a, 34a, 41b, 48a). Cynewulf makes the thematic equation precise: divine love tenders riches far surpassing the mundane wealth that would come to Juliana through marriage (*mæglufan*, 70a). All of this has been added to the *Acta*.

The ritual quality of the narrative and its effects on the characterization become apparent once the action begins. Without any hint that she must necessarily suffer because she refuses marriage with Eleusius, Juliana announces that no pain or torment can force her to acquiesce:

> "Swylce ic þe secge,   gif þu to sæmran gode
> þurh deofolgield   dæde biþencest,
> hætsð hæþenfeoh,   ne meaht þu habban mec,
> ne geþreatian   þe to sinhigan;

næfre þu þæs swiðlic   sar gegearwast,
þurh hæstne nið,   heardra wita,
þæt þu mec onwende   worda þissa."

(51a–57b)

"Likewise I say to you, if you through idols put your trust in a worse god,
vow a heathen tribute, you cannot have me, nor force me to be your wife.
You can never prepare a pain of hard torments so severe through violent
hatred that you can turn me from these words."

There has been no suggestion up to this point of possible torture for
Juliana if she does not obey her father's will. Her outburst represents
a certain knowledge of what will ensue, and prepares for those specific
torments she must undergo. This speech illustrates very well the double
perspective that informs the poem. Juliana in her role of canonized
saint, in her symbolic position as *ecclesia*, speaks here; she can defy her
temporal tormentors from an eternal standpoint that assures hers, the
saints', and the church's triumph over whatever adversities may have
to be endured. No strictly realistic approach to hagiography can ever
deal adequately with these mixed chronological modes, which embody
in narrative and dramatic form a Christian notion of time. The effect
is most similar to the complex intersection of the temporal and eternal
in *Christ II*, but here the characters enact the contrasts, not the shifting
perspectives. Again ironically, it is Eleusius, not Juliana, who bears the
pain. Afflicted with sexual desire (27b), Eleusius finds that her refusal
causes him great torment: *Me þa fraceðu sind / on modsefan mæste
weorce* ("Her insults are most painful to my mind," 71b–72b). Little
else could be expected, however, for this bridegroom "stained with
sins" (*firendædum fah*, 59a) from the outset. Once more these details
seem to be original with Cynewulf, including the additional ironic
notation that Eleusius and Affricanus *wæron begen / synnum seoce,
sweor ond aþum* ("they were both sick with sins, father-in-law and
son-in-law," 64b–65b). Here a model of human affection and family
ties—father and son by marriage—evolves into a corrupt coalition
(symbolized by the splendid heroic detail of their leaning spears
together before taking counsel [63b]) for which earthly treasure stands
as the analogue.

Yet more than merely being "wicked," disciples of Satan and thanes
in the *dryht* of hell, Juliana's opponents join in a parody of divinity.

Thus Affricanus replies to Eleusius's report of Juliana's recalcitrance:

> "Ic þæt geswerge   þurh soð godu,
> swa ic are æt him   æfre finde,
> oþþe, þeoden, æt þe   þine hyldu
> winburgum in,   gif þas word sind soþ,
> monna leofast,   þe þu me sagast,
> þæt ic hy ne sparige,   ac on spild giefe,
> þeoden mæra,   þe to gewealde.
> Dem þu hi to deaþe,   gif þe gedafen þince,
> swa to life læt,   swaþer leofre sy."
>
> (80a–88b)

"By the true gods I swear, so I may ever find grace from them, or, prince, your favor in the joyous cities, if these words are true, dearest of men, which you tell me, that I will not spare her, but, famous prince, will give her up to destruction, into your power. Sentence her to death, if that seems right to you, or let her live, whichever seems more suitable."

The various speeches in which Eleusius, Affricanus, and Juliana extol God or their gods all use the same evaluative terms, and so create a parodic vision of the false deities. The grace, favor, and power of which he speaks in this earthly context, as well as the joyous cities, burlesque God's true mercy and dominion of paradise. In the Latin *Acta* the heathen gods lack strong advocates. Their worship of the Roman pantheon is merely customary, and Juliana's mother, completely absent from the Old English poem, has no religious opinions of any sort. The epithets for Apollo and Diana may be respectful, but they hardly indicate religious fervor. In *Juliana*, on the other hand, the worship of idols is as fiercely defended as the worship of the Christian God, which is in keeping with all the polarities Cynewulf introduces.

As both a character and a symbol Juliana understands exactly the pattern of which she herself is a part. In her demands that Eleusius be converted to Christianity, the saint makes explicit the irreconcilable opposition between divine love and earthly lust, worldly treasure and heavenly reward. Stating anew that she will never submit to "married love" (*mægrædenne*, 109a) unless Eleusius "loves with sacrifices" (*lufige mid lacum*, 111a) her God, she severely changes the request of her Latin counterpart, who asks only that the prefect adhere to the

forms of Christian worship. And with a summary statement Juliana
scornfully connects these two motifs in a final dismissal of Eleusius's
suit:

> "He þa brydlufan
> sceal to oþerre   æhtgestealdum
> idese secan;   nafað he ænige her."
> (114b–16b)

"He must seek bridal love from another woman with his wealth; he shall have
none here."

Interestingly, Cynewulf here provides a minor, though original, ironic
juxtaposition that accords perfectly with Juliana's speech. Affricanus in
his ultimatum quoted above warns Juliana not to reject the *ece eadlufan* Eleusius proffers, and then Cynewulf continues with the formulaic presentation of Juliana as *seo eadge* ("the blessed one," 105a).
The irony seems deliberate with its contrast between *eadlufan*
("blessed love," "rich love," but in a pagan context) and *eadge* ("rich,"
"blessed," in a Christian context). Cynewulf manipulates the semantic
correspondences of the language itself to contain and reveal his thematic concerns much as he did in *Christ II*.

When Juliana's obdurate refusal leads to the first of her ritual torments, the dominant motifs also change, although the emphasis on love
and affection does not. This change marks off a clear division in the
narrative which closely resembles the "panel construction" noted in
both *The Fates of the Apostles* and *Christ II*, although the narrative
clarity in *Juliana* produces a simpler form. Still, the shift from the
opening panel which includes Juliana's initial confrontation to the torments of the second section allows Cynewulf to continue his series of
ironic comparisons between God's true love and Satan's perverted
affection (122b, 165a, 178, 195a, 219a–20a, 233b–35b). However,
Cynewulf momentarily suspends the association of the evil characters
with worldly treasure and turns instead to other images suggested in
the opening invocation. In her present extremity, Juliana requires first
and foremost protection from her God; the God whom Juliana loves is
above all her *mundbora* ("protector," 156a, 213a, 266b, 272b). So the
irony must cut even more deeply when her bridegroom informs her

that she will find "merciful protection" (*mildum mundbyrd,* 170) if only she will sacrifice to the pagan gods. And Eleusius's offer in *Juliana* differs markedly from the corresponding suggestion in the Latin. The Latin Eleusius has no special interest in the heathen religion, nor indeed much sense of what religion is at all. He tells Juliana that if she will only give in and go through the motions of the heathen sacrifice, he will gladly accept her God *(Domina mea Iuliana, consenti mihi & credo Deo tuo).*[33] And his final explanation to Juliana has all the earmarks of a middle-echelon bureaucrat's fearful caution: if the emperor hears about it, I will lose both my position and my head. The Old English Eleusius takes a radically different tack with Juliana; he is overcome by her beauty and radiance (166a–68b), but insulted (205b) when she will not accept "grace from the holy ones" (*hyldo to halgum,* 171a) and sacrifice to "the true gods" (*soþum gieldum,* 174b). For this Eleusius Juliana's intransigence is a matter of folly and delusion (*þurh þin dolwillen gedwolan fylgest,* 202). Her stance is "blasphemy" (*godscyld,* 204b), not merely a dangerous political position. Eleusius becomes a symbol of cruelty, one who easily accepts his role as a savage persecutor. He does not fear his earthly emperor, but acts as his willing deputy; the Latin Eleusius does fear his mortal emperor and so acts out of a cowardly sense of self-protection. His reaction prompts Juliana to raise a point on which Cynewulf builds a major and absolute conflict: *Et si tu times istum Imperatorem mortalem, & in stercore sedentem, quomodo me cogere potes immortalem Imperatorem negare?* ("And if you fear this mortal emperor, one who sits in dung, how can you compel me to deny the Immortal Emperor?").[34]

Those who wield the cruel power of the earthly *imperium* demand that Juliana be tortured, but this exacts from the saint an even firmer faith, a trust in the ultimate power of God her Protector. In fact, Cynewulf's Juliana has little in common with the Latin saint. For faced with the inevitability of torture and imprisonment, the Latin heroine cries out quite humanly to God for help and revenge:

"Domine Deus omnipotens, anima mea in exitu posita est, confirma me, & exaudi me, & miserere mei, & dolentibus circumstantibus mihi miserere: & praesta mihi misericordiam tuam, sicut & omnibus qui tibi placuerunt. Deprecor etiam te, Domine, ne deseras me, quia pater meus & mater mea dereliquerunt me: Sed tu Domine Deus meus suscipe me; & ne proiicias me a facie tua, & ne deseras me in isto tempore doloris."

"Lord God Almighty, my soul is at the point of death, give me strength, and
hear me, and be merciful to me, and pity me in these dolorous circumstances,
and give me your mercy, just as you have done to all who pleased you. Still
I entreat you, Lord, not to desert me, because my father and my mother have
abandoned me. But, my Lord God, receive me; and do not cast me away
from your face, and do not desert me in this time of trouble."[35]

On the other hand, the serenity of the Old English Juliana when faced
with the identical situation seems remarkable and is made possible only
by the double perspective and the ritual mode in which Cynewulf has
set this narrative. Rather than a plea for aid, the poet gives us a descriptive example of unflinching steadfastness:

> Hyre wæs Cristes lof
> in ferðlocan   fæste biwunden,
> milde modsefan,   mægen unbrice.
> Ða wæs mid clustre   carcernes duru
> behliden, homra geweorc;   halig þær inne
> wærfæst wunade.   Symle heo Wuldorcyning
> herede æt heortan,   heofonrices God,
> in þam nydcleafan,   Nergend fira,
> heolstre bihelmad;   hyre wæs Halig Gæst
> singal gesið.
>
>   (233b–42a)

The praise of Christ was firmly fixed in her heart; she was mild in spirit, a
power unbroken. Then was the prison's door, the work of hammers, closed
by a lock. The saint dwelt steadfast therein. Always in her heart she praised
the King of glory, the God of the heavenly kingdom, the Savior of men, in
the prison, surrounded by darkness. The Holy Ghost was her constant
companion.

Here again the difference between the Latin and the Old English
results, at least in part, from Cynewulf's layering of perspectives.
Juliana at this moment is not only herself but a saint in the process of
imitating Christ's passion. Wittig lists the parallels between the two
martyrdoms: "The saint is interrogated and beaten by her angry father
(89–129 and 140-3a); she is given over to Heliseus for judgment (158-
60a) and scourged a second time on his orders (186b-8); she is then
hung 'on heanne beam' ['on a high cross'] (227b-30) where she suffers
for six hours."[36] Wittig compares these events to Christ's seizure and

appearance before the Sanhedrin, His beating, His judgment at the hands of Pilate, who had Him scourged again, and His Crucifixion, lasting for six hours, according to Mark's Gospel. Finally, he notes, "Even the interrogations of Christ by the Chief Priest and by Pilate, concerned as they are with blasphemy and the rights of Caesar, are echoed by the dialogues of the poem."[37] There is no question about the accuracy of Wittig's parallels, but we must be reasonably cautious in defining their exact status. Cynewulf's technique never permits an unequivocal allegorical equation (such as Juliana equals Christ) unless he expresses it openly (as he does in *Christ II*). With the resemblance between Juliana's martyrdom and Christ's Passion we can only speak of an allegorical "effect," achieved by placing one perspective (the historical account of Christ's suffering) over another (the report of Juliana's torment). The two do not fall into the perfect alignment that Wittig's schematic outline tends to imply, although the correspondences are close enough that they must be examined and considered. Here too we find the double perspective: her torture is an imitation of Christ's but it is also uniquely her own; she is a saint and yet we see the course by which she becomes that saint. Cynewulf's strategy both fuses and separates two modes—the symbolic (here figural) and the literal (here abstractly dramatic). The results have perplexed more than one reader who treats only one mode at a time, but it is with the subtle alternation between the fusion and separation of modes that Cynewulf makes his most original contributions to the Juliana legend.

In the *Acta* Eleusius continues the torture of Juliana out of anger and embarrassment that she will not bow to his command and sacrifice to the pagan gods, that is, observe the outward forms of worship. The Old English Heliseus, however, operates in a different way; he is less interested that she perform the required tasks than that she "convert" back again to the true religion. And when he perceives that Juliana's resolve remains unshakable, he throws her into prison out of sheer exasperation that he has been unable to "turn her mind" (*mod oncyrran*, 226b). This prepares for the devil's sudden entrance (242b) and his long confrontation with the saint; for during the course of his confession the devil reveals that he conceives of himself as a missionary and teacher, one "skilled in evil" (*yfeles ondwis*, 244a) and "wise" or "trained in afflictions" (*gleaw gyrnstafa*, 245a). Like all the other characters in *Juliana*, this devil is more abstract than his Latin equivalent (who is named Belial). Juliana's triumph over him and his subsequent recital of his evil deeds involve far more than the listing of crimes committed, which is what the Latin records. Cynewulf's concerns are both theological and psychological, and he takes this opportunity to probe the workings of the mind falling under the power of sin. The prevalence of psychological details contrasts strikingly with the Latin source. Nero does not simply crucify Peter and Paul, he is "deluded" (*bisweac*, 302b) by the devil; Simon Magus does not just accuse these same apostles of being sorcerers, he is the victim of an extended psychological attack by a demonic teacher:

> "Eac ic gelærde
> Simon searoþoncum   þæt he sacan ongon
> wiþ þa gecorenan   Cristes þegnas,
> ond þa halgan weras   hospe gerahte
> þurh deopne gedwolan,   sægde hy drys wæron."
>
>   (297b–301b)

"Also I taught Simon with crafty thoughts so that he began to strive against Christ's chosen thanes, and attack the holy men with insult, through a profound delusion, he said they were sorcerers."

As James F. Doubleday has noted, Cynewulf is obviously interested in the psychology of sin and is acquainted with Gregory's four-fold division of the movement of the mind toward acceptance of evil. The devil's own confession of his *modus operandi* confirms this connection:

> "þæt ic him monigfealde   modes gælsan
> ongean bere   grimra geþonca,
> dyrnra gedwilda,   þurh gedwolena rim.
> Ic him geswete   synna lustas,
> mæne modlufan,   þæt he minum hraþe,
> leahtrum gelenge,   larum hyrað.
> Ic hine þæs swiþe   synnum onæle
> þæt he byrnende   from gebede swiceð,
> stepeð stronglice,   staþolfæst ne mæg
> fore leahtra lufan   lenge gewunian
> in gebedstowe."
>
>   (366a–76a)

"I am ready at once to bring against him manifold lusts of the mind, grim thoughts, secret errors, through a great number of delusions. I sweeten for him the lusts of sin, wicked affections, so that he quickly becomes attached to my vices, heeds my teachings. I inflame him with sins so strongly that in his burning he ceases from prayer and steps forth boldly; he can no longer remain firm in the place of prayer because of his love of vices."

The Gregorian analysis of the four stages of sin places *suggestio* first ("suggestion," 366a–68b), followed by *delectatio* ("delight," 369a–70a), *consensus* ("consent," 370b-71b), and *defensio audacia* ("bold defense," 372a-76a).[38]

The drama of this flamboyant contest depends on Cynewulf's conception of the encounter as a ritual series of attempts to "turn" *(ahwyrfan)* Juliana from her faith (327a, 360a, 381b, 439). In this the devil acts like Heliseus (or vice versa); he too describes his activity as a parodic missionary and teacher. The devil's final concession of defeat comes at the point where he recognizes Juliana's "wisdom." His last words before Juliana sends him back to hell contain these admissions:

> "ic to soþe wat
> þæt ic ær ne sið   ænig ne mette
> in woruldrice   wif þe gelic,
> þristran geþohtes   ne þweorhtimbran
> mægþa cynnes.   Is on me sweotul
> þæt þu unscamge   æghwæs wurde
> on ferþe frod."
>
> (547b–53a)

"I know truly that I never met a woman like you in the worldly kingdom before or since, one of bolder thought or more perverse among the race of women. It is clear to me that you are completely guiltless, wise in soul."

It can hardly be said that Cynewulf developed this complex pattern from his source: the Latin says only "we introduce error into his thoughts" *(facientes errorem in cogitationibus eius)* and "we introduce many thoughts into their hearts" *(multas cogitationes immittimus in corda eorum).*[39] Ironically, after all his effort to "turn" Juliana's heart from God, it is the devil who must "turn humiliated" back to hell *(heanmod hweorfan*, 390a). Despite his attempt to proclaim Satan's wisdom (he calls him "the wisest king of hell-dwellers [*snotrestan ... helwarena cyning*, 543b-44b]), this devil must finally confess that the pagan gods are inferior *(sæmran*, 361b). We recall that

Juliana had used the same adjective in her first speech denouncing her fiancé's and her father's proposals.

In addition to this pervasive concern with faith, wisdom, the mind, belief, and the psychology of sin, Cynewulf also extends other earlier motifs into this section; he strengthens the resolve of Juliana's faith, giving her a firmness and stability that mirror their divine archetypes (107b, 222a, 234b, 270b, 654). Juliana and the devil actually reverse roles in their transformation from Latin to Old English characters: in the Old English this anonymous minion of Satan begs Juliana to have mercy on him and not to let him die (*þæt þu miltsige me þearfen-dum, / þæt unsælig eall ne forweorþe,* 449a–50b); but in the Latin Juliana is the one who rolls her eyes toward heaven, pleading for mercy and life: "Iuliana autem ingemiscens amarissime exclamavit ad Dom-inum, & oculos suos levans ad caelum cum lacrymis dixit: 'Domine Deus caeli & terrae, ne deseras me, neque permittas perire ancillam tuam'"[40] ("Juliana, however, sighing most bitterly, cried out to God, and, raising her eyes to heaven, said with tears: 'O Lord God of heaven and earth, do not desert me, nor permit your handmaiden to die'").

Cynewulf also deepens the chasm that exists between God's love and Satan's hatred masquerading as affection (34a, 70, 104a, 114b, 220a, 328b, 370a); and relating both to this motif and the theme of wisdom, he adds to his source the idea that the devil works through craft and skill (244a, 290a, 298a, 302a, 359b, 392b, 480b, 494a, 575b) which both in cause and effect proceed from a terrible delusion (281ff., 301a, 302b, 326, 368, 460, 468ff.).

The action in *Juliana* throughout, and particularly in the combat with the devil, is mainly symbolic. Juliana's victory over the devil under no circumstances must be subjected to a realistic analysis. Too many critics see only the slight figure of a woman holding the devil himself "prisoner" while she shouts him into submission through the force of her contumacious rhetoric. But such a reaction is misguided. Juliana, as a person, does not hold the devil fast; rather, the firmness of her faith in God's truth and power, reiterated at crucial intervals, ren-ders the devil "powerless." In this spiritual battle of universal propor-tions, Juliana, firm in her faith, has seized the devil and held him *fæste* according to divine command (later to be ironically linked in our minds with the devil's "firm grip" which Juliana breaks). Quite unlike the Latin Juliana, who has to be told to keep her faith, the Old English saint hears God's command and acts without hesitation. Juliana may also represent here, in some partial way, both the church speaking against its greatest adversary and Christ reenacting His Harrowing of Hell.[41] Some details which seem displaced or unmotivated may indicate that Cynewulf did, if only intermittently, view Juliana and her actions as reflecting Christ's. When the devil admits defeat, his speech seems excessive, unless we see it as primarily a reference to Christ's Harrowing transposed to Juliana as a mystical member of Christ's body:

> "Næs ænig þara
> þæt mec þus bealdlice   bendum bilegde,
> þream forþrycte,   ær þu nu þa
> þa miclan meaht   mine oferswiðdest,
> fæste forfenge."
>
>   (518b–22a)

"There were none who thus boldly laid hands upon me, overwhelmed with miseries, before you who now have vanquished, firmly seized my great power."

As with all such figural interpretations, a certain amount of caution is warranted. Again Cynewulf uses a "layering effect," with significant, but incomplete, alignment of the parallel actions and characters.

Thematically, however, the references to the Harrowing of Hell are of real importance, for Christ's judgment and salvation accomplished in that action prefigure the general apocalypse that is to come. This raises the question of judgment, earthly, divine, and hellish (249b, 256b, 466b, 534a). For the devil, who "fixes his hope" (*hyht stapelie*, 437b) on Satan (just as Juliana does on God, 107), who warns Juliana to give in to escape the prefect's judgment, who trusts in the affection of his father (436b), must ultimately submit to a triple judgment himself: that of God, that of Juliana, and that of Satan. And he knows the outcome will be excruciating (339a–42a, 553b–56a), because he will suffer God's judgment through Juliana (466), and then the judgment of Satan, who lacks all mercy and affection (328b–29a). His entire confession becomes a parody of a Christian confession. Juliana, the poem's other "prisoner," has a parallel fate: she must endure the prefect's judgment on earth and God's in heaven, but the prefect's torture wins glorification in paradise for the saint, while the devil receives real torment for eternity. Cynewulf's emphatic heightening of the apocalyptic overtones in Juliana's *flytyng* with the devil prepares for the (usual) vision of judgment he includes in the runic epilogue.

The devil's rhetorical strategies in *Juliana* are considerably more
sophisticated than Belial's lame confessions in the *Acta*. Each of the
devil's long speeches has a different purpose and tone; the devil shifts
from boasting, to confession, back to defiance, and then to an obvious
pitch to obtain Juliana's pity. Cynewulf gives him a much expanded
plea in which he compares his plight to Juliana's; they occupy the same
position because they have "trusted" their fathers, and his sudden
switch to an acknowledgment of the true God and the grace He offers
is a transparent ploy to win sympathy. Cynewulf has also made precise
connections between this devil and all the wicked characters in the
poem. Thus all characters who encounter Juliana address her initially
in the same way. Her father greets her with

> "Đu eart dohtor min,   seo dyreste
> ond seo sweteste   in sefan minum,
> ange for eorþan,   minra eagna leoht,
> Iuliana!"
>
> (93a–96a)

"You are my daughter, the dearest and the sweetest in my heart, my only
one in the world, the light of my eyes, Juliana!"

Heliseus says, *"Min se swetesta sunnan scima, Iuliana!"* ("My sweetest light of the sun, Juliana!" 166a–67a); the devil poses this question:
*"Hwæt dreogest þu, seo dyreste / ond seo weorþeste Wuldorcyn-
inge, / Dryhtne ussum?"* ("Why do you suffer, the dearest and most
precious to our King of Glory, to our Lord?" 247a–49a). Paradoxically
they all recognize Juliana's true "value," though with each expression
of it, they intend to remove it. The parallels continue: in the devil's
description of Satan's rule of hell we recognize the model for Maximianus's imperial rule on earth, Heliseus's lesser government as prefect, and Affricanus's familial domination.

We cannot be sure that we have the exact words with which Cynewulf ended Juliana's struggle with the devil; a page or more of the
manuscript is missing at the point where the devil seems about to
depart. But enough remains to see the extraordinary difference
between the Latin and the Old English in their disposals of their
respective fiends. As already mentioned, the Latin Juliana merely takes
Belial out of the prison with her, drags him through the marketplace,

and throws him into a dunghill. The anonymous author apparently felt that the devil needs only a fitting punishment. Cynewulf's "conclusion" to this portion reverberates with ironic implications:

> Ða hine seo fæmne forlet
> æfter præchwile þystra neosan
> in sweartne grund, sawla gewinnan,
> on wita forwyrd. Wiste he þi gearwor,
> manes melda, magum to secgan,
> susles þegnum, hu him on siðe gelomp.
> (553b–58b)

Then the woman let him, after his time of punishment, seek the darkness in the black ground, the enemy of souls, in the destruction of torments. He, the messenger of evil, knew the more certainly to tell his companions, the servants of torment, what had happened to him on his journey.

Cynewulf emphasizes again the devil as teacher, *melda* ("messenger"), who rather than teaching is taught. He learns his sad lesson well *(wiste he þi gearwor)*, and the report he gives to his companions in hell of his "journey" must dwell on the specific details of defeat. There are three journeys, more or less analogous, in the poem: the devil's "mission" *(siðe)* to tempt Juliana, Juliana's "departure" *(endestæf*, 610b), and Cynewulf's *siðfæt* ("journey," 700a). The full significance of these analogies will be examined, but here we note the outcome of the devil's journey is definite and certain, however negative.

Following the devil's departure to the nether regions, the prefect, acting as judge *(se dema*, 594b), orders Juliana brought from prison to confront her final sentence, torture, and death. But an angel, shining in ornaments (564a), frees and protects Juliana *(gefreode ond gefreoðade*, 565a), and the fire surrounding her, rather than her faith, is turned away. Having survived the fire, she next is plunged into a pot of molten lead, which the prefect prepares on explicit instructions from his "teacher" *(Næs se feond to læt, / se hine gelærde*, 573b–74a). These qualifying images do not occur in the Latin. Now near the end of her life and torments, the saint enjoys one final symbolic meeting with her most dangerous persecutor, the devil. His sudden reappearance marks the termination of the ritual action in a manner that calls attention to the fact that it is indeed a ritual. With formulaic phrasing exactly repeated from the devil's earlier entrance (*Ða cwom sem-*

ninga, "Then came suddenly," 242b, 614b), Cynewulf allows the devil
to voice his cry for revenge against the already sanctified Juliana. The
devil's speech this time around contains some of his former rhetorical
tricks: he rants and screams in perfect imitation of the prefect who
shortly before has turned into a wild raging beast, tearing his hair and
gnashing his teeth because he has failed to execute Juliana (594b–
600a). Most of the devil's diatribe consists of charges that Juliana has
"tortured" him unmercifully, but his greatest pain results from her
having turned him into a "confessor" (*"þæt ic to meldan wearð"*,
621b). Cynewulf uses the same word here that he had before in por-
traying the devil as a "messenger" or "missionary" of evil, with obvious
ironic intent. Another major deviation from the Latin account seems
worth noting: in the Old English, the devil's plea for "requital" or
"reward" (*lean,* 622b) becomes a "song of misery" (*hearmleoð,* 615b),
"full of sorrowful dirges" (*ceargealdra full,* 618b). This demon, characterized before as skilled and crafty in evil, is the artisan of deceit and
delusion. But the triumphant Christian irony that is present throughout
the poem reduces his skill to abject impotence and his song to the lamentation of the eternally damned. Here and elsewhere the devil's cunning trickery recoils on itself; his end befits the craft that earned it.

Finally, two instances distinguish the singular visions of the *Acta* and
Cynewulf's poem. The first occurs in one of the devil's earlier speeches
to Juliana. As the devil recounts the means he has employed to turn
Christians from their faith, he mentions particularly his fear that the
Christian victims will run to church and repent their sins, begin *"orare,*
& sanctas Scripturas audire & communicare divinum mysterium. . . .
Quando enim Christiani communicant divinum mysterium, rece-
dentes nos sumus illa hora ab eis" ("to pray and to listen to the Holy
Scriptures and partake of the Divine Mystery. . . . For when Christians
partake of the Divine Mystery, in that hour we recede from them").[42]
The liturgical and eucharistic emphasis is patent, but Cynewulf's ren-
dition of the same general thoughts is quite different. He composes at
this interval the extended metaphor of the brave Christian's soul
assaulted by a shower of arrows against which the heroic warrior
defends himself with his holy shield, his spiritual armor (382a–89a).[43]
The second item is Juliana's valediction to the newly converted multitudes (641a–69a).[44] This speech, in which Juliana specifically states
that she "wants to teach" her beloved people (*"Forþon ic, leof weorud,*
læran wille," 647), serves as a recapitulatory coda of the poem's motifs.
Juliana admonishes the Christians of the world to "remember"

("*Gemunað*," 641a) God's power and splendor, to be fast in their faith and to establish their house on a firm foundation ("*fæstnian*," 649a, 654b), to trust in God's love and mercy, to hold peace and love among themselves. She concludes by asking that they pray to Christ, that the "Protector of angels" ("*Brego engla*," 666b) will be merciful to her. The corresponding Latin section contains some of these particulars, but has in addition a series of reminders for continued liturgic practice: "*Sed semper orate indeficienter in ecclesia sancta, & ad sanctas Scripturas intenti estote ... bonum est frequenter psallere, bonum est orare sine cessatione*" ("But always pray unceasingly in Holy Church, and be attentive to the Holy Scriptures ... it is good to sing psalms frequently; it is good to pray without cessation").[45] Cynewulf impresses upon his readers the diagrammatic spiritual allegory that Juliana's martyrdom embodies; the anonymous author of the *Acta* concerns himself with the need for Christians to follow a quotidian liturgy. In this difference rests the distinction between a credulous attitude toward the historicity of legend, including the moral lessons derived from it, and an abstract comprehension that perceives the figure behind the tale.

The deaths of both Juliana and Heliseus, juxtaposed neatly for the sake of ironic comparison, stand sharply opposed to one another. On the devil's suggestion that a word will suffice to dispatch the saint (623a–24a), Heliseus orders Juliana to be beheaded, and the idea of physical separation implies the conventional idea of death as a separation of soul and body: *Ða hyre sawl wearð / alæded of lice to þam langan gefean / þurh sweordslege* ("Then her soul was led out of her body to everlasting joy through the stroke of the sword," 669b–71a). But even in death Juliana is surrounded by a "great throng" (*sidfolc micel*, 692a; *micle mægne*, 690a). Heliseus and his band of men (672b), thirty-four in all, drown at sea; they plummet instantly to hell, wretched, "free from joys" (*hyhta lease*, 682a), an appropriate ironic tag, especially when we recall that Juliana has so often been called "free from sins" (*synna lease*, 614a). Assuredly, they too will bear an eternal burden of torment, though Cynewulf does not state this explicitly. What he does assert, quite apart from his source, comprises a forceful bit of Christian irony couched in the diction of Old English heroic ritual:

> Ne þorftan þa þegnas   in þam þystran ham,
> seo geneatscolu   in þam neolan scræfe,

> to þam frumgare   feohgestealde
> witedra wenan,   þaet hy in winsele
> ofer beorsetle   beagas þegon,
> æpplede gold.
>
> (683a–88a)

Nor was there any reason for those thanes in the dark home, that band of retainers in the deep grave, to expect from their leader allotted treasures, that they in the wine hall along the beer bench might receive rings, embossed gold.

Woolf finds this description creates a "grimly incongruous effect."[46] But this characteristic use of litotes represents the logical resolution of the treasure motif, connected as it has been to the evil power of the earthly imperium under satanic rule. Cynewulf has suspended this motif only to revive it at the most tellingly ironic moment.

Cynewulf takes both Heliseus and Juliana only as far as their graves. He omits the Latin narration of the disposition of Juliana's relics and substitutes a generalized statement that at her sepulcher God's praise has been raised up over the years unto this day (692b–95a). Instead of concentrating on any realistic or historical detail, Cynewulf deflects his view to ponder the world's end.

The shift to the personal and eschatological conclusion to *Juliana* comes in the middle of line 695: *mid þeodscipe. Is me þearf micel,* ("among people. There is for me great need"). The first half line refers back to the many who have raised Juliana's praise; in contrast Cynewulf's isolation emerges all the more poignantly. His ruminations on death and judgment have no complement in the Latin source (as is the case with each of his runic epilogues), nor do the several places in the poem that stress the beginning and end of time (111b–13a, 273b–74b, 497b–504a, 508b–10a). Death is his theme, his own as well as the common death to come at the Day of Judgment. His statement that praises have been raised over Juliana's grave "up to this day" (694b) awakens a keen awareness of that "great day" (*on þam miclam dæge,* 723b) when God will judge mankind. His care and anxiety in the face of death, his fear of justified damnation because of his "former deeds" (*ærgewyrhtum,* 702b and *iudædum,* 703a) thrust themselves urgently into his consciousness. His spiritual apprehensions may be conventionally expressed, but they are deeply felt. They explain much about his treatment of the Juliana legend.

One additional transformation from the Latin illustrates this point:

scattered here and there through the *Acta* are numerous references to biblical figures who served God faithfully—Abraham, Isaac, Joseph, John the Baptist, and a host of others. Cynewulf deletes them. Although lacunae in the Exeter manuscript occur in some places where the Latin includes these biblical persons, Cynewulf's usual habit of omitting them even where the Old English text is not mutilated indicates that this was his customary practice. A moralistic and exemplary perspective operates in the Latin life; the author sees Juliana in the tradition of the Christian hero, with the patriarchs and prophets attesting to her glory. Cynewulf does, of course, amplify the purely heroic element, but he also imagines Juliana's martyrdom within the scope of a symbolic, nontemporal history that does not require selective reference to items in the biblical chronicle. Juliana's life and death do not for Cynewulf point toward a liturgical ideal that reminds Christians to "sing psalms frequently," but toward a fearful meditation on how it will be in "that terrible time" (*in þa frecnan tid,* 724b) when the Stern King (704b), the "Judge of deeds" (*dæda Demend,* 725b), will manifest the power of His Imperium and reveal Himself as the only Judge from whose pronouncements the citizens of the earthly kingdom can neither escape nor appeal.

Yet the legend also proves to Cynewulf the "Ruler of powers" (*meahta Waldend,* 723a) is a Protector of the Just and a God of love and mercy. The final lines are a prayer, deliberately echoing Juliana's dying words, that God will grant him this grace. It is not only in the very last verses of the poem that Cynewulf carefully repeats words, images, and thoughts which recall Juliana's exhortation to her followers just preceding her death. As Juliana reminds them that they will not know what comes after the "departure hence" (*utgong heonan,* 661a), so Cynewulf says that he too is uncertain of his ultimate destination (*nat ic sylfa hwider, / eardes uncyðþu,* 700b–701a, "I myself do not know where; I am ignorant of the land"). Juliana leaves the host with the blessing of "peace" (*sibb,* 668b) before her head is severed from her trunk and her soul from her body; Cynewulf speaks likewise of death as a shattering of the "peace" or "relation" of a "united pair" (*sibbe toslitað sinhiwan tu,* 698), but his point of view is opposite to Juliana's. He cannot count on her secure reward. Further, the description of this "relation" as "the dearest of all" (*deorast ealra,* 697b) definitely recalls the "repeated use of the *seo dyreste* and *seo sweteste* forms of address used by the father toward his daughter . . . , and by the *Min se swetesta* remarks of the bartered bridegroom, Heliseus, to

Juliana."[47] They also conjure up the devil's salutation *seo dyreste* and *seo weorþeste*. For Cynewulf not only echoes the verbal aura which surrounds Juliana; he also ties himself by means of his words to the devil. Frese has demonstrated one instance of this frightening analogy; she compares the devil's petition to Juliana for mercy (539a–40b) with Cynewulf's triple appeal to God, Juliana, and his readers. Frese does not make the explicit connection between Cynewulf and the devil; she restricts herself to seeing these references as Cynewulf's "setting himself up as spokesman and representative of sinful mankind."[48] But the equation must be made: in this runic epilogue Cynewulf hovers uneasily between the saint and the devil, and the examples of the latter connection are as numerous as the former. Cynewulf laments that "it was too late a time" before he became ashamed of his evil deeds (*Wæs an tid to læt / þæt ic yfeldæda ær gescomede*, 712b–13a); the devil, however, "was not too late" in teaching Heliseus how to prepare Juliana's tortures (*Næs se feond to læt*, 573b). Rhetorical and psychological attitudes also serve to connect Cynewulf with the devil in precise contrast to Juliana. In his last appearance the devil "remembers the affliction" ("*Ic þa sorge gemon*," 624b) he suffered for an entire night when he confessed under Juliana's power; in his confessional epilogue Cynewulf "remembers all the torment, the wounds of sin," which he had while he lived (*Sar eal gemon, / synna wunde, þe ic sið oþþe ær / geworhte in worulde*, 709b–11a). The resemblances between the devil's and Cynewulf's diction are striking, and they become even more so when viewed against Juliana's advice to the converted to "Remember the Joy of warriors, the Splendor of glory, the Bliss of the saints" ("*Gemunað wigena Wyn ond wuldres þrym, / haligra Hyht*," 641a–42a). An obvious difference exists between Cynewulf's and the devil's torment and the three synonyms for joy in Juliana's phrase; another, more subtle change exists in the mood of the verb itself. Cynewulf and the devil speak in the first-person indicative, while Juliana uses the imperative form. Cynewulf thus shares with the devil an inordinate absorption in self. The devil's avowal of his crimes overflows with "I"; Cynewulf's epilogue does not present so extreme a case, but the sense of an "I" predominates. None of Juliana's speeches has a similar emphasis. Her references to herself are quickly passed by, because the central reference in every word she utters is always God. This cannot be said of the Latin Juliana, who more than once turns her words toward her own person. Cynewulf clearly intends that he himself should fit midway between the poles of the cosmic scheme he has wrought from the bare legend.

The runes in *Juliana* are encased in the description of the angry God actually judging, much like the runes in *Christ II*. But only in this poem does Cynewulf group runes together, and the interpretation of this unusual practice in *Juliana* is moot: Page's version CYN, EWU, LF of the runic section leaves all the letters untranslated.[49] Sisam would have each group represent the name *Cynewulf*.[50] Elliot performs some clever tricks and makes CYN mean "mankind," EWU mean "sheep," and LF stand for *lagu-feoh*, meaning "flood-bound wealth." He translates the passage (703b–9a): "Sadly the human race will depart. The King, the Giver of victories, will be stern when the sin-stained sheep await in terror what He will decree to them as life's requital according to their deeds. (Earth's) flood-bound wealth will quake; it will lie heavy with its burden of sorrow."[51] Page is probably correct, given our limited knowledge, not to hazard a solution. He notes that Elliot's solutions are open to many objections,[52] but can provide no satisfactory alternatives. Even if we must accept the obscurity of Cynewulf's runes, we need not hesitate to acknowledge the larger function of the runic epilogue. Once again he creates a series of relations between himself and the characters and themes of his poem. And of major importance in *Juliana* is the presence of characters representing such absolute dichotomies. Here Cynewulf's verbal strategies do not have to imply both connection with and dissociation from the apostles, as they did in *The Fates* and *Christ II*. By identifying himself with all the elements in *Juliana* he establishes the same perspective. This viewpoint inheres in the ritual drama as he has structured it.

Out of an undistinguished prose life, domestic in tone and sentimental in detail, Cynewulf has fashioned an abstractly conceptualized poem that reveals through ritual action and symbolic scheme Christian tenets adumbrating an ironic view of divine power and satanic fraud within temporal history. But once past the shoals of time, marked by the span of Juliana's mortal life, Cynewulf's vision expands. Unlike the devil's craft, which damns through deception, his poem demonstrates that God's redeeming mercy finally transcends temporal irony. *Juliana* demands a rigorous reading, for Cynewulf's concerns are death and apocalypse. Confronting these, he prays with a reverence that carries the genuine terror of the human sinner caught between devil and saint, though he is buttressed by the hope that his own poem has bestowed.

CHAPTER 5

Elene

I Sources

THE story of the Invention of the True Cross, although involving a Roman emperor and his mother, is Syrian in origin. Greek and Latin imitations of the Syrian legend quickly appeared, and Cynewulf depended on one of these Latin texts to write his Old English poem.[1] Narrative variants set off the Syrian tradition from both its Greek and Latin branches, and several details in Cynewulf's poem do not correspond to any of the existing Latin texts. The issue, then, of the exact source for *Elene* poses a small, but still unanswerable, question. Gradon maintains "that in a number of respects the St Gall manuscript 255 offers striking parallels with the text of *Elene*,"[2] but a printed edition of this manuscript is unavailable. The best and oldest edited manuscripts are found in Alfred Holder's late nineteenth-century edition of the *Inventio Sanctae Crucis*;[3] and many critics have used his text when comparing the Old English poem with its "source." In his essay on *Elene* Jackson J. Campbell writes: "we can be relatively sure that Cynewulf's source was some lost or unkown MS of this *Inventio* which combined the details in a way slightly different from any of the existing Latin MSS." Campbell goes on to say that the Holder edition of the legend "is probably as close as we can now get to Cynewulf's source."[4]

For literary critics the version of the *Acta Cyriaci* printed in the Bollandist *Acta Sanctorum* is a more convenient text to consult. E. Gordon Whatley claims that Cynewulf's source "must have been very like the version of the *Inventio Sanctae Crucis* known as the *Acta Cyriaci, Pars Una*, and edited by Johannes Bollandus, *Acta Sanctorum, Maius*, 1 (Antwerp, 1688), 445–48."[5] While acknowledging that the Holder edition uses older manuscripts than the Bollandist redaction, he nonetheless chooses the *Acta Cyriaci* for comparative purposes because of its widespread availability. The critical essay which follows likewise depends on this Latin text; therefore, in matters of detail no absolute statements concerning the relation of source and poem are possible.

II *Criticism*

Elene has usually been considered Cynewulf's best poem, though in granting this few critics are also willing to bestow any special literary quality. G. K. Anderson lumps *Elene* together with *Juliana* and then concludes, "as literary creations, they are not particularly distinguished."[6] Kenneth Sisam is somewhat more discriminating; he would "rank *Elene* as the most pleasing, though not the most vigorous or original, of the translations from Latin which form the bulk of Old English poetry."[7] Stanley B. Greenfield describes *Elene* as "the most epic of Cynewulf's poems in its tone and imagery";[8] but Gradon dismisses Cynewulf's achievement rather brusquely: "poetic circumlocution apart, there is little which is not found in some version of the *Acta Cyriaci.*"[9]

The question of order of merit seems best left aside. Yet *Elene* does represent the most refined example of the various techniques Cynewulf used in all his poems. The runic epilogues and "autobiographical" conclusions to his poems form the defining structures; by relating himself to the preceding narrative or thematic components he creates a complex analogy, and this leads him to see corresponding analogies quite undeveloped within the narratives he chances upon in his devotional readings. The kind of relational schemes he exploits in *Juliana* become, in *Elene*, more perfectly realized: the conversions of Constantine, Judas, and Cynewulf himself are three panels that contain three contrasting poetic, psychological, and religious perspectives on the "finding" of the Cross, that is the true Christian life.[10]

In bold outline, *Elene* has three main sections: the battle between Constantine and the Goths culminating in Roman victory; a short bridge section in which Elene journeys to Jerusalem; the long encounter between Elene, Judas, and the Jews; and Cynewulf's epilogue. Cynewulf constructs in *Elene* a serial plan of ordering action and theme. The first panel contains all the elements that will run throughout the work; Constantine's battle sets the thematic pattern for the whole, and each of the other panels reflects this pattern in turn. Yet each new version is greater in extension and more significant in import than the initial action, and each employs a distinctive narrative mode:

Constantine's battle and conversion is a historical narrative, Elene's confrontation with the Jews, a dramatic dialogue, and Cynewulf's runic conclusion, a confessional monologue.[11]

Constantine's battle with the Goths is an oft-anthologized piece, usually admired for its capturing of the Germanic warrior ethic. Indeed, the full description, quite original with Cynewulf, does fall completely within the Germanic oral tradition.[12] But his use of all those devices requires a thorough examination. He divides the battle into five sections and assigns to each a specific purpose: the assembling of the Romans parallels the drawing up of the Goths; the raising of the Cross on earth parallels the vision of the Cross in the sky; and, with the final section, all four preceding panels merge in Constantine's victory through the power of the Cross. Cynewulf again creates reflecting panels which both mirror one another and yet stand in sharp contrast. His formulaic descriptions of the Goths and the Romans advancing on opposite shores of the Danube are nearly indistinguishable; the same half lines occur in each (*abannan to beadwe,* "summon to battle," 34a, 42a); the beasts of battle gather (27b–30a; 52b–53a); troops advance, accompanied with the noise of weapons. But the distinguishing details are as important as the parallel elements, and they all point to a resolution in Constantine's favor. The Goths may have the greater troop, which causes Constantine great fear (56b), but Constantine's "section" has the raven, a sure sign of victory[13] (the Goths are given the eagle and the wolf), as well as the clamor of military instruments (54), presaging the trumpets of victory. The two panels treating the Cross (79a–98b; 99a–109a) function in a similar manner: the Cross first appears to Constantine in the heavens, and the angelic messenger who appears with it then returns "to the hosts of the pure" (*on clænra gemang,* 96a); Constantine's replica of the Cross is fashioned on earth to be carried "into the hosts of the fiends" or "against the hosts of the savage ones" (*on feonda gemang,* 108b; *on gramra gemang,* 118b). Structurally the entire battle section repeats on a miniature scale the principles of contrast and analogy that characterize the whole poem.

This double structuring also reflects the double perspective on Constantine himself; the supernatural hints of Constantine's inevitable victory intimate his soon-to-be-acquired spirituality. For in the beginning Constantine is the righteous, but pagan, king (*cyninga wuldor,* "the glory of kings," 5b; *riht cyning,* "true king," 13b). He has even been given rule over the nations by God (14b–15a), though at this point Constantine hardly represents the Christian emperor in God's service. Still he is unmistakably God's champion in a battle which takes on aspects of the cosmic struggle between good and evil. When the Goths lose they are seen as savage heathens falling to the ground (*hæðene grungon, / feollon friðelease*, 126b–27a). The gift of the vision itself becomes the most significant means by which Constantine acquires a touch of heavenly aura before he has in fact earned it.

The beginning of the pattern, then, is the battle. With Constantine the emotional state associated with this strife is fear; with Judas and Cynewulf this emotional ground will be broadened into a profound examination of error and sin. A revelation of the Cross and a conversion follow, and in the Constantine part the second action brings with it the second theme. In both source and poem the angel appears as "radiant" (*splendidissimus, hwit ond hiwbeorht*, 73a).[14] But Cynewulf expands this portion considerably. The *Acta Cyriaci* makes little of the revelatory nature of this event, something which Cynewulf twice emphasizes:

> Þa wearð on slæpe   sylfum ætywed,
> þam casere   þær he on corðre swæf,
> sigerofum gesegen   swefnes woma.
> (69a–71b)

Then to the emperor himself, famed for victories, it was revealed in sleep, where he slept among his band, a vision, the revelation of a dream.

With this revelation by "the beautiful messenger of glory" (*wlitig wuldres boda*, 77a) the "shadows of night broke" (*nihthelm toglad*, 78b). Constantine's vision is of the Holy Rood, "adorned with gold, shining in gems" (*golde geglenged; gimmas lixtan*, 90). Such revelation is another of Cynewulf's proclamations of the word. He refers to the angel (who is only a man, i.e., a male figure [*vir*] in the *Acta*) as a messenger four times (76b, 77a, 87b, 95b). The ornamented Cross (*frætwum beorht*, 88b), the bright light (92a), and the announcement form a complex in which the divine makes a triple earthly appearance. The same is true, though to a much lesser extent, of the Latin narrative; it is inherent in the legend *per se*. However, Cynewulf's "poetic elaborations" constitute a vision of the ultimate reality the Cross embodies; here the Cross is not just a holy relic with special powers to protect the emperor against the invading Huns. Cynewulf's first presentation of the Rood does not simply serve a military function, but symbolizes the whole universal Christian order. Constantine, Judas, and Cynewulf must *become* servants of the Cross through their conversions; however, in *Elene* this vision of the Cross shows what it *is* they must devote themselves to before, in fact, that Cross is found and transformed into the radiant Rood that appears to Constantine. The details of that vision differ from the Latin in these significant respects, and Cynewulf once again superimposes his characteristic double perspective. The temporal narrative of *Elene* depicts the finding and decking of the Cross, but the adorned eternal Rood has already appeared proleptically in Constantine's vision.

Cynewulf's deliberate contrast of this eternal Cross with the simple replica Constantine carries with him into battle underscores the point. And to the previous signs of victory, Cynewulf now adds this token of God as he composes the fifth and final section completing Constantine's struggle; the trumpets, the raven, and the beasts of battle join with the Cross to rout the enemy (109a–13a). The final effect on the heathens expectedly reverses the effect the vision had on Constantine: *cyning wæs þy bliðra / ond þe sorgleasra*, 96b–97a ("The king was the happier and the less sorrowful"). This joy becomes the army's general rejoicing after the Cross's second appearance causes the Huns to flee in panic and terror (130a–39b). The power belongs to the Cross; the careful patterning, to Cynewulf.

However righteous and deserving of victory Constantine may be, he is, nonetheless, ignorant. He returns to Rome naturally curious to discover what this "beautiful tree" (*wlitige treo*, 165b) signifies. Constantine has obtained a portion of God's grace previous to the battle, otherwise he would not be worthy to receive the vision. His reaction to the angels' command to look into the sky for a sign of victory (83b–85a) indicates a predisposition toward the Christian faith, for he looks up after he has "opened his heart" (*hreðerlocan onspeon*, 86b). Campbell comments appropriately that Constantine's opening himself to the vision demonstrates his "spiritual receptiveness."[15] His strife is mostly an imperial problem with a marauding army, though with overtones of a spiritual contest; his revelation is an unasked for manifestation of grace; his conversion is sudden, effortless, and essentially rational. When he assembles the wisest scholars in his kingdom to explain his vision, they cannot tell him what he requires. Cynewulf characterizes this assembly in precisely the same terms as the later assemblies (of varying sizes) which Elene will convene in Jerusalem:

> Heht þa wigena weard   þa wisestan
> snude to sionoðe,   þa þe snyttro cræft

þurh fyrngewrito   gefrigen hæfdon,
heoldon higeþancum   hæleða rædas.
(153a–57b)

The guardian of the warriors ordered then the wisest to come quickly to a
synod, those who skillful wisdom had learned through ancient writings, held
in their thoughts the councils of men.

Interestingly, the *Acta Cyriaci* only says that Constantine gathered all
the priests of all the religions (*convocavit omnes Sacerdotes omnium
deorum vel idolorum*).[16]
     The major difference between this first council and the numerous
Jewish assemblies is patent: without hesitation the "wisest" of the wise
among the Romans identify the tree as Christ's Cross (169a–71b), and
those Christians then living in Rome materialize with "light hearts and
rejoicing in soul" (*him wæs leoht sefa, / ferhð gefeonde*, 173b–74a)
to corroborate this identification. Cynewulf also plays on numbers in
a short series culminating with the story of Christ's mission. Some hints
of this pattern exist in the *Acta*, though Cynewulf gives it a more intricate and completed expression: the massive troops of the Gothic hordes
threaten to conquer the much smaller Roman band, but God reverses
the balance and the Goths are scattered, with only a few of the Hun-
nish army returning home (*lythwon becwom / Huna herges ham eft
þanon*, 142b–43b). Constantine's army in the process increases and he
returns (the phrase is repeated, *ham eft þanon*, 148b) with a "band of
thanes" (*þegna þreate*, 151b). The council of the wise men may not
contain multitudes, but it is certainly larger than the "few" Christians
who can relate to Constantine the gospel message (*þeah hira fea
wæron*, 174b). During the rest of the poem Cynewulf allows the final
variation to develop; like Constantine's returning army, the number of
Christians swells until at the end the whole Jewish nation and the
Roman empire brim over with new converts, a respectful liberty
Cynewulf takes with both history and his sources.
     Constantine now receives instruction in the Christian religion—they
speak "wisely of the spiritual mysteries" (*gleawlice gastgerynum*,
189)—and makes his conversion complete through baptism. Joy, which
has accompanied all acts of revelation and conversion, now belongs to
Constantine as a lasting gift (195b–96a), as he wishes to make known
God's law through the grace of the Holy Spirit (*ongan þa dryhtnes æ
dæges ond nihtes / þurh Gastes gife georne cyðan*, 198a–99b). The

work of the wise men, the Christians, and Constantine is a corollary to
the initial vision of the Holy Rood. They disperse through wisdom and
missionary zeal the influence of the original sacramental revelation.

Constantine's battle is prologue to the whole. The poem now moves
from earthly to spiritual struggle, for strife at the beginning of the
poem is transformed from a mere clash of national armies to the universal struggle, in which the ultimate enemy is Satan, not the Goths.
After his conversion, Constantine learns of the greater conflict between
Christ and Satan, and how Satan has led the human race astray. In
response Constantine sends Elene to find the Cross. It is she who now
shoulders the burden of strife as she journeys to Jerusalem to fulfill her
mission. She is a fit choice to undertake the task because from the
beginning she is the unmoved mover of the action, already a saint in
the Christian communion, endowed with the fortitude and courage of
the Christian soldier, and never questioning the veracity or relevance
of the Christian scheme in which she herself, like all the saints, works
as a flash "sent forth from the dark bosom of the mystery of God."[17]
The other Roman characters belong to the sullied world of strife and
battle, to the state where nation and individual soul are prey to Satan's
domination and need divine revelation to effect their conversion to
Christian truth. Some scholars reasonably identify Elene as a figure of
Ecclesia, the Church Militant, that spiritual body which Constantine
married to the secular imperium of Rome, for hers is a mission
accepted without hesitation or equivocation. Cynewulf uses the same
images and formulas for Elene's eagerness to accomplish her duty as
he did for the apostles:

> Elene ne wolde
> þæs siðfates   sæne weorðan
> ne ðæs wilgifan   word gehyrwan,
> hiere sylfre suna   ac wæs sona gearu,
> wif on willsið.
>
> (219b–23a)

Elene did not want to be reluctant concerning the journey, nor to despise the
command of the ruler, her own son, but she was ready at once, the woman
on the joyful errand.

The diction may be that of the Germanic heroic poem, but Elene, the "war-queen" (*guðcwen*, 254a) combines the Christian saint, the figure of Mary, and the church striving against the very evil that has kept the Cross hidden and the Jews in dark ignorance.

Elene's sea journey to Jerusalem, like Constantine's battle with the Goths, has frequently been lifted from its context; it is admired as another example of Anglo-Saxon "sea poetry." This connection between the battle and the sea journey does not occur in any of the possible sources, but it is appropriate. Manipulating the formulas of Germanic poetry, Cynewulf composes a "type-scene" to describe Elene's departure from the shores of the Mediterranean that closely resembles the drawing up of the Gothic army on the banks of the Danube. The almost excessive military imagery also equates the sea journey, not only with the Gothic expedition, but also with the spiritual battle in which Elene, representative Christian, will engage with Judas, delegate of the Jews. The battle preparations and the sea journey both function as parallel prefaces to a fierce encounter, and in each the battle soon begins to symbolize a spiritual contest of another order. However, Cynewulf reverses one element in the comparison between Constantine's battle and Elene's journey; he transposes agency and effect, as Elene's joyous readiness and active setting out replace Constantine's fear. The switch causes some of the tonal difficulties in Elene's ensuing dialogue with the Jews, for, as James F. Doubleday notes, "There is no scriptural model for the Christian as citizen in power. The primitive Church, of course, existed for the most part as an illegal organization. . . . The New Testament is filled with models and advice for the Christian acting in that situation; but there are no models, there is no advice, for the Christian ruler of a state."[18] But Cynewulf seems purposely to emphasize the military quality of Elene's journey. He shows Elene thinking martial thoughts and anticipating battle with the Jews as much or more as pursuing her religiously inspired archaeological mission:

> Wæs seo eadhreðige   Elene gemyndig,
> þriste on geþance   þeodnes willan,
> georn on mode   þæt hio Iudeas
> ofer herefeldas   heape gecoste,
> lindwigendra   land gesohte,
> secga þreate.
>
> (266a–71a)

The blessed Elene was mindful, bold in thought, of the prince's wish, eager in heart, that she the land of the Jews should seek, over battle-fields with a trusted troop of shield warriors, with a troop of heroes.

Such details and perspectives make a figural interpretation of Elene even more attractive. Only when we see the *guðcwen* as the Church Militant setting out to erase spiritual darkness and establish the True Faith can the various levels of imagery be joined in a coherent system. Elene need not, of course, carry this figural meaning in every detail or action; this typological equivalence serves as a characterizing silhouette, ever-present, but not always intruding into the narrative surface.

After the sea journey, Elene arrives in Jerusalem and immediately calls a council of the wisest men. In contrast to Constantine's earlier convocation, however, this council is not to interpret what has been revealed, but rather to reveal. And establishing a connection between the wisdom of men and the truth revealed of God, Elene specifically requests to meet *þa ðe deoplicost dryhtnes geryno / þurh rihte æ reccan cuðon* ("Those who knew how to expound most deeply the secrets of the Lord by true law," 280a–81b). Expounding the Lord's "right law" differs from expounding "Moses' law," which is all that the wisest of the Jews there assembled know how to do:

> Ða wæs gesamnod   of sidwegum
> mægen unlytel   þa ðe Moyses æ
> reccan cuðon.
>
> (282a–84a)

Then a mighty host was gathered from far ways who knew how to expound the law of Moses.

Cynewulf characteristically repeats a formula to call attention to the disparate aspects of situations which may seem parallel.

An omission from the source is of interest here. Cynewulf suppresses all reference to the Temple of Venus which had been erected on Calvary in the time of Hadrian. This temple had subsequently fallen in ruins and was covered with rubbish; in the Latin Elene has soldiers and peasants remove the accumulated debris. Why Cynewulf chose (if he did choose) not to include this must remain a matter of conjecture, although he does achieve certain effects thereby, and these can be spec-

ified. Again the source states that Elene devoted herself to studying the
Holy Scriptures; in *Elene* this devotion has been transferred to Constantine, who needs to "understand" the mystery of the religion to
which he has just converted. This displacement lends Elene an even
greater figural significance than she has in the *Acta* because she possesses saintliness prior to any action which may earn it. Another common explanation asserts that Cynewulf always omits the names of any
pagan gods found in his sources. While this is true, it does not give
sufficient reason for the change. The clearing of Venus's temple in the
Acta is an extremely awkward piece of narration: Elene enters Jerusalem and calls an assembly; they then remove the rubbish from the
temple. Then Elene calls another assembly to inquire about the burial
place of the Cross. Obviously two different narrative traditions are here
conflated in a piecemeal and unskillful way. By proceeding directly to
the second convocation, Cynewulf avoids this clumsiness of his source
and focuses even more directly on the great confrontation between
Christians and Jews, Elene and Judas, the church and the synagogue.
He moves swiftly to the spiritual scene.

The Lord's right law and the law of Moses are not opposites in
Elene, but the fatal error into which the Jews fall is to believe they are.
Cynewulf emphasizes in their confusion the Pauline distinction
between the letter and the spirit. The irony in Elene's confrontation
with the wise Jews is pungent, as she reveals in her excoriating tirade;
for these men who supposedly know most deeply God's secrets in reality know nothing, since they have not accepted the light of faith to
penetrate into the real mystery of divinity. (Cynewulf usually associates
the Lord's law with *geryne*, "mystery"). The wisdom of men is limited
and its clear contrast in *Elene* to the wisdom achieved from God's
bright revelation points up the monolithic structure of the Christian
truth. As with Constantine's council of sages, only the wisest of them
all, that is, the Christian soul, can "make known" or "reveal" the truth
of the vision; but here in the council of the Jews none can reply to
Elene's question.

We cannot read Elene's speech and fail to perceive that it has
divided aims. We expect Elene would demand to know the burial
place of the Cross, but another purpose takes precedence: Elene's
harangue prepares the Jews for their eventual conversion. By preaching to them, by informing them of their ignorance, error, and darkness,
she initiates the process which will soon produce the one Jew who does
indeed know, yet who must suffer and convert before the Cross can be

found. Had Cynewulf included the Temple of Venus section, this
effective strategy would have been blunted. In the corresponding section of the *Acta*, Elene does the expected and "diligently asked the
natives about the place where the holy body of our Lord and Savior,
Jesus Christ, had hung, fixed to the Cross" *(quaesivit diligenter locum,
in quo sanctum corpus Domini & Salvatoris nostri Jesu Christi pati-
bulo adfixum pependerat, ab incolis).*[19] In *Elene*, this encounter
becomes the first of the ritual and purgative meetings the Jews must
successfully endure to make them worthy of a Christian revelation.

The poem contains a complex series of imagistic correspondences.
They arise from the light of revelation which enabled Constantine to
know, and then to learn about the true mystery. Thus light, truth, and
wisdom accompany Christian revelation; darkness, error, and blind
ignorance remain the share of those who in the battle between Christ
and Satan still adhere to the dark light of the Fallen Angel. In Elene's
first encounter with the Jews, Cynewulf stresses spiritual mystery, that
which is hidden as opposed to that which is known and revealed. Present, too, is strife, the first element of the thematic pattern, for Elene
meets only recalcitrance and refusal on the part of the Jews. From her
exalted position as divine agent, Elene is the wisdom of the church
chastising the stupidity of the unconverted Jews, God's chosen race.
With little concern for protocol, she informs them at once:

> "Ic þæt gearolice   ongiten hæbbe
> þurg witgena   wordgeryno
> on Godes bocum   þæt ge geardagum
> wyrðe wæron   wuldorcyninge."
>   (288a–91b)

"I have completely perceived through the secret words of the prophets in
God's scriptures, that you were dear to the King of Glory in days gone by."

The Jews have consciously rejected God's wisdom: *"Hwæt, ge þære
snyttro unwislice, / wraðe wiðweorpon, þa ge wergdon þane"* ("Lo,
you unwisely and perversely have spurned wisdom when you cursed
Him," 293a–94b). Thus it is deeply ironic that she call them into council at all; in their utter error they perceive nothing of the revelation of
Christ's Godhead. Shortly afterward, Elene connects the light of wisdom to the truth of divine revelation in Christ's person:

> "Ge mid horu speowdon
> on þæs andwlitan   þe eow eagena leoht
> fram blindnesse   bote gefremede."
>
> (297b–99b)

"With filth you spat on the face of the one who gave you the light of your eyes as a remedy from blindness."

A hint of these descriptive images comes from the source: "you wronged Him who with His spit brought light to your eyes ... you assumed the light was darkness and the truth a lie" *(eum qui per sputum oculos vestros illuminavit ... injuriastis ... & lucem tenebras existimastis & veritatem mandacium).*[20] But the pattern is both more pervasive and more highly developed in the Old English poem.

Continuing to follow his source, Cynewulf has Elene point directly to the Jews' spiritual errors:

> "Swa ge modblinde   mengan ongunnon
> lige wið soðe,   leoht wið þystrum,
> æfst wið are."
>
> (306a–8a)

"So you, blind in heart, began to confound lying with truth, light with darkness, malice with mercy."

Elene's speech underscores the relationship between the themes of strife and revelation. For her, already imbued with the wisdom bestowed by a knowledge of the mysteries, only one course of action remains open—direct encounter in mortal strife with the forces of darkness and unwisdom. And during this strife the truth will be revealed, the radiant power manifested to those who in their hate and blindness reject the light. In other words, from the struggle proceeds the revelation, and from the revelation, the conversion. The revelation itself has two facets, the human and the divine. In a sacramental form God reveals to man, and man, then perceiving, makes known this wisdom to himself and others. In *Elene* this chain reaction is sharply etched in the later description of the passing of lore and wisdom through the generations of the Jews.

Her first meeting with the Jews having concluded, Elene sends them
on their way, imploring them to seek out the wisest of their race:

> "þa ðe eowre æ,   æðelum cræftige,
> on ferhðsefan   fyrmest hæbben
> þa me soðlice   secgan cunnon,
> andsware cyðan."
>
> (315a–18a)

"those who, strong in virtues, have foremost your law in their minds, who
know how to tell me trúly, to make known an answer."

The Jews, "skilled in law" (*æcleawe*, 321a), that is, the letter of the
Mosaic law, depart "gloomy hearted" (*reonigmode*, 320b), "oppressed
by terror, sorrowful with cares" (*egesan geþreade, / gehðum geomre*,
321b–22a). Realistic assumptions that Elene's diatribe have hurt their
feelings do not operate in this instance. The Jews' "emotional" state
must be read not as a psychological description but as a statement
about their spiritual condition. Their fear and trembling parallel Constantine's anxiety before the battle and Cynewulf's later dread of the
Last Judgment; the extremity of their terror also measures the depth
of their error. Those who will not voluntarily accept the Christian revelation are doomed to a state of eternal spiritual "depression." The
basic fear Cynewulf finds in his source, but the Jews' sorrow is his own.
Their sadness takes its place in the alternating pattern of fear and joy,
before and after revelation, already sketched.

With almost pitiful impotence the Jews reassemble, bringing with
them a thousand "wise men, those who most completely knew the
memory of former times among the Jews" (*ferhðgleawra þa þe fyrn-
gemynd / mid Iudeum gearwast cuðon*, 327a–28b). In the presence
of Elene, their racial impotence is absolute. Here Elene stands for
Ecclesia, and, without allowing them an opportunity to demonstrate
their wisdom, she gives them proof of their ignorance. With irony she
addresses these wise men thus: "*Gehyrað higegleawe halige rune, /
word ond wisdom*" ("Hear, wise men, the holy secret, words and wisdom," 333a–34a). The wise men's unwisdom then becomes the basic
catalog of her speech as she outlines the Messianic prophecies which
the Jews have ignored.

Of special interest are the "poetic elaborations" on two biblical texts
which Cynewulf spins from the brief selections in the *Acta*. Elene

quotes two famous Old Testament passages, universally taken as prophecies of Christ's birth and redemptive mission: "Unto you a child is born" (Isaiah) and "I have begotten and raised children, but they have spurned me. The ox knew his owner and the ass his master's stable, but Israel did not know me nor my people understand me" (Isaiah 1:2–3). The Latin text does not agree with the Vulgate, but the references are clear. In addition *Elene* has a portion of Psalm 25. Cynewulf's alterations are significant. First, he changes Isaiah's prophecy of Christ's birth from the simple *nascetur* to *acenned bið cniht on degle* ("a child will be born in secret," 339). The various temporal levels all converge here. Christ's birth is not "secret," but the redemption the birth signifies is a "secret mystery" which these Jews will not acknowledge. Cynewulf links the Incarnation to the Cross, also now hidden, because of the Jews' opposition, in a "secret" grave. And Cynewulf describes the children who have spurned their father as lacking forethought, wise understanding (*nahton foreþances, / wisdomes gewitt*, 356b–57a). Their stupidity seems timeless, stretching back into ancient history and up to "the day" of this poem (*oð þysne dæg*, 312b). This time, too, they depart "sorrowful in mind" (*mode cwanige*, 377b).

Elene's second meeting with a smaller group of Jews is very much like the first; her subsequent duels with them likewise resemble those which precede. Such "wearisome repetition in the narrative of Helena's struggle against the unbelief, and stubbornness of spirit, of the Jewish leaders,"[21] as Kennedy describes it, has troubled many readers. But once again this criticism rests on a pragmatic, realistic perspective toward the action, and such an attitude betrays a lack of sympathy for the poem's underlying principles. Elene's series of meetings with the Jews comprises a necessary ritual for conversion, just as Juliana's successive tortures reenacted Christ's sufferings and earned her sainthood. Ritual action is a major characteristic of hagiographic narrative. As noted before, the Jews must be educated before the Cross can be revealed; Elene here "evangelizes" the Jews[22] and we are not at liberty to question her choice of rhetoric or the force of the symbolic struggle.

In any narrative a certain degree of verisimilitude undeniably exists. The puzzled reactions of the Jews to Elene's tirades are not only an ethical characterization, but also a comprehensible response:

> Hie þa anmode   andsweredon,
> "Hwæt, we Ebreisce   æ leornedon
> þa on fyrndagum   fæderas cuðon
> æt Godes earce   ne we eare cunnon

> þurh hwæt ðu ðus hearde,   hlæfdige, us
> eorre wurde;   we ðæt æbylgð nyton
> þe we gefremedon   on þysse folcscere,
> þeodenbealwa   wið þec æfre."
>
> (396a–403b)

They then answered unanimously: "We learned the Hebraic law which our fathers knew in days past at God's ark; but we do not know exactly why you were thus harshly so angry at us. We do not know what transgression we have committed among this people, nor what terrible evil we ever did against you."

Literally, this is true; but Cynewulf strongly emphasizes the "knowing" of the Hebraic law, which deals only with the past, and their "not knowing" of Elene's purpose and anger. He does this to make the Jews' position unforgivable; they *should* know: thus Elene's repeating to them from their same "law" the passages prophecying the birth of Christ. That they are *anmode* ("unanimous") strengthens a Christian condemnation. However rational the Jews' appeal to common sense may be, Christians must reject it in the larger framework of divine history.

Ironically, the Jews are not actually unanimous in their disclaimer. Judas admits he comprehends precisely what Elene means. The focus now shifts from the Jews as a whole unit to Judas as a single character representing the race. Although no early medieval reader would side with the Jews, both legend and poem expose their pretended innocence. Judas goes directly to the issue of Elene's unspoken request:

> "Ic wat geare
> þæt hio wile secan   be ðam sigebeame
> on ðam þrowode   þeoda waldend
> eallra gnyrna leas,   Godes agen bearn
> þone orscyldne   eofota gehwylces
> þurh hete hengon   on heanne beam
> in fyrndagum   fæderas usse."
>
> (419b–25b)

"I know well that she wants to find the Tree of Victory on which the Guardian of men, God's own Son, free of all sins, suffered, when in days gone by our fathers through hate hanged Him, guiltless of every sin, on the high Beam."

Critics have commented that Judas, in this confession, seems to be almost "sympathetic" toward Christianity. That, however, misses the point. The absolute truth of Christianity is revealed here, not Judas's "sympathy." Even the recalcitrant Jew falls inevitably into Christian rhetoric when recounting the Crucifixion. Judas shares this *secret* with the members of his tribe, and the secret he divulges, though not the strategy he concocts for dealing with it, partakes of the same mystery that began with Christ's "secret" birth and will end with the revelation of the "secret" Cross. In such a context, truth majestically overrides ignorance.

The imagery attached to good and evil now includes what is hidden against what is revealed. The power of darkness, ignorance, and sin hide the Tree of Victory; its revelation would bring light, truth, and another victory over sin. As wisdom is concealed from the Jews, so the Cross is hidden from Elene. Judas, who does understand, discusses the situation with his countrymen, who professed innocence, in exactly these terms:

> "Nu is þearf mycel
> þæt we fæstlice   ferhð staðelien
> þæt we ðæs morðres   meldan ne weorðen
> hwær þæt halige trio   beheled wurde
> æfter wigþræce,   þylæs toworpen sien
> frod fyrngewritu   ond þa fæderlican
> lare forleten."
>
> (426b–32a)

"Now there is great need that we firmly fix our hearts so that we do not become informers of the murder, or of where that Holy Tree was hidden after the strife, lest the wise ancient writings be overthrown and our ancestral teachings renounced."

The theme of strife becomes directly involved with the counterthemes of revelation and knowledge. For purely racial and political purposes, Judas counsels resistance to Elene and Christ, lest the worldly imperium of the Israelites cease to prevail. Judas's confession and plotting are rife with irony. He attempts to keep hidden that which only God can reveal; and the spiritual method he proposes for achieving this end is the "firm fixing of the heart" *(ferhð staðelian)*. This formula has an automatic frame of reference: Cynewulf uses the phrase repeatedly in all his poems (except *The Fates*) in the context of faith and trust in God's redemptive scheme. That Judas should "appropriate" it for his own evil purposes reveals him to be more ignorant than he knows at precisely the point where he shows himself to know the truth. In fine, Judas's present behavior is an antitype of conversion, a turning toward lies in the most ironically impotent manner. The questions of psychological and political reality are secondary at best. And when the Jews reconvene before Elene, their claim that Judas "may make known the truth, / reveal the secret events" (*mæg soð gecyðan, / onwreon wyrda geryno*, 588b–89a) is absurd in its pretension and pathetic in its sterility.

Judas does not, of course, know where the Cross is hidden; we can believe his statement "I do not know that which I do not know" ("*ic ne can þæt ic nat*," 640b). But he can be faulted for his apostasy, his retreat from the light of revelation. Judas has received the truth of Christ's Incarnation from his own ancestors and has abandoned that knowledge for the darkness of the Jewish (in itself acceptable, by itself Satanic) law. Although the symbolic chronology setting forth Judas's lineage bears no relation to history—Judas is called the brother of Stephen, the Proto-Martyr—he has been given an account of Christ's life by his father, and the images in which he retells the story complement the general pattern:

> "þreo niht siððan
> in byrgenne   bidende wæs
> under þeosterlocan   ond þa þy þriddan dæg
> ealles leohtes leoht   lifgende aras,
> ðeoden engla   ond his þegnum,
> soð sigora frea   seolfne geywde,
> beorht on blæde."
>
> (483b–89a)

"three nights afterwards in the grave He waited, in the dark tomb, and then on the third day the Light of all light living arose, the Prince of Angels, the True Lord of Victories revealed Himself to His disciples, bright in glory."

The description of Christ's Resurrection, with its heavy stress on the revelation of light defeating the darkness of the grave, brings with it the concomitant theme of conversion; Judas's father at once reports two such radical changes from the Jewish law to the Christian dispensation. First, comes the conversion of Judas's "brother," Stephen, who "after a time received the bath of baptism, the bright faith" (*onfeng æfter fyrste fulwihtes bæð, / leohtne geleafan*, 490a–91a); and then the conversion of Stephen's adversary, Saul, who as Paul symbolizes the type of the converted Christian, the best of the teachers of the law (*ond him nænig wæs / ælærendra oðer betera*, 505b–6b). This momentary return to the Jewish past after the coming of Christ contains within it the pattern of the whole poem, and Judas's obstinance becomes thereby the more frightening. He has two models of the converting Jew right at hand. But Judas expressly and inexplicably rejects his father's warning never to commit blasphemy or give a "hostile answer against God's son" (*grimne geagncwide wið Godes bearne*, 525).

This arbitrary quality cannot be accounted for on any realistic grounds, forcing an interpretation of Judas's persistence on a figural level. He refuses simply because the Jews refuse. He is the embodiment of "hardness of the heart" (*duritia cordis*). Whatley writes that the Jews "were traditionally described . . . as 'hard-hearted,' *duri cordis*, in token of their ingratitude and their obstinate lack of faith in God's love for them, their disobedience to his Law and their unbelief."[23] In this respect Judas stands at the opposite pole to Constantine, who, although ignorant, nonetheless "opened his heart" to the revelation. Cynewulf has reversed the pattern exactly: Constantine is given a revelation, which causes him to seek out knowledge and then he converts; Judas has the knowledge, but he denies it. He must then convert (in a spiritual sense) *before* he can receive the revelation. Cynewulf describes this action thus:

> Heo wæron stearce,   stane heardran,
> noldon þæt geryne   rihte cyðan
> ne hire andsware   ænige secgan.
>   (565a–67b)

They were obstinate, harder than stones, they did not want to make known that secret truly, nor to give her any answer.

Constantine can be chosen of God since he never had access to the revealed truth; Judas must suffer since as a Jew he is one of the chosen people.

In the final meeting between Elene and the Jews, Elene presses them
to the extreme, until in desperation they give Judas up. They now
know he does possess the answers to her questions, and they eagerly
give him as a "hostage" (*gisle*, 600a) to save their own lives. Their
speech gives a fine example of Cynewulf's ironic perspective. In bold
outline he follows his source closely, which reads: "Because they were
afraid, they delivered Judas to her and said, 'Here is the son of a just
man and a prophet; he knows the law and its statutes. Lady, he will
carefully show you all your heart desires'" (*Qui cum timuissent, trad-
iderunt ei Judam, dicentes; Hic viri justi & prophetae filius est, &
legem novit cum actibus suis: hic, Domine, omnia quae desiderat cor
tuum ostendet tibi diligenter*).[24] Cynewulf's variations on this basic
idea produce a nearly comic effect:

> Ða wurdon hie deaðes on wenan,
> ades ond endelifes   ond þær þa ænne betæhton
> giddum gearusnottorne—   þam wæs Iudas nama
> cenned for cneomagum—   þone hie þære cwene agefon,
> sægdon hine sundorwisne,   "He þe mæg soð gecyðan,
> onwreon wyrda geryno   swa ðu hine wordum frignest,
> æriht from orde   oð ende forð;
> he is for eorðan   æðeles cynnes,
> wordcræftes wis   ond witgan sunu,
> bald on meðle;   him gebyrde is
> þæt he gencwidas   gleawe hæbbe,
> cræft in breostum;   he gecyðeð þe
> for wera mengo   wisdomes gife
> þurh þa myclan miht   swa þin mod lufaþ."
>
> (584b–97b)

Then they expected death, fire and the end of their lives—and thereupon
they entrusted one very wise in speeches (whose name was Judas among his
companions)—they there gave him up to the queen, they said he was very
wise: "He may make known the truth to you, reveal the secret events as you
ask him to do with words, the law from the beginning up to the end. He is
of a noble race on earth, wise in word-craft, and the son of a prophet, bold
in council. It is innate in him to have wise answers, skill in his heart; before
the multitude of men he will make known to you the gift of wisdom through
his great power, as your heart desires."

The Jews stumble all over themselves in these deliberately awkward
hypermetrical lines. Repetition, both within the speech proper and in

the reiteration of concerns from what has gone before, becomes excessive. The syntax at the beginning reflects the Jews' panic and confusion. All these stylistic devices are meant to reflect Cynewulf's ironic point of view: the density of the images associated with Judas's wisdom, skill, craft, and power creates a clear parody of true wisdom and power. These words form a conventional Christian matrix, but here they are parodically misapplied. And of special interest is their assertion that Judas's wisdom is "innate." As the recipient of the Christian message from his own ancestors and as a Jew, Judas should indeed have such inborn understanding. That he does not, despite the cascade of assertions to the contrary, necessitates his coming ordeal.

Judas's ignorance works entirely against him in his protracted dialogue with Elene, questioning not only its ultimate validity, but even its immediate purpose. Elene does not hesitate in making plain what his situation is:

> Elene maþelode   to þam anhagan,
> tireadig cwen,   "þe synt tu gearu,
> swa lif swa deað   swa þe leofre bið
> to geceosanne."
>
>   (604a–7a)

Elene, the glorious queen, spoke to the solitary man: "Two things are prepared for you: either life or death, as you desire to choose."

This variation on the "choice" passage in *Christ II* provokes a predictably reasonable, self-protective response from Judas, now aptly called an *anhaga*, with all the overtones of solitary "exile" that word carries in Old English poetic diction. Judas answers:

> "Hu mæg þæm geweorðan   þe on westenne
> meðe ond meteleas   morland trydeð,
> hungre gehæfted   ond him hlaf ond stan
> on gesihðe bu geweorðað,
> stearc ond hnesce,   þæt he þone stan nime
> wið hungres hleo,   hlafes ne gime,
> gewende to wædle   ond þa wiste wiðsæce,
> beteran wiðhyccge   þonne he bega beneah":—
>
>   (611a–18b)

"How would it happen to the one who in the wilderness treads the moorland, weary and without food, gripped by hunger, and to his sight both a loaf and a stone appear, hard and soft, that he would take the stone for protection against hunger, and not take the loaf, turn away to want and renounce the food, scorn the better, when he has both at his disposal?"

Judas has just outlined the Christian perspective, except, of course, that he does not understand it in those terms and does in fact "choose the hard" at first.[25] Judas remains obdurate even in the face of Elene's direct accusations: *"Wiðsæcest ðu to swiðe soðe ond rihte / ymb þæt lifes treow"* ("You strive too resolutely against the truth and right concerning the Tree of Life," 663a–64a). To atone for his struggle against *soð* and *riht* Elene gives Judas only one alternative, to reveal the hiding place of the Cross, to act in a human way that imitates the divine. Judas, whose friends have claimed he could "reveal the secret of events" *(onwreon wyrda geryno)*, must now make good on their promise. Cynewulf uses the same verb to link the two contexts: *"þu scealt geagninga / wisdom onwreon swa gewritu secgaþ / æfter stedewange, hwær seo stow sie, / Caluarie"* ("You must completely reveal with wisdom that place, even as the scriptures say, where the place is, Calvary," 673b–76a). With a final warning that he will be killed unless he stops lying and reveals the truth (689a–90b), Elene orders Judas placed in a dry pit *(in drygne seað, 693a)*. The struggle between these two reaches a climax over a point of revelation, of making known the location of Calvary and the Cross.

On one level, Judas's entombment is the final and most effective device Elene has at her disposal to force him into submission; on a second level, his "burial" has many symbolic overtones. In the most general way it parallels Christ's three days in the grave, especially Christ's Harrowing of Hell during those three days. Judas's grave becomes the dark physical sign of his ignorance, the depths to which his blindness has taken him, and the means as well of his salvation. This black cistern refers both backward and forward, for in addition to resembling Christ's tomb, Judas's pit also anticipates the grave in which the Cross itself is hidden. He who will become the human instrument by which the world's most sacred object will be revealed must suffer burial as an expiation before he can release the Cross from its own ancient sepulcher. The punishment not only suffices to force Judas into ending his strife with Elene, the church, and God, but also fills him with the desire to accept the new light of truth that his sojourn in darkness has provided. Revelation, truth, and recognition are all part of his confession from the deep pit:

> "ic adreogan ne mæg
> ne leng helan   be ðam lifes treo
> þeah ic ær mid dysige   þurhdrifen wære
> ond ðæt soð to late   seolf gecneowe."
>
> (705b–8b)

"I cannot endure, nor longer conceal [the truth] about the Tree of Life, though I was riddled with folly before and that truth too late myself recognized."

His own recognition of the light of truth replaces his spiritual blindness. From his descent into the depths of darkness comes his inner sight. Judas has undergone a baptism of the spirit during his seven days in the pit and in this he imitates Christ's Harrowing of Hell.[26] He has himself struggled with the devil and conquered, else he could not now equate his factual information with knowledge and truth. Once inimical to God, Judas becomes one of His chosen through the ordeal. The *duritia cordis* has been softened by his very choosing of the "hard."

Calvary understandably reverberates with meaning. Here at the place of the Crucifixion tradition locates the truths and mysteries of Christianity. In this place the struggle between good and evil reached its universal culmination at the moment when eternity vanquished time and sin through Christ. But since the Cross remains hidden, Satanic power still controls. Cynewulf is most explicit. The Holy Tree, he says, *þurh facensearu foldan getyned, / lange legere fæst, leodum dyrne, / wunode wælreste* ("through the treachery was enclosed in the earth, long fast in its resting-place, concealed from men, dwelt in its place of rest on the battle-field," 721a–23a). Calvary is a *wælreste* and a "battle-field," because the Cross remains concealed from men. Revelation frees men from evil, just as it will unlock the Cross from its grave where it has lain *under neolum niðer næsse gehydde, / in þeostorcofan* ("under the deep, below the abyss, hidden in the dark chamber," 831a–32a).

In propitiation for his past sins, Judas prays to God to reveal the Cross, *elnes oncyðig* ("revealing courage," 724a). After his baptism in the pit a spiritual courage replaces his fear and ignorance, thus tying him directly to Constantine, the brave emperor, who overcame his fear through the vision of the Cross. He contrasts in his prayer the light and glory of heaven with the *heolstorhofu* ("dark court," 763a) of the fallen angels cast down from the empyrean blaze. By renouncing his role in Satan's causes, Judas has acquired wise inner sight, and so he asks God to make known in wonders the Cross's burial place and to end the reign of darkness which has held it. In a telling repetition, Judas promises to "fix his heart more firmly" (*ond þy fæstlicor ferhð staðelige*, 796) on the crucified Christ if his prayers are answered. We might accuse Judas here of bargaining with God, if it were not for the contrast between this promise and his previous vow to do the opposite to keep the Holy Tree hidden. Judas has undergone a complete conversion.

The sign asked of God appears: *Ða of ðære stowe steam up aras / swylce rec under radorum* ("Then from that place a vapor rose up, like smoke under the skies," 802a–3a). Judas's success in his first attempt at a miracle allows Cynewulf to add "blessed" (*eadig*, 805a), an obvious Christian appellation, to the Jew who was skilled in law (*ægleaw*, 805a). And Judas explicitly calls attention to his hardness of heart, his constitutional disposition to be like a stone before he knew the truth: *"Nu ic þurh soð hafu seolf gecnawen / on heardum hige þæt ðu hælend eart / middangeardes"* ("Now I have learned myself through the truth, in my hard heart, that you are the Savior of the world," 807a–9a). The choice of images hardly seems fortuitous, for at this juncture Cynewulf has Judas refer to his supposed brother, Stephen, Proto-Martyr. Like his sources, this Judas asks to be remembered among the blessed as Stephen was, but it is his characterization of Stephen, especially in contrast to his immediately preceding self-portrait as hard-hearted, that hits the most striking note. What the Old English Judas recalls for the reader is that Stephen "held firm even though he was stoned" (*"Stephanus, heold þeah he stangreopum / worpod wære,"* 823a–24a). Judas did in fact choose the stone, not the bread, of his own rhetorical question and in consequence of that choice finds the way out of hardness to truth; this makes him conscious of the analogous paradigm Stephen's death presents: Stephen is firm (as opposed to Judas's obstinance), but he too receives stones that pave a path to everlasting glory. Judas hopes that the analogy is tight enough to merit both the unhistorical relationship and the same reward.

Cynewulf's characteristic technique of contrasted analogies is nowhere more evident than in the passage describing the discovery and the identification of Christ's Cross. Miraculous enough in itself, the

narrative can distract a modern reader, but Cynewulf's careful patterning shows that he is concerned with more than simple narrative.
The whole section divides into two parts—the finding of the three
crosses and the identification of the True Cross. It is replete with "arisings" of many sorts, as the sources are not, except in the barest detail.
Each section begins with the familiar echoic pattern: *Ongan þa
wilfægen æfter þam wuldres treo, / elnes anhydig, eorðan delfan*
("The one resolute in bravery began then joyful to dig in the earth for
the Tree of Glory," 827a–28b); and *Asetton þa on gesyhðe sigebeamas þrie / eorlas anhydige fore Elenan cneo* ("The resolute nobles
set then in her sight the three victory-beams before Elene's knee,"
846a–47b). At the end of each part there is a "rising" that reveals: first,
the three trees are "raised" out of the grave (*ond mid weorode ahof
/ of foldgræfe*, 843b–44a), then the True Cross is raised over the dead
boy who "arose" with soul and body reunited (883b–89a). As a result
of this miracle the gathered multitude "raises" a song of thanksgiving
and praise to God the Father (889b–93b) which parallels the song
raised before the identification of the Cross (*Gesæton sigerofe, sang
ahofon*, 867); this is also antithetical to the hostility which the Jews had
"raised against God's Son while He was living" (*hie wið Godes bearne
/ nið ahofun*, 836b–37a). The return to the earthly city at the close of
the first section stands in opposition to the sense of a heavenly realm at
the close of the second, now that the revelation is complete. The Jews'
hostility flows from their obedience to the teachings of the author of
sins (837–38) which Cynewulf contrasts with the true revelations
which have come "through holy books" (*þurh halige bec*, 852b). The
burial of the Cross in a "dark pit" and a "sorrowful house" (*in
þeostorcofan*, 832a; *in þam reonian hofe*, 833a) is both a result and
a reflection of the darkness of the Crucifixion, which Cynewulf relates
in section two: *rodor eall geswearc / on þa sliðan tid*, 855b–56a).
Finally Judas's joy remains constant in both sections (839a–42a, 874b–
75b) and prepares for the general rejoicing that concludes the entire
miraculous revelation. This sense of structure is profoundly typological
and incorporates into the poetry the same order which the two testaments themselves reveal. The Old and New Testaments are filled with
details that parallel each other, but, of course, the New Testament is
a fulfillment and transcendence of the Old. Cynewulf works this basic
pattern into the form and imagery of his poem; so, the Jews' hostility
"raised" against God's Son is counterpointed and transcended by the
song of victory "raised" by the discoverers of the instrument of that

hostility, the Cross. Or to look at the pattern in a slightly different perspective, we note that the first section moves from a concern with the hidden Cross, through a reference to the Crucifixion, to a return to the city, presumably for the purpose of taking counsel, while the second reverses this order, beginning with Elene's speech on what has been revealed through holy books, and then once more a reference to the Crucifixion, then ultimately to the treatment of the revealed Cross. In this description of the scheme, the pattern of reversals creates a cross in itself.

Judas now becomes the second character in *Elene* to undergo a conversion after a revelation of the Cross. Although he faced the added struggle of softening his hardness of heart, he still performs a function following his acceptance of Christianity similar to Constantine's. Cynewulf portrays Judas as a *rihtes wemend*, 879a, a "revealer of right" to the Jews. He possesses the wisdom of truth and can reveal that truth to save his people.

The test of Judas's newfound faith comes soon. Hearing of Judas's "apostasy" from the old religion, the "hell-devil" (900b) appears, leaping up, rising into the air in a kind of parody of the preceding rituals of "raising" (*þa þeær ligesynnig / on lyft astah lacende feond*, 898b–99b). Cynewulf conceives the ensuing debate in a highly schematic fashion; it is one which takes place between friend and fiend, the blessed and the bad, the sinning and the saved (*se feond ond se freond*, 953a; *tireadig ond trag*, 954a; *synnig ond gesælig*, 955a). The parallel speeches each delivers contain the same balanced antithesis. The devil rages against Christ's plundering of his possessions (907b–10a) and the broadening of His Kingdom as his own withers away (916b–18a). He specifically rejects the Cross and all it represents and threatens to "raise up" another king, usually taken as a reference to Julian the Apostate, who will destroy the faith (*ic awecce wið ðe / oðerne cyning, se ehteð þin*, 926b–27b). This devil possesses a sense of the irony of this reversal; through a Judas he once hoped to establish his kingdom, and now another Judas has betrayed him. With his new but profound wisdom Judas answers the devil and implicitly counters the devil's threat to raise up an apostate with a reference to the Mighty King's power both to cast down the strife the devil will raise up (940b) and to raise the dead with His word alone (*se ðe deadra feala / worde awehte*, 944b–45a). All the devil's "raising" becomes instead a fall into the abyss (942). The poem has returned full circle to the beginning of the thematic pattern where a new warrior has picked up the standard of the

Christian battle. In his argument with the devil Judas turns against Satan the points Elene had used against him. Judas now equates evil with ignorance and darkness: *"wite ðu þe gearwor / þæt ðu unsnyt-trum anforlete / leohta beorhtost"* ("Know you the more clearly that you in unwisdom have relinquished the brightest of lights," 945b–47a). This light Elene now perceives glowing in Judas's bosom.

The last section of the narrative is a continuation, a variation on the events just outlined. It serves as a coda to the double conversions of Constantine and Judas which have been effected by the Cross. Here Cynewulf departs most radically from all the extant versions of his possible sources: Judas's conversion and his subsequent baptism follow one another, not surprisingly, in the sources; but in *Elene*, Cynewulf inserts a long description of Elene's report to Constantine, his reaction, and his return command to erect a church on Calvary (a detail of Elene's mission which she takes *with* her in the Latin *Acta*). Cynewulf's reasons for this "interruption" seem deliberate and its effect increases the sense of balance between Constantine and Judas struck throughout the poem. Constantine and Elene represent Roman civilization and the Christian Imperium; Judas stands as the central figure of an old religion and a damned race. Thus Cynewulf finds it necessary to recount the rapid spread of the news, the tidings proclaimed through all the cities of the world; the True Cross has been found, taken from its hiding place where the Jews had tried to conceal it, and the discovery of the Cross has now become a vexation for them, the greatest of griefs (967a–79a).

Elene's decision to send a particular report to Constantine becomes yet another communication, a revelation of "the greatest of glad tidings" (*wilspella mæst*, 983b). For in *Elene* the discovery of the Cross is not simply an archeological event of some religious interest, but a triumphant victory for Roman Christianity over both the Jewish law and the Jewish race. Thus Cynewulf displaces Constantine's order to construct a church from the narrative beginning to this point in his poem; Cynewulf makes the actual building of the church the corporeal reality symbolizing Elene's spiritual victory over the synagogue. The "interruption," then, which seems to be Cynewulf's invention, contributes to the larger meaning of the poem. Not until the full implications of Roman Christianity's defeat of Jewish obstinance and error are realized literally and symbolically does Judas's formal conversion to the Christian religion fit into the pattern. Judas, we must remember, undergoes a conversion with a double aspect: he not only accepts the

Christian faith but also changes both his name and his position. From being Judas, stubborn leader of the wicked Jews, he becomes Bishop Cyriacus of the newly converted nation. The change requires a more encompassing, figural interpretation; Cynewulf explicitly glosses Judas's Greek name as "the law of the Savior" (*æ hælendes*, 1062a). Gordon Whatley has shown that Cynewulf takes great liberty with his translation of Judas's new name. "Cyriacus," he writes, "does not mean 'the law of the Savior.' It is the adjective from Greek *kurios*, 'lord,' and means 'of the lord.' Its Latin equivalent is *dominicus*, and the usual Old English translation of *dominicus* was, predictably, *dryhtenlic*."[27] The presence of an onomastic interpretation itself justifies such a figural reading; Cynewulf's purposeful distortion makes this reading imperative. And, as Whatley accurately summarizes, Judas's

baptism looks back at his old faith and blindness and sums up his former life in the uncompromising words *unriht æ* ["the wrong law"]. The consecration looks forward to his future as bishop of Jerusalem and leader of the new Christian community in the city. The whole spirit and essence of his new role and identity are summed up in the new name, Cyriacus, *æ hælendes*, and the long chain of occurrences of *æ* and *æriht* is here brought to a fitting climax.[28]

Elene and Judas once enacted the hostility between the church and the synagogue; now Constantine and Judas symbolize the dual aspect of perfect leadership in the early medieval theocracy. As emperor and bishop they control both the secular and the spiritual realms which contain the two great races of the world each converted within the scope of this poem's action. Each is charged with the building of a new church, a literal and a spiritual church, and in this church Judas Cyriacus can speak "with a new turn," i.e., "afresh" (*niwan stefne*, 1060a).

The search for the nails which held Christ to the Cross next occupies Elene. They are *in foldan gen / deope bedolfen* ("still in the earth, deeply buried," 1079b–80a). Like the Cross the nails are a "treasure under the earth still hidden, concealed from men" (*hord under hrusan þæt gehyded gen / duguðum dyrne*, 1091a–92a). As before, the powers of darkness rule what is concealed in the dark pit. But Elene has confidence "that her desire will once more be fulfilled concerning the wondrous matter by the power of the spirit" (*þæt hire þa gina gastes mihtum / ymb wundorwyrd willan gefylde*, 1069a–70b).

God answers her prayer for another revelation and the nails of the Crucifixion shine forth from their burial place:

> Ða cwom semninga   sunnan beorhtra
> lacende lig. . . .
> næglas of nearwe   neoðan scinende
> leohte lixton.
>   (1109a–10a; 1114a–15a)

Then came suddenly, brighter than the sun, a darting flame . . . the nails shining closely from below, radiant with light.

After this final revelation comes the final conversion, as the Jews with one voice announce their resolve to turn from error and follow God's truth. In their speech they hit upon the causal relation between the light of revelation and their conversion to the truth:

> "Nu we seolfe geseoð   sigores tacen,
> soðwundor Godes   þeah we wiðsocun ær
> mid leasingum.   Nu is in leoht cymen,
> onwrigen wyrda bigang;   wuldor þæs age
> on heannesse   heofonrices God!"
>   (1120a–24b)

"Now we ourselves see the sign of victory, God's true wonder, although we struggled against it before with lies. Now has the light come in, been revealed the course of events. For that may the God of the heavenly kingdom have glory on high!"

As a parallel to their action, Elene abandons herself to the joy of a renewed and deepened faith. This faith is described in imagery reminiscent of the earlier pattern; she kneels down "in radiant belief" (*leohte geleafen*, 1136a) to thank God:

> þæs þe hio soð gecneow
> andweardlice   þæt wæs oft bodod
> feor ær beforan   fram fruman worulde
> folcum to frofre;   heo gefylled wæs
> wisdomes gife.
>   (1139b–43a)

because she now knew the truth which long before from the beginning of the world had been preached as a comfort to people. She was filled with the gift of wisdom.

God's will has been revealed and fulfilled once again, but what function does this second discovery serve, and what does it symbolize? The answer seems clear: the two discoveries are necessary to bring about the two conversions, first of Judas and then of the Jews themselves. And in Cynewulf's handling of the second conversion, we perceive that it extends the process of renouncing error and darkness on the part of those furthest from the truth. In *Elene* the final conversion of the Jews is not so much an awed response to the revelation of the nails, as the logical working out of Cynewulf's structuring of the action and the accompanying pattern of religious imagery. Once the Jews themselves have capitulated to Christianity, then Cynewulf need only be concerned about the Day of Judgment. Indeed, for medieval Christians the conversion of the Jews became a standard sign of the approach of the Last Judgment and Cynewulf's strong emphasis on this event prepares for his eschatological ruminations in the "autobiographical" conclusion.

The disposal of the nails—they are used to make a bridle for Constantine's horse—is perhaps another in the series of actions with a figural significance. Cynewulf follows his source quite closely here and lets Elene learn from a wise man that this would be the appropriate course, for it would fulfill the words of the prophet Isaiah: "on that day what is in the horse's bridle will be called sacred to the Lord" (*In ille die quod est in freno equi sanctum Domini vocabitur*, 14:20).[29] This bridle becomes the permanent and sacred token of invincible men who share in the revealed truth; both the Latin source and the Cynewulfian version present it this way. This noble gift will bring success at war, victory in battle, safety in the fight, and "peace everywhere" (*sybbe gehwær*, 1182b). Whether the nails carry a more specific meaning is problematic. Campbell suggests that Cynewulf here follows Prudentius and Jerome in making the bridle represent the controls which must be placed on the flesh to restrain pride and lust. He concludes that the bridle is particularly appropriate for Constantine, for

As a Christian ruler his physical power must be limited by the knowledge that even secular affairs must be governed by divine principles. Whether the horse is taken as his own pride, or perhaps as the self-centered physical desires of secular humanity, the bodily suffering of Christ on the Cross, revealed by the nails, can conduce to both humility, and a healthy, controlled treatment of desire.[30]

One cannot quibble with Prudentius and Jerome, but it remains doubtful that either the Latin author or Cynewulf had these interpretations in mind. For both the bridle bestows on its owner victory, success in arms. War may acquire the symbolic reference, rather than the armor of invincibility used in its fighting. The main narrative returns near the end to the ever-present need of facing the enemy within the domain of time. Though Judas and his people see deeply with the light of faith, there are many who would oppose God's law, keep the truth of the Christian faith hidden in the occlusion of ignorance so they may persist in their error. Against such there is no rest from the battle for the Christian armed with the true faith; the strife against the devil is, by the devil's own admission, "perpetual" (*singal*, 905a).[31] The ending of the narrative, with its stress on the battle between good and evil, the struggle to close the doors of hell and to keep "heaven's unlocked, eternally opened" (*heofones ontyned,* / *ece geopenad,* 1229b–30a), reflects on the spiritual level the martial encounter between Constantine and the Goths. What was only a heroic skirmish in which a good king defeats a foraging host of marauders has been skillfully transformed into a war at the very portals of hell. And Judas, the recalcitrant, becomes Cyriacus, the bishop who heals both the sick and the despairing (1209b–17a).

The serial and schematic structure of *Elene* has not been easily perceived. Smithson's comments sum up a general attitude: "*Elene* is greatly weakened by the fact that there are three main protagonists."[32] Such a criticism assumes that a proper narrative has a believable plot and that a "unified" story outlines a network of causes and effects deriving from the action of a "main" character. A partial rebuttal to such an unsympathetic approach first appeared in Stanley B. Greenfield's suggestion that the poem's structure can best be described as a "series of revelations, outward miracles being matched by inner illuminations."[33] Although Greenfield did not go on to develop the full implications of his statement, or relate the revelations and illuminations to the autobiographical conclusion, his insight has proved the most solid base for the new reevaluation of *Elene*. Greenfield and all later critics who depend upon him perceive that the struggle in *Elene* is the cosmic war between good and evil and not the continuing confrontation of a

single hero and an enemy within a tightly controlled temporal framework of events. The poem is a connected series of historical, indeed
legendary, *exempla*, each repeating the same pattern of strife, revelation, and conversion. This pattern represents schematically both the
"history" of the events and the psychological response to them as a
series of souls move from explicable ignorance, calculated denial, or
the weakness of sin into a world of faith. As *Elene* progresses from
example to example, the context broadens and is spiritualized: the story
begins with the battle on the shores of the Danube; it ends at the doors
of hell.

What has now become an obvious and ingenious habit on Cynewulf's part—the way he weaves his runic signatures back into the narrative—was first discovered and described in *Elene*. For in this poem
Cynewulf is the fourth protagonist, the last in the series, who enacts
within his soul the thematic pattern he has so carefully constructed in
the narrative. The tone is confessional and is separated from the rest of
the poem by the striking introduction of heavily rhymed verses:[34]

> Þus ic frod ond fus,   þurh þæt fæcne hus,
> wordcræft wæf   ond wundrum læs,
> þragum þreodude   ond geþanc reodode,
> nihtes nearwe;   nysse ic gearwe,
> be ðære rode riht   ær me rumran geþeaht,
> þurh ða mæran miht,   on modes þeaht,
> wisdom onwreah;   ic wæs weorcum fah,
> synnum asæled,   sorgum gewæled,
> bitrum gebunden,   bisgum beþrungen,
> ær me lare onlag   þurh leohtne had,
> gamelum to geoce,   gife unscynde
> mægencyning amæt   ond on gemynd begeat,
> torht ontynde,   tidum gerymde,
> bancofan onband,   breostlocan onwand,
> leoðucræft onleac   þæs ic lustum breac,
> willum in worlde.
>
>   (1236a–51a)

Thus I, old and eager to depart because of this fragile house, have woven
with wordcraft and wondrously gathered, at times have pondered and turned
my thoughts in the anxiety of night. I did not know exactly the right about
the Cross before wisdom revealed a more spacious thought through its glo-

rious might in the thought of my mind. I was stained by my deeds, bound by sins, afflicted with sorrows, bitterly bound, pressed by troubles, before the Mighty King gloriously granted the lore to me as a comfort in my age, a noble gift bestowed, and poured it into my mind, revealed its beauty, enlarged it betimes, unbound the body, unwound the heart, unlocked the art of poetry. This I have used gladly, joyfully in the world.

Like Constantine and Judas, Cynewulf struggles against his own sin and ignorance (1242b–44a). As a sinner, Cynewulf has engaged in a personal battle against impinging evil. But before he wrote *Elene* he suffered in sorrow and sin:

> ic þæs wuldres treowes
> oft nales æne   hæfde ingemynd
> ær ic þæt wundor   onwrigen hæfde,
> ymb þone beorhtan beam   swa ic on bocum fand,
> wyrda gangum,   on gewritum cyðan
> be ðam sigebeacne.
>
> (1251b–56a)

Not only once did I have in my mind the Tree of Glory before I had revealed that wonder concerning that bright Beam, as I found the course of events in books, made known in writings concerning that Sign of Victory.

Though Cynewulf shares a strife-filled existence with the other characters, his wrestling is of an interior sort. Cynewulf transforms the poem steadily in this direction, from the military struggle of Constantine, through Judas's duel with Elene, to the inner world of psychological disruption and the chaos of sin in Cynewulf's heart. Cynewulf casts his battle with sin and error, however, in the past tense. He knows what his ignorance was, but his darkness has been lightened. He, too, has been privileged to witness a divine revelation, and with that revelation come wisdom and truth as they did in the narrative proper. And in his conversion Cynewulf seizes upon the Cross as a symbolic object to contain his faith.

Cynewulf's deliverance from the strife of sin and misery comes through the revelatory power of poetry working on his inner mind as he himself *wordcræft wæf* the poem. Besides the bright vision God also *leoðucræft onleac*. His conversion to the truth of the Cross occurs as he writes his own poem; the report of his conversion then becomes

an integral part of that poem, reflecting the thematic structure of the
narrative events and linking the autobiographical conclusion directly
to the entire work.

Elene is Cynewulf's own revelation to the world and to himself. By
revealing the truth of the Victory-Tree in the art of poetry, he removes
himself from the bonds and fetters which the domination of sin had
placed on his soul. To each of the personages in the poem the revelation of the Cross is different. Constantine finds it gratuitously in a
vision; Judas prays for a sign to deliver him from death; Cynewulf discovers it in the power of art to transform the soul of the poet and make
known to him the wisdom of faith.

The epilogue also, like the poem, is divided into three parts, each
marked by a distinctive style. Following the rhymed portion comes the
runic signature, which in turn is succeeded by Cynewulf's most extensive description of the apocalypse. Tone, style, and subject differ
entirely for each of these sections. And quite unlike his practice in
Christ II and *Juliana,* the signature does not become part of the vision
of judgment, but resembles instead the signature of *The Fates* in its
emphasis on mutability. The addition, however, of the autobiographical details makes this particular signature a more emphatic statement
of the poet's own deliverance from his sinful past, and the crucial
power of the Cross in effecting that spiritual liberation.

> A wæs sæcg oð ðæt
> cnyssed cearwelmum, | ᚻ · drusende
> þeah he in medohealle   maðmas þege,
> æplede gold · ᚻ · gnornode,
> · ᛉ · gefera   nearusorge dreah,
> enge rune   þær him · ᛗ · fore
> milpaðas mæt,   modig þrægde,
> wirum gewlenced.   ᚹ · is geswiðrad,
> gomen æfter gearum,   geogoð is gecyrred,
> ald onmedla. ᚾ · wæs geara
> geogoðhades glæm;   nu synt geardagas
> æfter fyrstmearce   forð gewitene,
> lifwynne geliden   swa · ᛚ · toglideð,
> flodas gefysde. | ᚱ · æghwam bið
> læne under lyfte.
>
>   (1256b–70a)

Until then the man was continually tossed by the waves of care. He was like
a flickering torch *(cen),* even though he received precious gifts of embossed

gold in the mead-hall. *Yr*, his comrade at need *(nyd)*, mourned, felt clamming sorrow, secret oppression, where formerly the mettled steed *(eh)* galloped, measured the mile-long paths, splendid in its filigreed trappings. With the years delight *(wynn)* has faded, youth with its former pomp is changed. Once the radiance of youth was ours *(ur)*. Now the old days have passed away in the fullness of time, life's joys departed as water *(lagu)* ebbs away, the floods driven along. For every man beneath the heavens wealth *(feoh)* is transitory.[35]

But the split between the revelation of the poet's identity and its connection with what is both "past and passing" is a new technique for Cynewulf. "He" is now simply the "man," who has watched his life and the world disappear; whereas the "I" is *frod ond fus* ("wise and ready," 1236a) for the final departure from earthly existence, from the very ideas of time and the past. It is almost as if Cynewulf's "conversion" through the Cross allows him to be outside himself, to be disembodied and watch his earthly form and the name which accompanies it pass away with the rest of temporal reality.

The poem is composed in structures of threes: the conversions of Constantine, Judas, and Cynewulf, Judas's three encounters with Elene, the three discrete sections of the epilogue, the three divisions of humanity at the Judgment seat (1286b–306a).[36] All these correspond to the three states of being the poem examines—a sinful past, a "converted" present, and an unknown future—and to the three ways of knowing which the poem forces each character to adopt—the literal, the allegorical, and the anagogical. Just as the action moves from literal battle to eternal and spiritual struggle, so each of the characters goes from either an ignorance or a hostility toward the letter to an acceptance of the all-permeating eternal truths contained in the Cross. The fates of men at Judgment are likewise analogous: the righteous will eventually be absorbed into the world of pure spirit, the unrepentant will be tortured by the "grip of fire-coals" (*in gleda gripe*, 1302a), and those for whom salvation eventually may be possible will be "purified and melted" (*amered ond gemylted*, 1312a) "like refined gold," (*swa smæte gold*, 1309b); that is, in a world apart from time they will be permitted one last chance for conversion. All these considerations in the epilogue are logical extensions of the meanings present throughout. The Cross is the great mediating symbol, the means by which worldly reality takes on spiritual truth. It is through the Cross as symbol (the allegorical way of knowing) that Constantine, Judas, and Cynewulf come to contemplate and finally to understand the anagoge in all three of its divisions. Cynewulf's focus on the apocalyptic resolution of earthly struggle takes the poem the furthest possible distance into the spiritual realm. For some the integument of mortal flesh dissolves into the blaze of fiery judgment; for others the body is assumed into heaven:

> forðan hie nu on wlite scinaþ
> englum gelice,   yrfes brucaþ,
> wuldorcyninges   to widan feore.
>   (1319b–21b)

Therefore they now shine in beauty, like the angels, enjoy the heritage of the King of Glory, forever.

There is in *Elene* more than one saint. Each of the characters is, in one way or another, a "sign." As Thomas Merton writes: saints "are meant to be deeply significant flashes sent forth from the dark bosom of the mystery of God. For the saint does not represent himself, or his time, or his nation: he is a sign of God for his own generation and for all generations to come."[37] The poem, too, becomes, like the Cross, a holy object making the invisible visible and revealing to all men the truth of that sacramental vision.

CHAPTER 6

Cynewulf's Style and Achievement

I General Commentary

SINCE Cynewulf is the single poet with whom we can connect a
considerable body of Anglo-Saxon poetry, critics have persistently
attempted to describe his style and to compare him with other more
famous poets. Cook's estimate, despite his opening disclaimer, gives a
fine example of this aggrandizement by comparison:

> In grasp, in variety, in narrative skill, in the development of a difficult
> thought, in architectonic power, Cynewulf is hopelessly inferior [to Dante];
> but in compunction, gratitude, hope, love, awe, and tenderness, he belongs
> to the same order; and in his sense of the sublime and the ability to convey
> it to his readers, he need not shrink from a comparison with either Dante or
> Milton, in other words, with the very prophets of the sublime among the poets
> of Christianity.[1]

The temptation to judge and evaluate poets and poetry looms so large
in the history of literary criticism that Cook's excessive praise need not
surprise us. But a curious logical circularity operates here. Cynewulf is
worth studying as a historical figure. Since there are no other poets to
study from this period, Cynewulf is especially worth our efforts. Having expended so much effort in studying this poet, his work must be
greatly worth it: therefore, Cynewulf is, in some ways, kin to Dante
and Milton. The confusion of process and product in Cook's logic mir-
rors the attitudes of a whole generation, whose statements flow not only
from faulty reasoning, but also from a severely distorted picture of
what this "Cynewulf" actually composed. Cook's rhapsodic strains
seem less absurd when we remember how many poems he and others
thought Cynewulf wrote.

The early critics' misapprehensions about the canon produced a
flood of correspondingly mistaken comments on Cynewulf's "style."
Good critical observation becomes mixed with mere impression. Wit-

ness ten Brink. He saw a "conscious art" in Cynewulf's poetry, along
with the strong imprint of Latin syntax and rhetoric. He also believes
that Cynewulf's stylistic inheritance, however, causes a predictable
"diffuse treatment" of his sources, and, as a Christian, Cynewulf writes
necessarily in a "subjective" style.[2] Nineteenth-century German and
German-trained writers characterized all Old English poetry as "subjective," though it is difficult to discern just what they meant by this
term. Comments on the "personal" quality of Cynewulfian poems
occur frequently, inspired undoubtedly by the "I" speaker in the runic
epilogues.[3] The poems themselves, of course, are not personal at all.
The personal and the subjective merge in Richard Heinzel's feelings
about Cynewulf as a poet. He thinks Cynewulf's descriptions hover
above his objects, that he omits details essential to the narration, and
that this comes from his idealistic orientation and his "melting soft-
ness."[4] A certain truth hides somewhere in these foggy notions, though
to communicate a surer sense of Cynewulf's "poeticalness" requires
greater precision, even on the purely descriptive level.

W. P. Ker makes a more obscure comparison between Cynewulf and
the Italian poet, Marino (1569–1625), revealing perhaps a more accurate perception about the Old English poet than his contemporaries
managed. Ker writes:

His style is distinguished by a sensitive use of language, a rhetorical grace,
not unconscious: he is a correct poet. . . . The danger in his verse is that
fluency and sweetness may be carried too far. Like Alcuin, he is sometimes
over-gentle. Grimm's phrase about the autumnal beauty of *Andreas* and
Elene remains in the mind; there is not much promise in them. It would not
be misleading to compare Cynewulf with Marini [*sic*], if it were not that
Marini's faults have been exaggerated by critics. There is the same regard for
melody, the same sort of effusive eloquence in both poets. . . . [Cynewulf's]
interest is in the expansion and decoration of the theme, more than in the
action itself or the characters.[5]

Of all the late Victorian and Edwardian critics, Ker gives us the most
cogent description of Cynewulf's style. Not many picked up Ker's
characterizations of this style, and a good many later scholars revert to
earlier opinions. Kenneth Sisam's deeply conservative comments hark
back to ten Brink in their emphasis on the stylistic influence of Latin
on Cynewulf's poetry. His brief summary deserves attention, although
his prejudices against the innate stylistic qualities of Germanic verse
impair his evaluations.

This is the style of a man trained to read and write Latin, to admire the orderly progress of a Latin sentence, and to prefer its clarity to the tangled profusion of the native style. We have seen that Cynewulf took the matter and arrangement of his poems from Latin, and borrowed the new ornament of rhyme from Latin. The same great influence guided his treatment of alliterative verse, which in his best passages reaches its highest level of ease, refinement, and adaptability.[6]

Each of these comments is instructive; each strains after a way of defining and describing what Cynewulf's poetry is like, what makes it identifiably his own and no other's. But bias, lack of rigor, vague impressionism, and, frequently, misidentification of the Cynewulfian poems, reduce the value of such pronouncements and make them more interesting as historical dicta than as reliable statements about Cynewulf's works.

During the 1940s two scholars made separate attempts to put the related questions of canon and style into a clearer and more focused perspective. While in both instances the methodologies have become easy targets, the conclusions reached and the explications offered en route deserve consideration. S. K. Das's work takes two distinct approaches to the problem of Cynewulf's style and its relation to the canon: (1) a detailed grammatical-metrical analysis of all the "Cynewulfian" poems, and (2) an attempt to distinguish between the genuine and the spurious works using purely literary speculations.[7] Das's complex metrical investigations produce the answer many had long suspected—that Cynewulf wrote only the four poems he signed. In the second half of his book, Das, however intelligently, unfortunately returns to the belletristic methods inherited from his nineteenth-century predecessors. But his judgments carry the weight of one who has long pondered the works he writes about. He sees the universal theme of good versus evil, the devil versus the holy soul, Christianity versus paganism in all Cynewulf's poems. Traditional though it may be, this theme, he comments, "forms the warp and woof of the very conception of his poetry." And since this is not the case with other poems in the Cynewulfian group, Das questions "whether there was the existence of anything like a 'Kynewulf Kreis' or the 'School of Cynewulf.'"[8] Das points to Cynewulf's habitual emphasis on abstract ideas, a trait so marked that his ideas reach "a region of pure abstraction such as we do not find in any of the Unsigned Poems."[9] Beauty, melody, and religious devotion aside, a significant aspect of Cynewulf's art is his interest in ideas and in the forms appropriate to express them—an aspect Das here hits upon.

Although based on some rationalistic and classical criteria inappropriate for the Old English aesthetic, Claes Schaar's wide-ranging study still represents the culmination of the stylistic investigations into Cynewulf's style. Schaar's various concerns and biases manifest themselves even in a listing of the topics he covers: (1) the poet's ability to distinguish between vital and subordinate epic matter (here Schaar's classical prejudices come straight to the fore); (2) the reflection of this distinction in syntax—whether the clauses are compound or complex; (3) the distribution of paratactic and hypotactic structures; (4) the use of "essential" and "unessential" variation. Applying these categories to the many poems in the "Cynewulfian group," Schaar finds obvious differences between the signed poems and all the others. He concludes, for example, that only Cynewulf had a keen intuition on what is important "epic matter" and what is not. And related to this capacity is Cynewulf's use of the compound/complex series: in the genuine poems "Compound series are reserved for descriptions of incidents and actions important to the plot. . . . In the study of the use of the complex series we can notice . . . that it is especially common in speeches. Prayers, explanations, and results of action also employ the complex series."[10] Such is not the case with the other "Cynewulfian" poets. In *Andreas,* Schaar remarks, the compound series is used "indiscriminately" and the complex series occurs only rarely.[11] Schaar's survey of parataxis and hypotaxis leads him to the same point: Cynewulf knew how to relate important matter importantly and how to subordinate the rest in the correct syntactic constructions.[12] As for variation, Cynewulf again comes out ahead; unlike the other scops, he makes spare use of "loose" variation, thus avoiding diffuseness, monotony, and achieving a greater concentration and precision.[13] And yet finally, Schaar's opinions, however valid in reaffirming the conservative view of the canon, come to sound much like those expressed from the end of the nineteenth century on. He writes:

Cynewulf's style . . . is distinguished by elaborateness combined with moderation and variety. He is dependent on vernacular tradition, but he is not overwhelmed by it. In Elene the poet is at his ripest and richest, and this epic . . . contains much of the best poetry in Old English poetical literature on the whole. There is much excellent poetry in Juliana and Christ II as well, but the former poem is less mature and has a certain epic meagreness. In Christ

II the poet is somewhat overwhelmed by the rhetoric of Gregory. The *Fata Apostolorum* is inferior in quality to the other poems.[14]

It is interesting to watch Schaar move from a series of precise and meticulous comments on syntax, diction, variation, and heroic vocabulary to such essentially meaningless declarations as these. Presented with this summary no student could possibly derive a sense of what Cynewulf's style, his essential poetic quality, could be. Once more we face the frustrating tension caused by an overabundance of facts and a lack of good synthesizing commentary on them.

The burden of "evaluation" has lain heavy on all Old English poetry. Holding that, aside from *Beowulf* and the elegies, the rest of the poetic remains from early England are paltry at best, critics have given free rein to their unfortunate impulse for judging—arranging and rearranging hierarchies of Old English poems. Thus Schaar's last words on the comparative values of Cynewulf's individual works. At this point John Ellis's strictures on evaluation in literary criticism may well be worth calling to mind: "General summary value judgments are practical in nature, and not instruments of analysis and knowledge. . . . The structural properties of highly valued texts may be many and various, and must be sought empirically, not speculated about. They are in no sense criteria of value."[15] Ellis's comment applies particularly to Schaar, who sees his mission plainly until he takes on the role of the judge. He realizes that Cynewulf's style must be thrown into relief against two related backgrounds: (1) the entire tradition of Germanic verse as practiced locally by the Anglo-Saxon scops, and (2) the particular poetical milieu that emerged in the late eighth century as the older Germanic patterns began to assimilate the rhetoric, aesthetic habits, and perspectives of Latin antiquity. No stylistic commentary on any Anglo-Saxon poem can ignore these two powerful and convergent influences, and Cynewulf is, perhaps, the most extreme example of the lettered scop, whose basic diction is yet formulaic.[16] But this historical necessity of reaching a firm position on the canon has produced only a vague sense of the differences among the various "Cynewulfian" styles.

This marked variety suggests that for Cynewulf each poem was a conscious experiment, that within the limits of his inherited stylistic traditions and the restrictions of his own habitual manner of expression, Cynewulf attempted something quite different in each work and did so in a distinctly individual way. The rigid conventions of its oral-formulaic system often seem to reduce every Anglo-Saxon poem to an identical stylistic mode. But given Cynewulf's striking transformations of his Latin sources, we should not be shocked to discover that his styles are equally distinct. Each poem is a radical exercise in perspective and each uses traditional formulas to create a singular work of poetic art.

II The Fates of the Apostles

Although the relation between *Andreas* and *The Fates of the Apostles* has long been a subject of dispute (the two poems follow one another in the Vercelli manuscript), it is not our purpose to enter that discussion. Yet the opening of *The Fates* does closely resemble the opening lines of both *Andreas* and *Beowulf* (which the author of *Andreas* himself was imitating). Here are the three beginnings.

Fates

> Hwæt! Ic þysne sang   siðgeomor fand
> on seocum sefan,   samnode wide
> hu þa æðelingas   ellen cyðdon,
> torhte ond tireadige.   Twelfe wæron,
> dædum domfaeste,   dryhtne gecorene,
> leofe on life.
>
> (1a–6a)

Lo! I wrought this song travel-weary, sick at heart, gathered from far and wide how the nobles showed bravery, bright and glorious. There were twelve, glorious in deeds, chosen by the Lord, loved in life.

Andreas

> Hwæt! We gefrunan   on fyrndagum
> twelfe under tunglum   tireadige hæleð,
> þeodnes þegnas.   No hira þrym alæg
> campraedenne   þonne cumbol hneotan,
> syððan hie gedaeldon,   swa him dryhten sylf,
> heofona heahcyning,   hlyt getaehte.
>
> (1a–6b)[17]

Lo! We have heard in far-off days of twelve glorious heroes under the stars, thanes of the Prince. Nor did their glory fail in warfare when banners clashed together, after they had dispersed as the Lord Himself, the High King of the heavens had shown them by lot.

Beowulf

Hwæt, we Gardena   in geardagum,
þeodcyninga   þrym gefrunon,
hu ða æþelingas   ellen fremedon!

(1a–3b)[18]

Lo! We have heard of the glory of the kings of the Spear-Danes in days of yore, how the nobles performed brave deeds.

This juxtaposition of texts occasions several interesting questions: Did the collator of the Vercelli manuscript place *The Fates* after *Andreas* because of the similar subjects and opening lines? Is Cynewulf echoing *Andreas* with his first lines or *Beowulf* (lines 3 in both *The Fates* and *Beowulf* are nearly identical)? Is Cynewulf imitating a specific Old English poem at all or simply writing in the classic heroic style of Germanic verse? What effect does he intend this epic style to have?

Much of the critical frustration with *The Fates of the Apostles* stems from the unacknowledged feeling that the poem does not turn out to be what it seems at first to promise. For the opening lines of *The Fates*, the prologue as we have described it, place the poem firmly within the tradition of epic poetry. Its short length makes it more akin to the earlier short lay than the full-blown epic, represented by *Andreas* and *Beowulf*. To state the case negatively, it lacks the "amplitude" which one scholar uses as the criterion to distinguish between brief lay and extended epic.[19] Cynewulf avoids the fullness of the late epic style in *The Fates*, returning to the cryptic technique of the heroic lay.[20] We note, too, the relative absence of variation in *The Fates*, a common, even necessary, item for the epic.[21] After the opening fifteen lines and except for one or possibly two instances, the variation which occurs treats only eternal life or Christ (lines 20, 26b–28a, 31b–33a, 48b–49a, 81a–82a, 117a–18a). And the single important exception dwells on the vanity of worldly treasures contrasted to the joys of eternal life (83b–84a). The weight thus given to an obvious theme by such stylistic choice is evident, and the epic variations, usually connected with the actor, are now associated with the result of action. Cynewulf's use of variation tips the balance to the side of an abstract possibility rather than concentrating on an event. The effect does not become antiheroic, but rather transcends secular heroism.

In *The Fates of the Apostles* repetition replaces variation and the allusiveness of the brief lay begins to resemble the deliberately cryptic styles of the enigma and of gnomic poetry. Repetition itself, of course, produces a feeling of simplicity and the many kinds of repetition in *The Fates*—words and formulas, rhetorical patterns, structural devices, events, and themes—create the impression of a simplicity in the extreme. Yet, as we have noted, the one embellishment on this base line is the comparatively decorative variation on the vision of eternal life. The aesthetic assumptions underlying the style of *The Fates* all concern reduction and compression, assumptions which are common, in one degree or another, with the styles of the brief lay, the riddle, and the gnome, with *The Fight at Finnsburg*, the shorter riddles, and *Maxims I* and *II*. If the exercise in stylistic sparseness and its concomitant affinities with gnome and riddle were not apparent before the runic epilogue, they become patent in Cynewulf's pointed reference to riddles at the end of the runes: *Nu ðu cunnon miht / hwa on þam wordum wæs werum oncyðig* ("Now you may see who has been revealed to men in these words," 105b–6b). This sentence follows the paradigm of many a concluding line to an Anglo-Saxon riddle. In this poetic environment a careful critic does not search for the broad stroke, but for the telling single detail. As the compression becomes more intense, the poetry becomes more constricted. So we observe Cynewulf's play with rhyming tricks—Nero's *nearwe searwe*, for example, an intensification of rhyme within the formula that often offends modern standards of taste. Or, we note the ordinarily smooth metrical pattern suddenly interrupted by the following line, burdened with extra syllables in the first half, leaving both the predicate and the thematic referent effectively isolated and suspended in the second half: *Ne þreodode he fore þrymme ðeodcyninges* ("Nor did he fear the might of a temporal ruler," 18). Or again, we may comment upon the visual and metrical embodiment of the action in *lætan me on laste lic, eorðan dæl* ("leave behind me the body, the earthly part," 94). This line alone breaks the steady correspondence in phrasal/clausal and metrical alignment, and in this break the "body" does literally get "left behind." Or, we can point to the ironic reversal that occurs unremarked in these lines: *Æðele sceoldon / ðurh wæpenhete weorc þrowigan, / sigelean secan* ("Through weapon-hate the nobles had to *suffer torment, seek the victory-reward*," 79b–81a, my italics).[22] But

Cynewulf is not merely being clever. Each of these different stylistic ploys refers back to a part of the main idea—the vanity of the world, the permanence of heaven, and the irony which comes from contemplating the abyss between them.

In *The Fates of the Apostles* Cynewulf conjoins the styles of epic, riddle, and gnome to produce a heroic enigma; but compared to any of the various possible Latin analogues, the style of *The Fates* has an amplitude nonexistent in the martyrologies. A familiarity in Latin Christendom with the deaths of the twelve apostles is reflected in all versions. As imitations of Christ's own death, their martyrdoms are inevitable. So the emphasis in both the analogues and in Cynewulf's poem shifts from the apostles' suffering to their reward. Yet despite the traditional heroic diction, other stylistic traits—those appropriate to the enigma—inhibit a full development of the heroic ethos and concentrate instead on both what is beyond heroism, and what heroism implies for less courageous men. Cynewulf, therefore, does not exploit the received, typical heroic style, since the importance of action *per se* fades into the awesome mystery that the apostles all became, in their different ways, Christ Himself, leaving mankind, here the "I" or Cynewulf, to ponder their beatific deaths. The aspects of the heroic style remaining in *The Fates* properly suggest the apostles' heroic martyrdoms; but the conscious use of riddle devices explains a paradox that their deaths bring eternal glory, that the instruments of hate yield to the joys of heavenly reward, and that man alone, Cynewulf, wanting the strength of the saints, lies caught in the puzzle of this transitory existence (Cynewulf puts his name actually "in" the openly riddle-like runic signature). The style and techniques of the riddle combined with the already allusive qualities of the brief heroic lay finely express Cynewulf's meditation on the meaning of the apostles' fates, for thus he comments on a series of acts without seeming to do so. The style contains the paradox that Cynewulf explores. If many facets of the poem are cryptic, it is because Cynewulf here attempts to encapsulate the mystery.

The double epilogue and the final exhortation have altered styles. In the first two instances Cynewulf deals with his own spiritual dilemma and requests prayers; in the last, he directs his attention outward to humanity, exhorting us all to pray for the apostles' reward. The rhetoric of prayer differs from that of the heroic lay or the riddle, and in these sections Cynewulf moves away from his previous compressed and cryptic style to a more continuous syntax associated with the style of direct address; the poem's symbolic action he describes in the past tense; the call for specific action now necessitates the imperative. The styles shift accordingly, though the metrical simplicity and the syntactic clarity remain unchanged. The looser style reflects the greater emotional urgency of present need, compared to the firm assurance of past heroism and consequent reward.

III   Christ II

The diverse lists which perhaps served as sources for *The Fates of the Apostles* cannot, in a strict literary sense, be said to have a style; and if they contribute to the style of *The Fates* in any way it is only to the starkness of that poem. In *The Fates* Cynewulf turns not primarily to Latin texts for his stylistic models, but to the styles inherently associated with several of the ancient Germanic poetic genres. When we move on to *Christ II*, we encounter a different situation. First, there is no possible model from the Germanic tradition on which Cynewulf could have drawn to compose this poeticized sermon; second, the style of his source, Gregory's sermon, is that of Latin homiletics through and through. Indeed, *Christ II* represents a major departure from the whole previous tradition of Anglo-Saxon poetry, since it is undoubtedly the first meditative poem based on a Latin homily. We might suspect, therefore, that Gregory's style would thoroughly permeate the Cynewulfian version. Curiously, this is not so. In style, as in perspective and interpretation, Cynewulf remolds Gregory's Latin, creating an entirely new artifact.

The difference reveals itself immediately. Whereas Gregory begins the ninth section of his homily with a straightforward question—"This is the first question we must ask"—Cynewulf opens by urging the "famous man" to meditate. Gregory then proceeds to answer his question in a series of questions and responses, each of which implies a kind of dialogue with the homily's actual audience. The public circumstances of composition affect the rhetorical movement. And the interchange of dialogue lends itself naturally to antithesis, including the paradoxes these antitheses contain—ascent/descent; exaltation/humiliation. The opening of Gregory's ninth section reflects the style of the advocate; he examines each piece of evidence carefully and moves logically step by step to the inevitable resolution. Gregory has, to take a modern view, a lawyer's mind and a lawyer's style.

Gregory's curt, logical, and antithetical clauses give way to a series of Cynewulfian involuted and periodic sentences. If there is a trace or more of Latin influence on Cynewulf's style, it does not go back to Gregory, but to more distant models of the complex period. The expansion in the number of subjects indicates the greater degree of complexity. Gregory: at the *Lord's* birth, there were *angels,* but not in white robes. Cynewulf: *famous man,* think about the *Lord's* birth, when He chose *Mary* to come into the world, and *angels* were there, but not in white robes. Cynewulf certainly did not find the six subordinate clauses, five with a different subject and temporal reference, in the lawyer's brief Gregory composed. A glance at Cynewulf's first sentence with an eye to these details is instructive:

> Nu ðu geornlice   gæstgerynum,
> mon se mæra,   modcræfte sec
> þurh sefan snyttro,   þæt þu soð wite
> hu þæt geeode,   þa se ælmihtiga
> acenned wearð   þurh clænne had,
> siþþan he Marian,   mægða weolman,
> mærre meowlan,   mundheals geceas,
> þæt þær in hwitum   hræglum gewerede
> englas ne oðeowdun,   þa se æþeling cwom,
> beorn in Betlem.
>
> (440a–49a)

Famous man, now earnestly seek with searchings of the spirit, with mindcraft through the wisdom of the heart, so that you may know truly how that happened, when the Almighty was begotten in purity, when He chose the protection of Mary, the best of maidens, the glorious Virgin, that there robed in white garments angels did not appear, when the Prince came, the Child to Bethlehem.

Our own biases will determine whether Cynewulf's version is judged adequate or clumsy,[23] but there is no doubt that Cynewulf here attempts something almost unrelated to Gregory's purpose. The difference lies in the two authors' respective modes of thinking and structuring, and their attitudes toward antithesis, juxtaposition, and parallelism. Gregory's logical approach is essentially mathematical—he places the contradictory items in a formula and, going through the correct manipulations, comes up with an answer. Gregory is intellectually outside the objects of his concern, and treats them as counters to be managed according to prescribed rules. For Cynewulf logical operations either do not appeal or suffice, and he is inside the object, seeking a way to reexperience the "narrative." Contradictions resolve themselves in a vision of simultaneous states, rather than in the logical product of linear formulas. Thus the intricate series of subordinate clauses in his opening sentence.

Many of the connections Gregory makes strike a modern reader as obscure, even bizarre. The interrelatedness which Christian exegetes could find between the two testaments never ceases to amaze the uninformed. But this strangeness does not invalidate the mode of thought, which remains logical, linear, and dependent on formulas. Cynewulf, on the other hand, does not make distinctions and antitheses to display his ingenuity. He explores both difference and resemblance, juncture and disjuncture; and he uses repetition in its many guises to provide the means for uniting the disparate.

In the first half of *Christ II*, there is a sense of constant return, of a movement bound by stasis. Through repetition Cynewulf brings the story and the focus back again and again to the same point. But the repetition in *Christ II* does not serve exactly the same purpose it did in *The Fates*, where, given the enigmatic tone of the poem, the repetitions create a riddling tone to express a mystery where none exists on the surface. The mystery of the Ascension in *Christ II* is plainly there before the Apostles' (and the readers') eyes, and so the intensity of repetition produces other effects. In one sense it works against the narrative, for the forward movement describes Christ's actions, but the constant verbal returns apply only to the human responses to that action. Thus the text incorporates both a picture of divine release (movement, the Ascension) and human captivity (stasis, the insistent return through repetition to the same place).

Within these larger considerations the style of *Christ II* is smooth and simple. It is true that the complex sentence has a function here that was absent in *The Fates;* still the regular coincidence of metrical unit with syntactic unit proceeds nearly undisturbed throughout. Rarely does Cynewulf compose run-on lines, though three instances which follow the same pattern are interesting to examine. All three come near the beginning and involve variation: *his þegna gedryht / gelaðade, leof weorud* ("He summoned His band of thanes, the beloved troop," 457b–58a); *þær him tacna fela tires brytta / onwrah, wuldres helm* ("there the Giver of Glory, the Protector of Wonder revealed many signs to them," 462a–63a); *ond þæt word acwæð waldend engla, / gefysed, frea mihtig* ("and that word spoke, the Ruler of Angels, about to depart, the Mighty Prince," 474a–75a). Whether the occurrence of these three examples within eighteen lines has any significance or not cannot be proved. The variation once characterizes the apostles, twice Christ. Variation later is reserved for Christ and heaven, as in *The Fates*. The specific construction here thrice repeated does of course have an effect: with its metrical displacement of the verb from its subject through the breaking of the syntax, in the first two cases the verb receives inordinate stress: "summoned," "revealed." This emphatic syncopation underscores the emotional tension of the preparation for the climactic event, the Ascension itself, and the release comes with Christ's long speech to His disciples in which He commands them to evangelize the world.

The complicated, often involuted, meditation on the Ascension comprises the first half of *Christ II;* the second half concentrates on the many lessons to be derived from the Ascension. This first section concluded with the speech of a herald within heaven's gates as he announces Christ's triumphant return with His spoils from the Harrowing of Hell. The Herald's speech is a fine example of Cynewulf's subtle and sophisticated technique. In twenty-eight lines he brings to a climax Christ's Ascension into heaven by a complex interweaving of rhetorical, syntactical, metrical, and sound effects. First, the alliteration: the twenty-eight lines employ only ten different alliterating sounds, and the relation of these sounds to one another reduces the number even further. [g], [d], and [k] account for nine lines; the rest are all vowels, semivowels, aspirants, or sibilants. [h] occurs five times, [w] three, [f] three, [s] two, [l] one and there are four vowels. The impression made by this special collocation is evident; the sounds of the passage embody the great excitement and the breathless enthusiasm the herald must feel at being the first witness to this event. And the alliteration varies between breath sounds and stops, rather than other continuants, increasing the listener's impression of a torrent of excitement punctuated with deep catches. That this pattern is more than intuitive or accidental becomes obvious in the last line: *lufu, lifes hyht, ond ealles leohtes gefea* ("love, hope of life and the joy of all light," 585). Cynewulf's switch to [l] alliteration (reinforced by the same sound in *ealles*) both continues the sound pattern of the previous lines and brings it to a climactic conclusion. This final line serves the same syntactic and metrical end: the additive series departs radically from the precise correspondence of meter and syntax that has obtained before. And the rush that alliteration, meter, and syntax combined give the herald's speech comes abruptly to a halt as the breaks in line 585 require a slow, deliberate, even ponderous reading. Love, the hope of life, and the joy of all light are the radiant effects of Christ's Ascension, and their importance here is heightened by all the devices of sound and meter at Cynewulf's disposal, as well as their logical placement at the end of the speech.

Rhetoric, too, contributes to this unrestrained climax. The speech begins *"Hafað nu se halga helle bireafod"* (*"Now has the Holy One plundered hell,"* 558). A pattern of present becoming future and then crystallizing in the eternal (as best as that can be expressed in human language limited by temporal forms) follows from this with repeated insistence: *"Nu sind forcumene"* ("Now are overcome," 561a); *"Wile nu gesecan"* ("Will now seek," 571a); *"Nu ge geare cunnon"* ("Now you entirely know," 573b); *"nu ge fromlice"* ("Now you quickly," 575a); *"Wile in to eow"* ("Will in to you," 577a); and again the climactic change, *"Wær is ætsomne"* ("A covenant is in common," 583b). Christ's Ascension and the description of it through the herald's reactions give way to an eternal decree and a restoration of the covenant the Ascension effected. All the stylistic details reinforce, indeed carry, this profound assertion, an assertion that transcends literal statement and so portrays the harmony of this eternal peace.

Cynewulf opens the second half of *Christ II* with a return to a common opening formula: *Hwæt, we nu gehyrdan* ("Lo! we have now heard," 586a) and in so doing signals his structural intent. His poem divides neatly into two sections—the curious "spiral" narrative of the Ascension and the moral exhortation. The structure and consequently the style of *Christ II* differ completely from Gregory's ordering, which moves in a series of distinct paragraphs, each discussing the Ascension from another perspective. Gregory's structure is additive; Cynewulf's is typically modeled on the diptych. As Cynewulf means the second half of *Christ II* to be direct in its explications of the Ascension, so he likewise finds a new style to convey his altered approach. The remaining homiletic portion reveals many of the devices that characterize Cynewulf's most easily recognizable stylistic habits. Immediately following the change in line 586 comes the well-known rhyming portion in which Cynewulf outlines the choices man now has before him: *swa helle hienþu swa heofones mærþu* ("either the infamy of hell or the glory of heaven," 591). Alliteration, anaphora, antithesis, end rhyme, internal rhyme, and assonance combine to create a sequence so consciously and abstractly patterned that its significance in the logical order cannot be missed. Further echoes of this technique occur throughout: the gifts of men passage with its patterned *sum* series (664a–81a), the "leaps" passage with its extended use of anaphora (720a–38a), and one of the several admonitions for right living to be drawn from the Ascension with its complex series of parallel relative clauses:

> > Is us þearf micel
> þæt we mid heortan   hælo secen,
> þær we mid gæste   georne gelyfað
> þæt þæt hælobearn   heonan up stige
> mid usse lichoman,   lifgende god.
> > (751b–55b)

There is great need for us that we seek salvation with our hearts where we earnestly believe with our spirits, so that the Saving-Son, the Living God, may rise up with our body.

Under these more obvious set pieces run several rhetorical structures that keep the poem's argument moving in a continuous line. Again Cynewulf resorts to repetition, and the effect is that of an anaphoric series, but one interrupted and interwoven. As in *The Fates* the formulas with which Cynewulf chooses to begin his sections themselves become an identifiable pattern marking out through rhetorical signposts the major stops in the larger rhythm: *Hwæt*, again in line 627a; *Bi þon* (633a, 650b, 691b, 712a); *Ðus* (686a, 744a); *Forþon* (756a, 766a, 815a). We can easily derive a sense of Cynewulf's rhetorical concerns simply by noting these words so appropriate for demonstration and argument and by remarking their regular recurrence.

Cynewulf's experiment in *Christ II* is to find stylistic equivalents for the two differing modes which dominate their respective halves. This he does through a combination of narrative structuring and highly wrought verbal contrivances. The final section represents a departure from all that has preceded; the turn at the end of a Cynewulfian poem, however, is a mark of its authenticity. He abandons the distancing words (*Ðus, Forþon, Bi þon*) that enabled him to outline a sermon on the Ascension with a clear rhetorical sequence to focus on the immediate present: *Nu is þon gelicost* ("Now is that most like," 850a). This concluding paragraph insists on the "now" of the sinful Christian's present experience and then concludes with a final reference back to the Ascension as a historical, a completed and past, event: *þa he heofonum astag* ("when He ascended into the heavens," 866b). Having receded into memory by the end, the Ascension stands as a pledge, but not an assurance, of salvation. The trepidation this raises in the sinner's heart finds expression in the elaborate simile Cynewulf spins on the topos of the sea journey, of death as a voyage to another port. Metaphor has now replaced the preceding symbolic modes and the vehicles Cynewulf has used to express them. The choice is radical, for while the topic may be ancient, its sudden introduction at the end of *Christ II* suggests that faced with death's reality the poet relies on the visionary world of metaphor rather than the logical world of rhetoric. In the extended simile Cynewulf attempts to replace the ever-present reality of the Ascension, now that it is "finished," with a poetic symbol to match his homily.

IV   Juliana

Rosemary Woolf writes of *Juliana:* "The sparse imagery and the conventional heroic terms are only minor adornments to a poem in which emotional overtones and stylistic variations are reduced to a minimum. *Juliana* clearly comes at the end of a period. Though it parades remnants of the old heroic style, the spirit and general effect are deficient. There could be no poetic progress from it: beyond lie monotony or prose."[24] Woolf's description may be to the point, but several of her underlying assumptions are built on shaky foundations. First, we can make no certain statements either on the chronological placement of *Juliana* within the Cynewulfian canon, or within the whole problematic chronology of Old English poetry. To assert that the style of *Juliana* is either the cause or effect of anything else creates relations where none can be proved to exist. Second, Woolf assumes that "the old heroic style" has definite qualities, though she does not state what they are, and that *Juliana* represents a serious falling away. *Juliana* has always been a troublesome poem for modern critics. In matter as in style, the poem appears weak, diluted, grotesque—in short, a failure. Perhaps several generations of critics may not be wrong, yet a more careful examination of what Cynewulf actually does with the style of *Juliana* seems in order.

   With this venture into pure hagiography, Cynewulf, whatever his success, attempted to create several effects. Whether we like those effects, or whether they contribute meaningfully to the poem's narrative, are different questions. Woolf describes the style in *Juliana* correctly as more like that of "prose than in any other Old English poem of this type." The important qualities are "clarity and directness, simplicity and smoothness."[25] Of course, the style does not exactly conform to prose norms, for, as in the other poems examined, there is a strict observance of alliterative rules and a nearly perfect correspondence between syntactic and metrical units. And again when Cynewulf does interrupt those units, however slightly, he does so with the choice he usually makes—complementary verb, plus variation on the subject: "*þu me furþor scealt / secgan, sawla feond*" ("You shall tell me further, enemy of souls," 347b–48a). Variation is, in fact, more prominent in *Juliana* than in *The Fates* or *Christ II*. The relative profusion has prompted more than one critic to comment on its empty, mechanical effect. Writing in imitation of classical epic style, Cynewulf draws upon both this device and the characterizing diction from the Germanic tradition more heavily than in any of his poems. Incongruous to critics with a realistic bent, the result nevertheless forces an examination of the dissonance.

In *Juliana* Cynewulf distills the epic style as he understood it and could recreate it. Thus reduced to its simplest elements, the style strikes some as having lost its power to portray a valid heroic ethos. But we may also argue that this distilled version of epic style parallels in its stark simplicity the highly diagrammatic narrative structure that Cynewulf imposed on the Latin account. Cynewulf holds a radically simple conception of the Juliana legend, but this must not be confused with a crudely simplistic view. And unlike his practice in *The Fates* and *Christ II*, Cynewulf does not divide the poem into distinct sections, each with a different style, or introduce at specific points obvious stylistic punctuations. None of these typical devices appears here. Rhyme is absent, except for what may be occasional, or even accidental, instances (76a–77b, 463a–64a). He repeats a pun on *rod/rodor* ("cross"/"heavens") twice (305, 447).[26] *Juliana* lacks any elaborate series of the verbal tricks that crop up periodically in *The Fates* and *Christ II*; though one Cynewulfian trait does occur frequently—the repetition of alternating formulas opening successive paragraphs: *Him þa seo eadge ageaf ondsware* ("Then the blessed one gave him answer," 105); *Hyre þa þurh yrre ageaf ondsware* ("Then he in anger gave her answer," 117); *Him þa seo eadge ageaf ondsware*, 130; *Ða wæs ellenwod, yrre ond reþe* ("Then he was furious, angry and wrathful," 140); *Him seo unforhte ageaf ondsware* ("The fearless one gave him answer," 147); *Hy þa þurh yrre Affricanus* ("She then in anger Affricanus," 158). These examples represent bold alternation, but not the sense of antithesis which similar repetitions of opening formulas produce in his other poems. The panels do not stand in implicit opposition, commenting on one another by their placement. Instead Cynewulf gives the force of dramatic interchange directly to the characters, and the alternating formulas only increase the reader's awareness of the absolute antipathies being enacted.

Except at the highest level, *Juliana* is not a comforting poem; indeed, most saints' legends are not to the modern, skeptical, nonreligious reader. This tale dwells on violent emotions, hatred, cruelty, torture, and death. The stark simplicity of the style not only supports the abstract structuring of the action, but also lays it bare in an even harsher way. Cynewulf does not permit escape from the violence of this universal collision between good and evil. The distillation concentrates the effect. So too does the particular use of certain constructions. With greater frequency than in his other works, or than in other Anglo-Saxon saints' lives, Cynewulf composes sentences based on these patterns: through *x* something was brought about, or, something happened so that *x* was the result. The prevalence of these relative clauses of result adds to the impression that the poem's style is prosaic. The clauses give full explanations and thus move back from the cryptic style which a mere accumulation of alliterative half lines without connectives or subordinating devices produces. Cynewulf seems especially interested in agency and result, the interrelationship of doer and deed. Both action and style identify this concern. Such a description of the poem's highly individual style cannot easily erase the many disappointments that others have felt. What is boldly plain and strikingly abstract for one becomes mindlessly mechanical, frustrating, and barren for another. But that Cynewulf attempted to harmonize the style of *Juliana* with his own schematic interpretation of the legend seems sure. His success will depend on a critic's predisposition toward such projects in the first place. Cynewulf's style in *Juliana* is as unrelentingly simple as the heroine herself, and few have found her attractive. The experiment is extreme enough to have provoked this negative response.

V   Elene

The influence of specific Latin sources on the style of Cynewulf's poems is difficult to describe, in part because we cannot identify the exact Latin text Cynewulf may have used. With the exception of Gregory's homily and probably Bede's Ascension hymn, the texts of the other sources are only proximate versions of the manuscripts Cynewulf had before him. And even in cases where we can identify the texts, Cynewulf makes major thematic, structural, and stylistic alterations. With these caveats in mind, we may still look at the Latin accounts of Juliana and Helena to explain some of the stylistic divergences between Cynewulf's two Anglo-Saxon adaptations. Both Latin saints' lives open with a conventional formula, placing the action in the historical reign of the appropriate emperor. Thus the Latin *Acts of Juliana: temporibus Maximiani Imperatoris, persecutoris Christianae religionis, erat quidam Senator in ciuitate Nicomedia, nomine Eleusius, amicus Imperatoris*[27] ("In the days of the Emperor Maximianus, a persecutor of the Christian religion, there was a senator in the city of Nicomedia named Eleusius, a friend of the Emperor"). Compare this beginning with the first sentence of *The Acts of Saint Cyriacus: Anno ducentesimo tricesimo tertio, post passionem Domini nostri Jesu Christi, regnante venerabili Dei cultore magno viro Constantino, in sexto anno regni ejus, gens multa barbarorum congregata est super Danubium, parati ad bellum contra Romaniam*[28] ("In the two hundred and thirty-third year after the Passion of our Lord Jesus Christ, in the sixth year of the reign of Constantine [a great man and reverent worshipper of God], a large barbarian host gathered beyond the Danube, prepared to wage war against the Roman Empire"). The simple, indeed fairy-tale, style of *The Acts of Juliana* contrasts sharply with the more intricate style of *Cyriacus*, with its several subordinate clauses, one of which interrupts the main narration to characterize Constantine. On the whole the style of *Cyriacus* can hardly be called complex, sophisticated, or elegant; but in comparison to that of *The Acts of Juliana*, it is considerably more elaborate. Some of its complexities are downright blunders: clauses imbedded within clauses until all notion of an initial referent becomes lost. Inevitably aspects of these two Latin styles have at least a general effect on Cynewulf's own poetic reworkings. The colloquial simplicity of *The Acts of Juliana* becomes the radically abstract simplicity of Cynewulf's *Juliana*, and the more consciously literary style of *Cyriacus*, its attempt to capture a higher style of Latin historical writing, influences Cynewulf as one of his several stylistic models for *Elene*.

In more than one instance Cynewulf clearly straightens out a syntactical clumsiness from his source; he has no interest in being complex for its own sake. Amplification and symmetry distinguish Cynewulf's

main adjustments to the Latin. While retaining the Latin author's sense
of a rhetorical style that requires a series of subordinate clauses, Cynewulf separates one clause from another, one point of focus from
another with care, and so consistently avoids the Latin confusions. The
beginning of Cynewulf's *Elene:*

> Þa wæs agangen   geara hwyrftum
> tu hund ond þreo   geteled rimes
> swylce þrittig eac   þinggemearces
> wintra for worulde   þæs þe wealdend God
> acenned wearð   cyninga wuldor
> in middangeard   þurh mennisc heo
> sodðfæstra leoht;   þa wæs syxte gear
> Constantines   caserdomes
> þæt he Romwara   in rice wearð
> ahæfen hildfruma   to hereteman.
> Wæs se leodhwata   lindgeborga
> eorlum arfæst,   æðelinges weox
> rice under roderum;   he wæs riht cyning,
> guðwearð gumena.   Hine God trymede
> mærðum ond mihtum   þæt he manegum wearð
> geond middangeard   mannum to hroðer
> werþeodum to wræce   syððan wæpen ahof
> wið hetendum.   Him wæs hild boden,
> wiges woma.
>
>   (1a–19a)

Then in the course of years two hundred and thirty-three winters had passed,
counted in number of allotted time, since ruling God, the Glory of kings had
been born into the world in human form, the Light of the righteous. That
was the sixth year of Constantine's rule, since he, the battle prince, had been
raised up in the kingdom of the Romans as the war-leader. The protector of
his people, the warrior, was gracious to men. The kingdom of the prince pros-
pered under the heavens. He was a true king, the war-guardian of men. God
confirmed in him glories and powers, so that to many men throughout the
world he was a joy, but a misery to nations when he raised up weapons against
his enemies. Battle was announced to him, the tumult of war.

This passage again illustrates Cynewulf's habitual process of mind and
the stylistic patterns this mode of thought determines. First, he separates the two temporal references—the two hundred and thirty-three

years since the birth of Christ and the six years of Constantine's reign—
making them independent subjects. Having done that, he finds there
a convenient opportunity to introduce a stylistic parallel between Jesus
and Constantine through extended variation: the several attributes of
Christ in glory are matched by the strengths and virtues of Constantine's reign as emperor (lines 4b–7a and 13b–17a). The parenthetical
Latin statement about Constantine's piety (a proleptic judgment, since
the story itself narrates Constantine's conversion to Christianity) Cynewulf puts in its proper place within the description of Constantine. So
he completes the symmetrical balance. Finally, Cynewulf sets the
action, not so many years after the Lord's Passion, but so many years
after His birth, thus laying the groundwork for the variational series
on light, truth, and glory which carry such weight in the rest of *Elene*.
Cynewulf focuses his attention on pattern and design, on balance and
symmetry, so that whatever syntactical complexities he introduces, the
outline of the greater structure always dominates. Even though he may
imitate some of the Latin stylistic qualities, his departures from the
Latin model are more significant and typical.

Certainly no deviation from a Latinate style could be greater than
the first section of *Elene*, Constantine's war with the Goths. As we
commented before, the three panels of *Elene* have three characteristic
modes—historical narrative, dramatic dialogue, and monologue.[29] And
the heavily formulaic diction of epic poetry subdues any Latin element
present in the first panel. It is more than a matter of certain themes—
the beasts of battle, for example. Cynewulf's stylistic experiment in this
section has no parallel in any of his other works. The purity of his
recreation makes it a conscious imitation, but his effort is paradoxically
almost too successful. Again Cynewulf takes the essential qualities of
a style and reduces them to their most intense effect. Particularly in
the battle scenes, where he depends most heavily on the older models
of the epic lay, Cynewulf moves away from a complex literary style
derived from Latin prose, and resorts instead to a direct, staccato
description. Even without regard to the punctuation which modern
editors have invented, the great number of very short sentences, many
taking up only one half-line, suggests not only the clash of battle, but
also the antithesis of the balance and rhythm with which he began and
which embodies a sense of harmony. The harshness of his syntactical
patterns in this section, his abrupt piling of clause upon clause, stands
as the stylistic equivalent of a chaos not to be resolved until after the
span of the entire poem. Then at that point Cynewulf can turn to

rhyme. A kind of rhyme (anaphora) does, however, exist in the deliberate repetition of word and pattern in this first section: *For folca
gedryht; For fyrda mæst* ("Advanced the host of people," 27a;
"Advanced the greatest of armies," 35a). But this repetition describes
a confusion that the style likewise projects. Constantine's vision interrupts the short burst of the epic style and returns to the more continuous line associated with Cynewulf's Latinity. Yet no sooner has the
vision departed and the battle itself begun than Cynewulf once more
composes in a style which impresses with its bluntness: *Stopon
stiðhidige, stundum wræcon, / bræcon bordhreðan; bil in dufan, /
prungon præchearde* ("Steadfast they marched, pressed forward at
times, broke shields, blades pierced in, strong in battle they hastened
on," 121a–23a). Just as Cynewulf perceived a scheme in the legend of
the Invention of the Cross and then structured his poem to explore that
scheme, so he seems to identify specific styles with each of the panels
in that structure. Styles and segments stand juxtaposed and they outline
steps in a progression from chaos to harmony.

Cynewulf's favorite pun on *rod/rodor* runs throughout the poem,
occurring at every point where the context permits the allusion. But
more important is his putting aside of the abrupt epic style and his
corresponding change to the dramatic dialogue between Elene and
Judas. The basis of these separate styles exists already in the Latin
source; however, Cynewulf's expansions and remoldings are distinct
enough to credit him with an original perspective on the possibilities
of sharp stylistic variation paralleling his thematic and structural patterns. All the elaborate fluency of the complex sentence missing in the
battle section returns now full force in Elene's and Judas's dialogue,
especially in the saint's lengthy instructions. Balance, control, careful
subordination, rhythmic patterning of the syntax, and the sense of a
higher style appropriate for a symbol of the Church Militant dominates
Elene's rhetoric. The barest bones may be present in the Latin, but
Cynewulf's fleshing out creates a different style with a different force.
Compare this brief outburst from the Latin with the Cynewulfian
expansion:

Latin

sed quia repellentes omnem sapientiam, eum qui volebat de maledicto vos
redimere maledixistis, & eum qui per sputum oculos vestros illuminavit
immundis potius sputis injuriastis, & eum qui mortuos vestros vivificabat in

mortem tradidistis, & lucem tenebras existimastis & veritatem mendacium, pervenit in vos maledictum quod est in lege vestra scriptum.[30]

"Rejecting all wisdom, however, you cursed Him who wanted to redeem you from the curse; you wronged Him who with His spit brought light to your eyes, spitting filthily instead on Him; you betrayed into death the man who brought life to your dead; you assumed the light was darkness and the truth a lie; accordingly, the curse which is written in your law has come upon you."

Old English

> "Hwæt ge þære snyttro   unwislice,
> wraðe wiðweorpon   þa ge wergdon þane
> þe eow of wergðe   þurh his wuldres miht,
> fram ligcwale   lysan þohte,
> of hæftnede.   Ge mid horu speowdon
> on þæs andwlitan   þe eow eagena leoht
> fram blindnesse   bote gefremede,
> edniowunga   þurh þæt æðele spald
> ond fram unclænum   oft generede
> deofla gastum.   Ge deaþe þone
> deman ongunnon   se ðe of deaðe sylf
> woruld awehte   on wera corþre
> in þæt ærre lif   eowres cynnes.
> Swa ge modblinde   mengan ongunnon
> lige wið soðe,   leoht wið þystrum,
> æfst wið are,   inwitþancum
> wroht webbedan;   eow seo wergðu forðan
> sceðþeð scyldfullum.   Ge þa sciran miht
> deman ongunnon,   on gedweolan lifdon
> þeostrum geþancum   oð þysne dæg."
>   (293a–312b)

"Lo, you angrily threw away wisdom in your stupidity when you cursed Him who thought to redeem you from the curse, from fiery torment, from imprisonment through the might of His glory. You with filth spat on the face of the one who restored the light of your eyes, gave you the remedy from blindness, and afresh saved you through that noble spittle from the unclean spirits of devils. You then began to condemn to death the one who before had raised up many of your race from death itself in the presence of men. So you, blind in heart, began to mix lying with truth, light with darkness, envy with mercy;

you contrived slanders with your malice. Therefore the curse harms you for
your sinfulness. You began to condemn the radiant power, and have lived in
error, with dark thoughts, to this day."

The differences are immediately apparent: the short series of antithetical expletives in the Latin become in *Elene* a precise balance of long
rhythmic units with parallels and contrasts carefully varied to reach a
rhetorically effective climax. Such differences can not be explained by
reference to Cynewulf's prolixity; they demonstrate a new way of con-
ceiving the basic narrative.

The influence of Latin style remains strong throughout *Elene*. A
direct imprint from the Latin can easily be detected in the following
section, though Cynewulf manages to thread his way through the tortured passage with less involution than the Latin author:

Latin

Et nunc, Domine, si tua voluntas est regnare filium Mariae, qui missus est a
te (nisi autem fuisset ex te, non tantas virtutes fecisset: nisi vero tuus puer
esset, non suscitares eum a mortuis) fac nobis, Domine, prodigium hoc.[31]

"Now, Lord, if it is your will that Mary's Son, who was sent by you, shall
reign—unless He came from you, He would not have performed such great
miracles; unless He was your Son, you would not have raised Him from the
dead—give us a sign, Lord."

Old English

"Gif þin willa sie,   wealdend engla,
þæt ricsie   se ðe on rode wæs
ond þurh Marian   in middangeard
acenned wearð   in cildes had,
þeoden engla—   gif he þin nære,
sunu synna leas   næfre he soðra swa feala,
in woruldrice,   wundra gefremede
dogorgerimum   no ðu of deaðe hine
swa þrymlice,   þeoda wealdend,
aweahte for weorodum   gif he in wuldre þin
þurh ða beorhtan   bearn ne wære—
gedo nu, fæder engla,   forð beacen þin."
                                    (772a–83b)

"If it be your will, Ruler of angels, that He will rule, the one who was on the Cross, and through Mary was born into the world in the form of a child, the Prince of Angels (if He were not your Son, void of sins, never would He have performed so many of true miracles in the world in the course of His days; nor would you, Ruler of Man, have awakened Him from death so gloriously before the people, if He had not been your Son in glory through the fair Virgin), do now, Father of Angels, show forth your sign."

This passage follows the Latin original so closely that it makes certain the written mode of Cynewulf's text; he could not have composed such a passage using only his oral formulas and arranging them in a specific performance. The formulaic half-lines, however, permit small segments to stand alone and thus the reader can assimilate the many subjects of this complex sentence more readily.

In more than one place the dialogue takes on a conversational tone unusual in Old English poetry and most unlike the formal declarations in *Juliana*, though this too may be derived from the Latin and it characterizes Judas's response more than Elene's:

> "Hu mæg ic þæt findan   þæt swa fyrn gewearð
> wintra gangum?   Is nu worn sceacen
> tu hund oððe ma   geteled rime;
> ic ne mæg areccan   nu ic þæt rim ne can;
> is nu feala siðþan   forð gewitenra,
> frodra ond godra   þe us fore wæron
> gleawra gumena;   ic on geogoðe wearð
> on siðdagum   syððan acenned
> cnihtgeong hæleð;   ic ne can þæt ic nat
> findan on fyrhðe   þæt swa fyrn gewearð."
>
>   (632a–41b)

"How can I find that which existed so long ago in the passage of years? A great many have now hastened away, two hundred or more have been counted. I cannot make a reckoning, since I don't know the number. Many old and good men, wise men, have passed away who lived before us. I was born in later days afterwards into the band of young retainers, a young warrior. I do not know that which I do not know, how to find in my heart that which happened so long ago."

The irregular and unpatterned repetition in Judas's disclaimer imitates the abrupt shifts in ordinary conversational rhythms. In contrast to

Judas's awkward style (before his conversion) stands Elene's controlled rhetoric:

> "ge þæt geare cunnon
> edre gereccan   hwæt þær eallra wæs
> on manrime   morðorslehtes,
> dareðlacendra   deadra gefeallen
> under bordhagan;   ge þa byrgenna
> under stanhleoðum   ond þa stowe swa some
> ond þa wintergerim   on gewritu setton."
>
>   (648–54b)

"You that clearly can tell me forthwith, what was the number of all the men in the slaughter, of dead spear-men fallen under the shield-wall. You have set down in writing the graves under the cliffs, and also the place and the number of years."

The patterned repetition in Elene's speech suggests her lofty stations—social, political, and theological.

Apart from occasional examples of repetition, anaphora, and other common devices, Cynewulf does little in the main section of *Elene* to call attention to the style of his poem *per se*. Reaching the personal monologue at the conclusion, however, he resorts to rhyme with an intensity that has caught the notice of every reader. It is unparalleled in Old English poetry (excepting the curious *Riming Poem*). The stylistic shift introduces both a new persona and a sense of the importance of poetic creation that would be boastful were it not for the pervasive sadness of the confessional tone. Interestingly, Cynewulf chooses to discuss his craft within the passage where he most obviously demonstrates that art, where the surface tricks capture the attention and call demanding attention to themselves. Not all the rhymes are perfect, even if corrected for the Anglian dialect; one line in the middle of the sequence is unrhymed; and then Cynewulf drops the rhyme completely at a seemingly arbitrary point. Besides rhyme, the passage also gives us Cynewulf's most expanded use of variation. He writes that he was stained with sin and then continues that idea with four variations; again, God's grace unlocks the art of poetry through seven variations. Cynewulf abandons rhyme just at the moment when he begins to speak, once more, of the Cross. The intensity, the self-consciousness of his stylistic experiment seems connected with personal statement; the focus on the Cross requires an altered style. Although we may not be able to recreate unerringly Cynewulf's intentions, we can be sure that he moves consciously from one style to another in observation of a strict sense of decorum.

Cynewulf's bold experiment at the end of *Elene* helps to define what an Anglo-Saxon notion of decorum might encompass. The length and complexity of *Elene* give Cynewulf ample space to try his several stylistic innovations and combinations. For each section he chooses one general stylistic mode, appropriate to its theme and action and different from each of the others. The styles of *Elene* also reflect the Cynewulfian technique of juxtaposed perspectives. Through those several panels, views, and styles Cynewulf portrays the perfection Christianity envisions, seen from a human position where imperfect fragments mar its purity. Through the serial turnings in *Elene*, and the conversions these enact, the fragments, with their differing styles, merge into one final apocalyptic vision of a heavenly world, a world beyond perspective and beyond the necessity of a decorum that such perspectives impose on style.

VI   *Cynewulf's Achievement*

Much of the assessment of Cynewulf's work suffers from the need to make him more important than he is. As the single author whose name can be connected with specific Anglo-Saxon poems, he already occupies a significant place in English literary history. It comes with the accident of manuscript transmission. While Cynewulf is a poet of ability and interest, the exaggerated comparisons between him and, as Cook would have it, Dante and Milton, obscure his actual talents rather than clarify his position in the range of European literature. Ker's remarks on the resemblance Cynewulf bears to Marino also stretch too far to find a kindred poetic spirit, but Ker hits upon a truth which must not slip by. Like Marino, Cynewulf is a mannerist poet. Certainly we do not thus connect Cynewulf with any historical school of mannerist poetry, as we do Marino; but by his interest in experimenting with the decoration of poetic surfaces, Cynewulf falls within the most general definition of that term. Cynewulf's immediate Latin predecessors are undoubtedly responsible for this stylistic trait. The extraordinarily elaborate and self-conscious style of Aldhelm's Latin poetry and prose, to take the most obvious example, may have been available to Cynewulf and also admired by him. On the subject of Aldhelm's style, Peter Hunter Blair writes: "His most popular works were a poem on virginity and a prose treatise on the same subject. His poem began with an elaborate double acrostic in which the initial and final letters of the lines formed one and the same hexameter verse, reading the initial letters downwards and the final letter upwards. In such mental gymnastics lay his chief delight. . . ."[32] We can see here some of the same idiosyncracies that mark Cynewulf's poetic habits, though Cynewulf never "progressed" to the Aldhelmian extremes.

Cynewulf's attention to poetic surfaces remains one of his greatest contributions to Anglo-Saxon poetry. This concern derives from a more than casual acquaintance with Latin poetry, including, perhaps, the classics of Roman literature and certainly other early medieval Latin works. We assume that the practice of poetry by its very nature implies an attention to surfaces; what distinguishes Cynewulf's poems from those written in Anglo-Saxon before him is the degree of self-consciousness involved. Striving for effect, Cynewulf consistently makes his mannerisms verbal focal points. Compare Cynewulf's several handlings of the *sum*-series with that of *The Wanderer*-poet. J. E. Cross sees the *sum*-series as an Old English "equivalent of a 'figure of diction' derived from pre-Christian Greek and Latin rhetorical teaching but available to the Englishmen in the works of Latin Christian writers who accepted the stylistic methods of the old rhetorical schools to present their arguments."[33] While Cross believes all *sum*-series in Old English poetry ultimately come from Christian Latin sources, the differences between *The Wanderer* and Cynewulf's poems are striking (for a translation of the second passage, see p. 62)

The Wanderer

> Sume wig fornom,
> ferede in forðwege;   sumne fugel oþbær
> ofer heanne holm;   sumne se hara wulf
> deaðe gedælde;   sumne dreorighleor
> in eorðscræfe   eorl gehydde.
>
> (80b–84b)[34]

Some war took off, carried away. One a bird carried off over the high seas; the grey wolf shared one with death. A dreary-faced noble hid one in an earth grave.

Christ II

> Sumum wordlaþe   wise sendeð
> on his modes gemynd   þurh his muþes gæst,
> æðele ondgiet.   Se mæg eal fela
> singan ond secgan   þam bið snyttru cræft
> bifolen on ferðe.   Sum mæg fingrum wel
> hlude fore hæleþum   hearpan stirgan,
> gleobeam gretan.   Sum mæg godcunde
> reccan rhyte æ.   Sum mæg ryne tungla
> secgan, side gesceaft.   Sum mæg searolice
> wordcwide writan.   Sumum wiges sped
> giefeð æt guþe,   þonne gargetrum
> ofer scildhreadan   sceotend sendað,
> flacor flangeweorc.   Sum mæg fromlice
> ofer sealtne sæ   sundwudu drifan,
> hreran holmþræce.   Sum mæg heanne beam
> stælgne gestigan.   Sum mæg styled sweord,
> wæpen gewyrcan.   Sum con wonga bigong,
> wegas widgielle.
>
> (664a–81a)

In *The Wanderer* the repetition remains only an aspect of the gnomic style, another aphorism expressing the mutability of all earthly things. In *Christ II*, we note first the rhetorical expansion and then the careful patternings and balances, the alternation in the length of the segments, the double structuring within the passage, signaled by changes in the case of *sum*, and both the repeated and altered verbs paired with *sum*, when it is the subject. Cynewulf's self-conscious devotion to the perfecting of the surface identifies his training in Latin grammar and rhetoric; and whatever *The Wanderer*-poet's acquaintance with similar materials may have been, he uses them in a different way.

This example seems especially instructive because the disparity between Cynewulf's approach and that of other Old English poets is here more subtle. Yet these are the same practices that manifest themselves boldly in the myriad of attention-calling devices we have already detailed: the runes, rhyme, puns, anaphora, and the expert restructuring of his sources. But Cynewulf finds in the verbal pattern a means of expressing his particular ideas. His is not the ultimate failure of the mannerist poet, to become so enchanted with complexity and ingenuity (as some think Aldhelm did) that any reason for such display vanishes. Cynewulf subordinates his attraction to verbal and rhetorical tricks to a strong overriding sense of structure and perspective. The occasional mannerism serves a specific purpose in a greater scheme. And this harmonizes with Cynewulf's basic habits of mind, a process which we have described as discontinuous. Cynewulf brings an item— an action, character, statement, panel, or rhetorical device—into focus for the moment, but then abandons it after it has served the immediate purpose. He creates continuity out of the assemblage of these discontinuous items as he molds them into precise and total structures. The pieces that constitute the finished structures do not, therefore, always resemble each other, or even seem to come from the same quarry.

Literary historians have often remarked that Cynewulf introduced an entirely new subject matter into Anglo-Saxon poetry. Kemp Malone sums up this common point:

The work of Cynewulf marks a new stage in the history of English religious poetry. This had begun with paraphrases of biblical story. It now went on to themes more pointedly didactic. Cynewulf himself versified exemplary deeds of saints and a sermon on the ascension. We do not know whether he took the lead in departing from Caedmon's themes, or whether he was following someone else. In any case, the school which goes by his name greatly widened the scope of vernacular verse.[35]

After Cynewulf, Anglo-Saxon taste preferred poetic saints' lives and sermons. Malone correctly reminds us that we do not know whether Cynewulf was personally responsible for this major historical change, though we can perceive that it coincides with Cynewulf's poetic activity. Even *Judith*, a late ninth- or early tenth-century paraphrase of an Old Testament story, bears little resemblance to the early Caedmonic poems and draws instead on the Anglo-Saxon hagiographical tradition for most of its distinctive features. To have been a part of, indeed perhaps the initiator of, such a deep change within a national literature bestows importance. Further, this change becomes the pattern for vernacular literatures throughout Europe a century or two later. While we can imply no cause and effect, we must remember that to be in the vanguard of what emerges as a universal cultural displacement is no small indication of a poet's intuitive powers.

Inheritor of a poetic style which was suited to expressing full narratives, Cynewulf turned it in several different directions. The style itself derives from a rhetoric of praise, the Germanic (and universal) need for a ceremonial poetry to endow heroes with fame. Its epideictic origins remain even in Cynewulf's relatively late poetry, and not infrequently does the description of an evil character betray the enthusiasm which the original style was designed to carry for those who deserved it. But before Cynewulf, Old English poets did not treat abstract thoughts in the nature of theological deliberations. With Cynewulf, we turn to prose as a new source for the inspiration of poetry; for the biblical origins of the early Caedmon poems can hardly be said to depend on prose, as the sacred text holds a position beyond the categories "prose" and "poetry." The only poetic source which seems to have influenced Cynewulf is Bede's Ascension hymn and this influence is more general than specific. Cynewulf makes, then, a particular combination—that of an ancient heroic style with Latin didactic prose. Here again, Cynewulf is apparently the first vernacular writer to move a national literature in this direction, and the results are occasionally discordant. But the discord is functional, if not deliberate. It may also be intentional, though that cannot be proved. Yet the effect contributes to the sense of irony that pervades Cynewulf's poems. This irony is not one that denigrates the heroes it portrays. It is a Christian irony and depends upon the many paradoxes of that religion for its full force. Not all Christian poems, in Old English or any other language, are perforce ironic, as Cynewulf's are. His irony follows his sense of structure, which though it may not be as "architectonic" as Dante's or Milton's, is still one of the clearest and surest in early medieval literature. His art of juxtaposing panels, of repeated sections mirroring each other in successive, though changing, modes creates a system of parallels and comparisons in which evident disparities—good and evil, human and divine, time and eternity—span a range of ironic possibility. Some of these ironies are obvious and heavy, some quite subtle. But nonetheless it is Cynewulf's ironic point of view that distinguishes in part his hagiographical exercises from those which follow. Perhaps his personal epilogues, however autobiographical they may or may not be, are at the base. For the world is not only divided into heaven and earth, but into heaven, the perfect from earth, and the imperfect on earth. The ever-present awareness of his own imperfection silhouettes the lives of his saints against an even brighter background, one that only widens the cleft between him and his symbolic characters of perfection. Faced with this chasm, the two extreme polar reactions are cynicism or faith, and their expressive modes, some form of invective or prayer. Cynewulf's choice is evident to all.

We have only begun to acknowledge the complexity of his poetic structures. Assuming that he started with rude and naive subjects, earlier critics logically deduced that the poems likewise were obvious and simplistic. Cynewulf's sources, with the exception of Gregory and Bede, are open to this charge; Cynewulf's poems are not. For his changes in the received structures do not merely rearrange details; they are absolute. He imposes his own order on the material, and his ability to perceive new structural possibilities in rough matter bespeaks a mind finely attuned to formal properties and not just to the bare sequences of events.

With Cynewulf we see the first example of processes that established themselves firmly in the history of English poetry: the reworking of foreign literatures in the native language, and the consequent attention to form, genre, surface, and technique. French was to provide a major influence on some English writers; Latin, on many. Cynewulf's predecessors in Anglo-Saxon poetry have a beauty and a greatness of their own; certainly they paid attention to their art. But Cynewulf took his task to be the weaving of one literature into another, and the result is a new clarity for Old English poetry.

Cynewulf's efforts may have had little effect on later poets, other than those who came immediately after and still composed in Anglo-Saxon. What he discovered, however, sets the pattern for what author after author had to rediscover in the following centuries. In this sense Cynewulf can be called the first classical poet in the English language. He employs his skill in God's service, and the art itself comes from a welding of an early medieval concept of classical rhetoric with Germanic diction. The characteristic Cynewulfian irony may stem more from this curious joining than from either his theology or character. If Cynewulf did not succeed in creating a cosmos to match Dante's or Milton's, he nevertheless gave to Anglo-Saxon poetry an ideal of craft and form that is the best gift of the classical tradition.

Notes and References

Chapter One

1. For a good summary of oral-formulaic studies, see Andreas Haarder, *Beowulf: The Appeal of a Poem* (Aarhus: Akademisk Forlag, 1975), pp. 178–204.
2. See Daniel G. Calder, "The Study of Style in Old English Poetry: A Historical Introduction," in *Old English Poetry: Essays on Style*, ed. Calder (Berkeley: University of California Press, 1979), pp. 33–34.
3. Jakob Grimm, ed., *Andreas und Elene* (Cassel: Fischer, 1840), p. 167. This and all subsequent translations are mine, unless otherwise noted.
4. John M. Kemble, "On Anglo-Saxon Runes," *Archaeologia* 28 (1840):360–64.
5. Ibid., pp. 362–63.
6. "Maier's Transcript and the Conclusion of Cynewulf's *Fates of the Apostles*," *Journal of English and Germanic Philology* 56 (1957):572.
7. Ibid., p. 573.
8. "Collation der altenglische Gedichte im Vercellibuch," *Zeitschrift für Deutsches Altertum und Deutsche Literatur* 33 (1889):70.
9. Albert S. Cook, ed., *The Christ of Cynewulf* (Boston, 1909), p. lxxii. For information on Cynewulf's identity and dates I depend entirely on Cook and also Charles W. Kennedy, *The Earliest English Poetry* (London, 1943); Kenneth Sisam, "Cynewulf and His Poetry," *Proceedings of the British Academy* 18 (1934, for 1932):303–31; Rosemary Woolf, ed., *Juliana* (London, 1953); and P. O. E. Gradon, ed., *Cynewulf's "Elene"* (London, 1958).
10. Heinrich Leo, *Quae de se ipso Cynevulfus (sive Cenevulfus sive Coenevulfus) poeta Anglosaxonicus tradiderit* (Halle: Hendelius, 1857).
11. The quotations are from Gradon's edition. I have changed "wynn" to "w," "yogh" to "y," and "7" to "ond."
12. Kennedy, p. 199.
13. Cook, pp. lxxii–lxxvi.
14. Gradon, p. 13.
15. Sisam, p. 304.
16. Gradon, p. 14.
17. Cook, p. lxviii.
18. See ibid., pp. lxviii–lxix.
19. Sisam, p. 306.
20. See Gradon, p. 14 and Sisam, p. 306.
21. See Gradon, pp. 22–23 and Sisam, pp. 327–28, n. 13.

22. *Old English and Middle English Poetry,* Routledge History of English Poetry, no. 1 (London: Routledge and Kegan Paul, 1977), p. 292.

23. Henry Bradley, *The Academy,* March 24, 1888, p. 197. Napier's brief notice concerning the runes in *The Fates* appeared in *The Academy,* September 8, 1888, p. 153 and later in *Zeitschrift für Deutsches Altertum und Deutsche Literatur.*

24. *Anglo-Saxon Poetic Records,* III, p. lv.

25. Henry Morley, *English Writers,* vol. 2 (London: Cassell, 1888), pp. 218–19.

26. Bradley, p. 197.

27. "The Cynewulfian Runes of the First Riddle," *Modern Language Notes* 25 (1910):235–41.

28. Sisam, p. 311.

29. S. K. Das, *Cynewulf and the Cynewulf Canon* (Calcutta, 1942), and Claes Schaar, *Critical Studies in the Cynewulf Group,* Lund Studies in English, no. 17 (Lund, 1949).

30. "The Lacuna in the Text of Cynewulf's *Ascension* (*Christ II,* 556b)," in *Studies in Language, Literature and Culture of the Middle Ages and Later,* ed. E. Bagby Atwood and Archibald A. Hill (Austin, 1969), p. 219.

31. Woolf, p. 19.

32. Ibid., p. 7.

33. Schaar, p. 261.

34. Dolores Warwick Frese, "The Art of Cynewulf's Runic Signatures," in *Anglo-Saxon Poetry: Essays in Appreciation,* ed. Lewis E. Nicholson and Dolores Warwick Frese (Notre Dame, 1975), pp. 312–13.

35. See Tupper, p. 37; *Monumenta Germaniae Historica, Auctores Antiquissimi,* vol. 15 and Tatwine, *Corpus Christianorum,* vol. 133.

36. T. A. Shippey, *Old English Verse* (London, 1972), pp. 156–58.

37. See H. P. R. Finberg, *The Formation of England 550–1042* (London: Hart-Davis MacGibbon, 1974), pp. 100–102.

38. Ibid., p. 99.

39. Frank M. Stenton, *Anglo-Saxon England,* 2d ed. (Oxford: Clarendon Press, 1950), p. 190.

40. Sisam, p. 312.

41. See Michael J. B. Allen and Daniel G. Calder, trans., *Sources and Analogues of Old English Poetry: The Major Latin Texts* (Cambridge; D. S. Brewer, 1976) for a general survey of the kinds of source materials that were at the Anglo-Saxons' disposal; see also J. D. S. Ogilvy, *Books Known to the English, 597–1066* (Cambridge, Mass.: Mediaeval Academy of America, 1967). For the grammatical and rhetorical education of the Anglo-Saxons, see the two articles by Jackson J. Campbell, "Knowledge of Rhetorical Figures in Anglo-Saxon England," *Journal of English and Germanic Philology* 66 (1967):1–20 and "Learned Rhetoric in Old English Poetry," *Modern Philology* 63 (1966):189–201.

Chapter Two

1. See, for example, Gregor Sarrazin, "Die *Fata Apostolorum* und der Dichter Kynewulf," *Anglia* 12 (1899):375–87 and J. Bourauel, "Zur Quellen- und Verfasserfrage von *Andreas, Crist* und *Fata*," *Bonner Beiträge* 11 (1901):101–107. The text of the poem is taken from *Anglo-Saxon Poetic Records*, II.

2. René Aigrain, *L'Hagiographie* (Paris: Bloud and Gay, 1953), p. 11.

3. Sisam, p. 327, n. 13.

4. *Andreas and The Fates of the Apostles* (Oxford, 1961), p. xxx.

5. *Clavis Patrum Latinorum*, ed. E. Dekkers and A. A. Gaar, *Sacris Eruditi*, no. 3, rev. ed. (Bruges: C. Beyaert; The Hague: Martinus Nijhoff, 1961), p. 2031.

6. See Richard Adelbert Lipsius, *Die Apokryphen Apostelgeschichten und Apostellegenden*, vol. 1 (Braunschweig: C. A. Schwetschke und Sohn, 1883), p. 213.

7. *Andreas and The Fates of the Apostles* (Boston, 1906), p. xxx.

8. See George L. Hamilton, "The Sources of *The Fates of the Apostles* and *Andreas*," *Modern Language Notes* 35 (1920):387.

9. Ed. Krapp, p. xxxii.

10. Ibid., p. xxxii.

11. Hamilton, "The Sources" and Ruth Perkins, "On the Sources of the *Fata Apostolorum*," *Modern Language Notes* 32 (1917):159–61.

12. Sisam, p. 327, n. 13.

13. See Daniel G. Calder, "*The Fates of the Apostles*, the Latin Martyrologies, and the Litany of the Saints," *Medium Ævum* 44 (1975):219–24.

14. See J. E. Cross, "Cynewulf's Traditions About the Apostles in *Fates of the Apostles*," *Anglo-Saxon England* 8 (1979):163–75 for a far-ranging investigation of the backgrounds.

15. Schaar, p. 34.

16. *Anglo-Saxon Poetic Records*, II, p. xxxviii.

17. "Form and Meaning in Cynewulf's *Fates of the Apostles*," *Papers on Language and Literature* 5 (1969):115–22.

18. Ibid., p. 116.

19. Ibid., p. 119.

20. "*The Fates of the Apostles*: Imagery, Structure, and Meaning," *Papers on Language and Literature* 10 (1974):120.

21. Ibid., p. 123.

22. "*Se giddes begang* of *The Fates of the Apostles*," *English Studies* 56 (1975):387.

23. Ibid., p. 389.

24. Hieatt, p. 123.

25. Calder, "*The Fates*," p. 221.

26. R. K. Gordon, trans., *Anglo-Saxon Poetry* (London: J. M. Dent, 1926; New York: E. P. Dutton, 1927), p. 178.

27. See "The Penitential Motif in Cynewulf's *Fates of the Apostles* and in His Epilogues," *Anglo-Saxon England* 6 (1977):105.

28. *Patrologia Latina* 82.287ff. This reference is cited in Warren Ginsberg, "Cynewulf and His Sources: *The Fates of the Apostles*," *Neuphilologische Mitteilungen* 78 (1977):112–13.

29. Ginsberg, pp. 111–12.

30. This last point is made by Hieatt, p. 123.

31. Ed. Brooks, p. xxxi.

32. Sisam, p. 327, n. 13.

33. Kennedy, p. 232.

34. See the pseudo-Alcuin litany, *Patrologia Latina*, 101.591–96.

35. See Morton Bloomfield's remarks in his review of Stanley B. Greenfield's *A Critical History of Old English Literature*, in *Speculum* 41 (1966):331.

36. Gordon, pp. 179–80.

37. "Cynewulf's Runes in *Juliana* and *Fates of the Apostles*," *English Studies* 34 (1953):197.

38. *An Introduction to English Runes* (London, 1973), pp. 205–6.

39. Frese, "Cynewulf's Runic Signatures," p. 321.

40. See Randolph Quirk, "Poetic Language and Old English Metre," in his *Essays on the English Language: Medieval and Modern* (Bloomington, Ind.: Indiana University Press; Harlow: Longmans, 1968), p. 11.

Chapter Three

1. "Cynevulfs Crist," *Zeitschrift für Deutsches Altertum und Deutsche Literatur* 9 (1853):204.

2. See Peter Clemoes, "Cynewulf's Image of the Ascension," in *England Before the Conquest: Studies in Primary Sources Presented to Dorothy Whitelock*, ed. Peter Clemoes and Kathleen Hughes (Cambridge, 1971), p. 294.

3. See Clemoes, passim, and George Brown, "The Descent-Ascent Motif in *Christ II* of Cynewulf," *Journal of English and Germanic Philology* 73 (1974):1–12.

4. *The Christ of Cynewulf* (Boston, 1900), pp. 116–18.

5. See Pope, pp. 214–19.

6. Cook, p. xvi; his discussion continues to p. xxv and my summary is based entirely on his work.

7. Ibid., p. xvii.

8. *Anglo-Saxon Poetic Records*, III, p. xxvi; see also Brother Augustine

Philip, "The Exeter Scribe and the Unity of the *Christ*," *Publications of the Modern Language Association of America*, 55 (1940):903–9.

9. "Unity of Cynewulf's *Christ* in the Light of Iconography," *Speculum* 23 (1948):426–32.

10. "God's Presence through Grace as the Theme of Cynewulf's *Christ II* and the Relationship of this Theme to *Christ I* and *Christ III*," *Anglo-Saxon England* 3 (1974):97.

11. Ibid., p. 99.

12. Ibid., pp. 100, 101.

13. Frese, "Cynewulf's Runic Signatures," p. 333.

14. Ibid., p. 330.

15. Brown, p. 1, n. 1.

16. *Patrologia Latina*, 76.1217–18.

17. *Patrologia Latina*, 76.1218.

18. *A Critical History of Old English Literature* (New York: New York University Press, 1965), p. 129. The text of the poem is taken from *Anglo-Saxon Poetic Records*, III.

19. In line 446a Cynewulf refers to Mary as *mærre* and again in line 456a he applies this same adjective to Christ *(se brega mæra)*. It seems obvious that Cynewulf had this word on his mind when he composed this section; and it seems unlikely that he would have applied the same laudatory description he uses for Christ and Mary to a contemporary, however "illustrious." Gregory, of course, as a saint and founder of the English church would have deserved such an appellation.

20. See R. W. Adams, "*Christ II:* Cynewulfian *Heilsgeschichte*," *English Language Notes* 12 (1974):78, for comments on the use of *beorn*.

21. The entire patristic tradition behind Christ's descent and ascension is fully explored by Brown in the article cited in note 3 above.

22. "Figurative interpretation" of the "word" is the central concern of the article by Oliver J. H. Grosz, "Man's Imitation of the Ascension: The Unity of *Christ II*," *Neophilologus* 54 (1970):398–408. While I agree wholeheartedly with Grosz that the word and its interpretation are of signal interest in this and in all Cynewulf's poems, I do not agree with many of the specific interpretations in Grosz's essay.

23. Chase makes this text the principal theme of the whole poem; he maintains that all of Cynewulf's changes from his source are made to give prominence to this idea (passim). God's presence through grace is a cardinal point in Christian theology but there are other thematic considerations in *Christ II* in addition to this theme which Chase does not treat.

24. Brown, p. 9.

25. Peter Clemoes sketches the pictorial and iconographic tradition behind this scene in his article, "Cynewulf's Image of the Ascension," pp. 293–304.

26. This point was first made by Pope, p. 216.

27. Ibid., p. 217.

28. Ibid.

29. The connection between the Harrowing of Hell and Christ's entry into heaven has a long history; see Brown's article.

30. *Rhythm and Cosmic Order in Old English Christian Literature* (London: Cambridge University Press, 1970), p. 12.

31. Chase, p. 92.

32. *Patrologia Latina*, 76.1218.

33. Ibid.

34. Cook, p. 141; *Patrologia Latina*, 76.899.

35. See J. E. Cross, "The Old English Poetic Theme of 'The Gifts of Men,'" *Neophilologus*, 46 (1962):66–70.

36. Ibid., p. 68. For an English translation, see Allen and Calder, p. 155.

37. Grosz, p. 406.

38. Ibid., p. 401.

39. *Patrologia Latina*, 76.1218.

40. Ibid.

41. Ibid., 76.1219.

42. This interpretation agrees in principle with that expressed by Chase, i.e., that the important element in *Christ II* is the presence of grace as a gift of the spirit, but the actual comparison of Gregory and Cynewulf at this point and the analysis based upon it differ markedly; see Chase, pp. 93–95.

43. *Patrologia Latina*, 76.1219.

44. See Roberta Frank, "Some Uses of Paronamasia in Old English Scriptural Verse," *Speculum* 47 (1972):226.

45. Grosz, p. 403.

46. *Patrologia Latina*, 76.1219.

47. See my article, "*Guthlac A* and *Guthlac B:* Some Discriminations," in *Anglo-Saxon Poetry*, ed. Nicholson and Frese, pp. 65–80.

48. Page's translation.

49. Frese, "Cynewulf's Runic Signatures," p. 314.

50. Ibid., p. 328.

51. *Patrologia Latina*, 76.1219.

Chapter Four

1. I am completely dependent for this section on two works: *Juliana*, ed. Woolf, pp. 11-17; and S. T. R. O. d'Ardenne, ed., *þe Liflade ant te Passiun of Seinte Iuliene*, Early English Text Society, no. 248 (London: Oxford University Press, 1961, for 1960), pp. xviii–xxiv.

2. *Acta sanctorum, Februarius*, vol. 2, ed. Johannes Bollandus and Godefridus Henschenius (Antwerp: Ioannes Meursus, 1658), 873–77.

3. "Saints' Lives," in *Continuations and Beginnings: Studies in Old English Literature*, ed. E. G. Stanley (London: Nelson, 1966), p. 44.

4. d'Ardenne, p. x.

5. Greenfield, p. 111.

6. Woolf, "Saints' Lives," p. 45.

7. Ed. Woolf, p. 19. The text of the poem is taken from this edition. I have changed "wynn" to "w," "yogh" to "y," and "7" to "ond."

8. See Woolf, "Saints' Lives," pp. 43–44.

9. Ibid., p. 48.

10. William Strunk, Jr., ed., *Juliana* (Boston, 1904), p. xl.

11. Woolf, "Saints' Lives," pp. 40–41.

12. See *Les Légendes hagiographiques*, 4th ed. (Brussels: Société des Bollandistes, 1955), p. 23; cf. pp. 88–89.

13. See Bertram Colgrave, ed., *The Earliest Life of Gregory the Great* (Lawrence: University of Kansas Press, 1968), p. 131; see also Charles W. Jones, *Saints' Lives and Chronicles in Early England* (Ithaca: Cornell University Press, 1947), pp. 57–64.

14. "Typology and Iconographic Style in Early Medieval Hagiography," *Studies in the Literary Imagination* 8 (1975):16.

15. Ibid., p. 21.

16. Joseph Wittig, "Figural Narrative in Cynewulf's *Juliana*," *Anglo-Saxon England* 4 (1975):55.

17. *The Theory of Literary Criticism: A Logical Analysis* (Berkeley: University of California Press, 1974), p. 102.

18. *The Guest-Hall of Eden: Four Essays on the Design of Old English Poetry* (New Haven, 1972), p. 102.

19. *Form and Style in Early English Literature* (London: Methuen, 1971), p. 126.

20. See, for example, James M. Garnett, "The Latin and the Anglo-Saxon *Juliana*," *Publications of the Modern Language Association of America*, 14 (1899):279–98.

21. Shippey, p. 125, uses the term "polarisation" to describe the Old English *Andreas*-poet's handling of his source.

22. "Characterization in the Old English *Juliana*," *South Atlantic Bulletin* 41 (1976):14.

23. Wittig, pp. 50–55.

24. Ibid., p. 51.

25. Shippey, p. 171.

26. *Acta sanctorum, Februarius*, vol. 2, p. 874.

27. For an excellent discussion of "Religious Laughter," see V. A. Kolve, *The Play Called Corpus Christi* (Stanford: Stanford University Press, 1966), pp. 124–44.

28. The pervasive irony in *Juliana* would be classified by D. C. Muecke

as that which occurs within a "closed ideology" (*The Compass of Irony* [London: Methuen, 1969], pp. 125–28 and passim).

29. *Acta sanctorum, Februarius*, vol. 2, p. 873.

30. See Schaar, p. 30.

31. Garnett mentions that the characterization of the heathens as wealthy has been added by Cynewulf (p. 289); he does not pursue the matter, however.

32. See Woolf's remarks in her edition, pp. 13–15; and in "Saints' Lives," p. 46.

33. *Acta sanctorum, Februarius*, vol. 2, p. 874.

34. Ibid.

35. Ibid.

36. Wittig, p. 42.

37. Ibid.

38. "The Allegory of the Soul as Fortress in Old English Poetry," *Anglia* 88 (1970):504.

39. *Acta sanctorum, Februarius*, vol. 2, p. 875.

40. Ibid., p. 875.

41. See Wittig, pp. 43–47.

42. *Acta sanctorum, Februarius*, vol. 2, p. 875.

43. See Doubleday's article for an exploration of the patristic background of this image.

44. For an interesting explication of that portion describing the soul as a house buffeted by storms, see Kenneth A. Bleeth, "*Juliana:* 647–52," *Medium Ævum* 38 (1969):119–22.

45. *Acta sanctorum, Februarius*, vol. 2, p. 877.

46. Ed. Woolf, p. 19.

47. Frese, "Cynewulf's Runic Signatures," p. 316.

48. Ibid., pp. 318–19.

49. Page, p. 210.

50. *Studies in the History of Old English Literature* (1953; reprint ed., Oxford: Clarendon Press, 1962), pp. 21–22.

51. Elliot, p. 202.

52. Page, p. 211.

Chapter Five

1. For a good discussion of this question, see Gradon's ed. of *Elene*, pp. 15–22.

2. Ibid., p. 19.

3. Alfred Holder, ed., *Inventio Sanctae Crucis* (Leipzig: B. G. Teubner, 1889).

4. "Cynewulf's Multiple Revelations," *Medievalia et Humanistica* 3 (1972):258.

5. "Old English Onomastics and Narrative Art: *Elene* 1062," *Modern Philology* 73 (1975):109, n. 6.

6. *The Literature of the Anglo-Saxons* (New York: Russell and Russell, 1962), p. 128.

7. Sisam, "Cynewulf and His Poetry," p. 308.

8. Greenfield, p. 113.

9. Ed. Gradon, p. 20. The text of the poem is taken from this edition. I have changed "wynn" to "w" and "yogh" to "y."

10. A number of articles has appeared within the last decade all commenting on this same pattern. Since one of my own essays is among them, I have not, in what follows, tried to distinguish carefully who says what on small details. The essays fall into two groups, with the first being mainly "literary," i.e., concerned with themes and images without a great deal of reference to the patristic background. These include, in order of publication: Robert Stepsis and Richard Rand, "Contrast and Conversion in Cynewulf's *Elene*," *Neuphilologische Mitteilungen* 70 (1969):273–82; John Gardner, "Cynewulf's *Elene*: Sources and Structure," *Neophilolgus* 54 (1970):65–76; Daniel G. Calder, "Strife, Revelation, and Conversion: The Thematic Structure of *Elene*," *English Studies* 53 (1972):201–10; Ellen F. Wright, "Cynewulf's *Elene* and the *singal sacu*," *Neuphilologische Mitteilungen* 76 (1975):538–49. The second group, which has examined the poem from a more historical viewpoint, has two subdivisions. In addition to purely literary concerns, division one sees *Elene* as a poem about the conflict between the church and the synagogue: Thomas D. Hill, "Sapiential Structure and Figural Narrative in the Old English *Elene*," *Traditio* 27 (1971):159–77; J. Campbell's article cited above in note 4; and Catharine A. Regan, "Evangelicalism as the Informing Principle of Cynewulf's *Elene*," *Traditio* 29 (1973):27–52. The articles in division two concern themselves with aspects of the background other than the church/synagogue debate: Whatley's article cited above in note 5; also Whatley, "Bread and Stone: Cynewulf's *Elene* 611–618," *Neuphilologische Mitteilungen* 76 (1975):550–60; and Varda Fish, "Theme and Pattern in Cynewulf's *Elene*," *Neuphilologische Mitteilungen* 76 (1975):1–25. There is a great deal of overlap among all these articles and unless a critic has a most specific point, I have not noted individual contributions at every turn.

11. This last point is made by Fish, p. 5.

12. Donald K. Fry has made a complete analysis of the oral-formulaic element in this part: "Themes and Type-Scenes in *Elene* 1-113," *Speculum* 44 (1969):35–45.

13. See ibid., p. 41.

14. Latin quotations are from the *Acta sanctorum, Maius*, vol. 1, ed. Godefridus Henschenius and Daniel Papebrochius (Antwerp: Ioannes Meursius, 1680), p. 445.

15. J. Campbell, "Cynewulf's Multiple Revelations," p. 281.

16. *Acta sanctorum, Maius*, vol. 1, p. 445.

17. Thomas Merton, *The Last of the Fathers: Saint Bernard of Clairvaux and the Encyclical Letter, "Doctor Mellifluus"* (New York: Harcourt, Brace, 1954), p. 27.

18. "The Speech of Stephen and the Tone of *Elene*," in *Anglo-Saxon Poetry*, ed. Nicholson and Frese, p. 122.

19. *Acta sanctorum, Maius*, vol. 1, p. 446.

20. Ibid.

21. Kennedy, p. 219.

22. This is the basic assumption of Regan's article.

23. Whatley, "Bread and Stone," p. 555.

24. *Acta sanctorum, Maius*, vol. 1, p. 446.

25. Whatley, "Bread and Stone," p. 553.

26. See Jean Daniélou, *The Bible and the Liturgy*, Liturgical Studies, no. 3 (Notre Dame: University of Notre Dame Press, 1961), on the relation between the Harrowing of Hell and Baptism.

27. Whatley, "Old English Onomastics," pp. 110–11.

28. Ibid., p. 115.

29. *Acta sanctorum, Maius*, vol. 1, p. 447.

30. J. Campbell, "Cynewulf's Multiple Revelations," p. 274.

31. See Wright's article for an interpretation of the poem from this point of view.

32. George A. Smithson, *The Old English Christian Epic*, University of California Publications in Modern Philology, vol. 1 (Berkeley: University of California Press, 1910), p. 323.

33. Greenfield, p. 114.

34. Many of the rhymes are imperfect and it has long been an accepted theory that by restoring the West Saxon text to its Anglian "original," the rhymes can be made more perfect. See Chapter I; but note also H. L. Rogers, "Rhymes in the Epilogue to *Elene:* A Reconsideration," *Leeds Studies in English* 5 (1971):47–52, who questions this assumption.

35. The translation of the runic signatures is Page's, p. 208.

36. See Carleton Brown, "Cynewulf and Alcuin," *Publications of the Modern Language Association of America*, 18 (1903):308–34.

37. Merton, pp. 26–27.

Chapter Six

1. Cook, p. xcv.

2. Bernhard A. K. ten Brink, *History of English Literature*, trans. Horace M. Kennedy, vol. 1 (New York: H. Holt, 1889), pp. 55–56.

3. See, for example, Stopford A. Brooke, *The History of Early English Literature* (New York: Macmillan, 1914), p. 427 and M. Benedick Smith,

"Old English Christian Poetry," in *The Cambridge History of English Literature*, vol. 1, ed. A. W. Ward and A. R. Waller (New York: G. P. Putnam's Sons, 1907), p. 69.

4. Richard Heinzel, *Über den Stil der altgermanischen Poesie*, Quellen und Forschungen, no. 10 (Strasbourg: Karl J. Trübner, 1875), pp. 43ff.

5. W. P. Ker, *The Dark Ages* (1904; reprint ed., London: Nelson, 1955), pp. 262–63.

6. Sisam, "Cynewulf and His Poetry," p. 315.

7. Das, *Cynewulf and the Cynewulf Canon*.

8. Ibid., p. xvii.

9. Ibid., p. 236.

10. Schaar, p. 127.

11. Ibid., pp. 131–32, 134.

12. Ibid., pp. 170–71.

13. Ibid., p. 233.

14. Ibid., pp. 325–26.

15. Ellis, p. 102.

16. See Robert E. Diamond, "The Diction of the Signed Poems of Cynewulf," *Philological Quarterly* 38 (1959):228–41. On the influence of Latin letters see two articles by J. Campbell, "Knowledge of Rhetorical Figures" and "Learned Rhetoric."

17. The quotation is from *Anglo-Saxon Poetic Records*, II.

18. The quotation is from Friedrich Klaeber, ed., *Beowulf and the Fight at Finnsburg*, 3d ed. (1936; reprint ed., New York: D. C. Heath, 1950).

19. See A. Campbell, "The Old English Epic Style," in *English and Medieval Studies Presented to J. R. R. Tolkien on the Occasion of His Seventieth Birthday*, ed. Norman Davis and C. L. Wrenn (London: Allen and Unwin, 1962), pp. 19ff.

20. See Alois Brandl, *Englische Literatur: A. Angelsächsische Periode*, Hermann Paul's Grundriss der germanischen Philologie, vol. 2, pt. 1, 2d ed. (Strasbourg: Karl J. Trübner, 1901), pp. 988ff.

21. See A. Campbell, p. 20.

22. This example is mentioned by Shippey, p. 167.

23. Cf. Das: "He does not look away from his theme to cast such glances at outside nature as other Anglo-Saxon poets frequently indulge in, but through excess of emotion goes on lengthening his sentence periods, elaborating and giving a finishing touch to his ideas, raising them to their highest excellence so that on occasions his sentence-structure becomes clumsy" (p. 154).

24. Ed. Woolf, p. 19.

25. Ibid., p. 17.

26. See Frank, p. 226.

27. *Acta sanctorum, Februarius*, vol. 2, p. 873.

28. *Acta sanctorum, Maius*, vol. 1, p. 445.

29. See Fish, p. 5.

30. *Acta Sanctorum, Maius,* vol. 1, p. 446.

31. Ibid., p. 447.

32. *An Introduction to Anglo-Saxon England* (Cambridge: Cambridge University Press, 1956), p. 326.

33. "On *The Wanderer* Lines 80–84: A Study of a Figure and a Theme," in *Vetenskaps Societen i Lund Årsbok* (1958–1959), p. 77.

34. The quotation is taken from T. P. Dunning and A. J. Bliss, eds., *The Wanderer* (London: Methuen; New York: Appleton-Century-Crofts, 1969).

35. "The Old English Period (to 1100)," in *A Literary History of England,* ed. Albert C. Baugh (New York: Appleton-Century-Crofts, 1948), pp. 74–75.

Selected Bibliography

PRIMARY SOURCES

BROOKS, KENNETH R., ed. *Andreas and The Fates of the Apostles.* Oxford: Oxford University Press, 1961.

COOK, ALBERT S., ed. *The Christ of Cynewulf: A Poem in Three Parts.* 2d ed. Boston: Ginn, 1909.

GRADON, PAMELA O. E., ed. *Cynewulf's Elene.* London: Methuen, 1958.

HOLTHAUSEN, FERDINAND, ed. *Cynewulf's Elene.* 4th ed. Heidelberg: C. Winter, 1936.

KRAPP, GEORGE PHILIP, ed. *The Vercelli Book. ASPR II.* New York: Columbia University Press, 1932.

————, and Dobbie, Elliott Van Kirk, eds. *The Exeter Book. ASPR III.* New York: Columbia University Press, 1936.

STRUNK, WILLIAM, JR., ed. *Juliana.* Boston: D. C. Heath, 1904.

WOOLF, ROSEMARY, ed. *Juliana.* London: Methuen, 1955.

SECONDARY SOURCES

ANDERSON, EARL R. "Cynewulf's *Elene*: Manuscript Divisions and Structural Symmetry." *Modern Philology* 72 (1973):111–22. Anderson claims that the poem's structural design is not to be found in the narrative development, but in the manuscript divisions, which are arranged symmetrically on each side of the central encounter between Elene and Judas.

BOREN, JAMES L. "Form and Meaning in Cynewulf's *Fates of the Apostles*." *Papers on Language and Literature* 5 (1969):115–22. The author finds a rhetorical pattern in which the description of each of the apostles' fates contains a locative, a nominative, and an instrumental element.

BROWN, GEORGE H. "The Descent-Ascent Motif in *Christ II* of Cynewulf." *Journal of English and Germanic Philology* 73 (1974):1–12. A good investigation of the Greek and Latin commentaries on the Ascension.

CAMPBELL, JACKSON J. "Cynewulf's Multiple Revelations." *Medievalia et Humanistica* 3 (1972):257–77. One of the several essays that sees the poem as structured around the serial revelations of Constantine, Judas, and Cynewulf himself.

CHASE, COLIN. "God's Presence through Grace as the Theme of Cynewulf's *Christ II* and the Relationship of this Theme to *Christ I* and *Christ III*." *Anglo-Saxon England* 3 (1974):87–101. Chase believes that Cynewulf

184 CYNEWULF

altered Gregory's homily to focus attention on the gifts of God's grace, and that the three *Christ* poems are united by this common theme.

CLEMOES, PETER. "Cynewulf's Image of the Ascension." In *England before the Conquest: Studies in Primary Sources Presented to Dorothy Whitelock*, edited by Peter Clemoes and Kathleen Hughes, pp. 293–304. Cambridge: Cambridge University Press, 1971. An interesting essay on the possible influences of contemporary art and liturgical practice on *Christ II*.

DAS, S. K. *Cynewulf and the Cynewulf Canon*. Calcutta: University of Calcutta Press, 1942. A complex metrical examination of the signed and the unsigned poems, along with some impressionistic literary comments, proves that Cynewulf wrote only the four signed poems.

DIAMOND, ROBERT E. "The Diction of the Signed Poems of Cynewulf." *Philological Quarterly* 38 (1959):228–41. Illustrates that much of Cynewulf's diction is oral-formulaic.

EARL, JAMES W. "Typology and Iconographic Style in Early Medieval Hagiography." *Studies in the Literary Imagination* 8 (1975):15–46. An important article which explores the relation between typology and iconography and the ways in which they explain the lack of realism in medieval saints' lives.

ELLIOT, R. W. V. "Cynewulf's Runes in *Christ II* and *Elene*." *English Studies* 34 (1953):49–57.

———. "Cynewulf's Runes in *Juliana* and *The Fates of the Apostles*." *English Studies* 34 (1953):193–205. Two important, though controversial, attempts to decipher the runes in the signature passages.

FISH, VARDA. "Theme and Pattern in Cynewulf's *Elene*." *Neuphilologische Mitteilungen* 76 (1975):1–25. A historical interpretation which divides the poem into three panels, each with its own style: historical narrative, dramatic dialogue, and monologue.

FRESE, DOLORES WARWICK. "The Art of Cynewulf's Runic Signatures." In *Anglo-Saxon Poetry: Essays in Appreciation*, edited by Lewis E. Nicholson and Dolores Warwick Frese, pp. 312–34. Notre Dame: University of Notre Dame Press, 1975. An excellent essay which demonstrates how Cynewulf connects himself to the poems he writes through his runic signatures.

FRY, DONALD K. "Themes and Type-Scenes in *Elene* 1–113." *Speculum* 44 (1969):35–45. An examination of the battle in *Elene* from the point of view of oral-formulaic criticism.

GARDNER, JOHN. "Cynewulf's *Elene*: Sources and Structure." *Neophilologus* 54 (1970):65–76. Gardner sees the poet as placing himself in the position of Constantine and Judas. The theme of the poem, he believes, is the contrast between the universal Christian ethic and the Germanic heroic ethic.

GROSZ, OLIVER J. H. "Man's Imitation of the Ascension: The Unity of *Christ II.*" *Neophilologus* 54 (1970):398–408. Grosz holds that man imitates Christ's Ascension by his willingness to understand the figurative meanings of signs.

HIEATT, CONSTANCE B. "*The Fates of the Apostles:* Imagery, Structure, and Meaning." *Papers on Language and Literature* 10 (1974):115–25. Argues against Boren's structural division and creates another based on a numerological analysis.

HILL, THOMAS D. "Sapiential Structure and Figural Narrative in the Old English *Elene.*" *Traditio* 27 (1971):159–77. Hill asserts that the poem is concerned with the contrast between the letter and the spirit, the Old and the New Law, and between Judas and Elene as figures of the synagogue and the church.

HOWLETT, D. R. "*Se giddes begang* of *The Fates of the Apostles.*" *English Studies* 56 (1975):385–95. Another attempt to create a numerological structure for the poem, this one based on the "Golden Section."

KENNEDY, CHARLES W. *The Earliest English Poetry.* London: Oxford University Press, 1943. A general history of Old English poetry, with a good chapter on Cynewulf. Kennedy is better on backgrounds and previous scholarship than he is on the poems proper.

LEE, ALVIN A. *The Guest-Hall of Eden: Four Essays on the Design of Old English Poetry.* New Haven: Yale University Press, 1972. A study of Old English poetry with a mythological bent, but one which contains some good perceptions on the nature of saints' lives.

MILDENBERGER, KENNETH. "Unity of Cynewulf's *Christ* in the Light of Iconography." *Speculum* 23 (1948):426–32. An unconvincing try to make one poem out of the three parts of *Christ* by relating it to various works of art which indicate that the threefold association of Advent, Ascension, and Last Judgment was known in Cynewulf's time.

PAGE, R. I. *An Introduction to English Runes.* London: Methuen, 1973. The best text now available as an introduction to this difficult subject.

POPE, JOHN C. "The Lacuna in the Text of Cynewulf's *Ascension* (*Christ II,* 556b)." In *Studies in Language, Literature and Culture of the Middle Ages and Later,* edited by E. Bagby Atwood and Archibald A. Hill, pp. 210–19. Austin: University of Texas Press, 1969. Pope demonstrates that a seeming confusion in the middle of *Christ II* is due to a missing leaf in the manuscript, and he recreates the general movement of this portion by reference to the source, Bede's Ascension hymn.

REGAN, CATHARINE A. "Evangelicalism as the Informing Principle of Cynewulf's *Elene.*" *Traditio* 29 (1973):27–52. Believes the poem is about the church and its mission to lead men to salvation through acceptance of the Cross.

RICE, ROBERT C. "The Penitential Motif in Cynewulf's *Fates of the Apostles* and in His Epilogues." *Anglo-Saxon England* 6 (1977):105–20. Rice describes the poem as a meditation on death and judgment in the tradition of purgatorial and penetential motifs.

ROGERS, H. L. "Rhymes in the Epilogue to *Elene:* A Reconsideration." *Leeds Studies in English* 5 (1971):47–52. Disputes the standard assumption that by substituting Anglian forms the rhymes in *Elene* can be perfected.

SCHAAR, CLAES. *Critical Studies in the Cynewulf Group.* Lund Studies in English, no. 17. Lund: C. W. K. Gleerup, 1949. The most important study of the canon. After extensive syntactic and stylistic analyses, Schaar decides that Cynewulf wrote only the four poems he signed. Some of Schaar's methods have been criticized, but there is a wealth of information to be found in this large book.

SHIPPEY, T. A. *Old English Verse.* London: Hutchinson, 1972. A general study with a good chapter on Cynewulf.

SISAM, KENNETH. "Cynewulf and His Poetry." *Proceedings of the British Academy* 18 (1934, for 1932):303–31. A very important lecture given to the British Academy, establishing Cynewulf's dates, origin, and canon.

STEPSIS, ROBERT, and RAND, RICHARD. "Contrast and Conversion in Cynewulf's *Elene.*" *Neuphilologische Mitteilungen* 70 (1969):273–82. The first of the new critical essays to appear on this poem, it discusses the imagery of good and evil, light and darkness, the hidden and the revealed.

WHATLEY, GORDON. "Bread and Stone: Cynewulf's *Elene* 611–618." *Neuphilologische Mitteilungen* 76 (1975):550–60. Explores the Christian overtones of "hardness of heart" *(duritia cordis)* in a particular passage.

———. "Old English Onomastics and Narrative Art: *Elene* 1062. *Modern Philology* 73 (1975):109–20. Discusses Judas's surname, Cyriacus, "the law of the Savior," as a significant thematic element in the poem.

WITTIG, JOSEPH. "Figural Narrative in Cynewulf's *Juliana.*" *Anglo-Saxon England* 4 (1975):37–55. A convincing demonstration that Juliana sometimes reflects Christ and the church in her actions.

WOLPERS, T. *Die englische Heiligenlegende des Mittelalters.* Tübingen: M. Niemeyer, 1964. The standard work on medieval English saints' lives.

WRIGHT, ELLEN F. "Cynewulf's *Elene* and the *singal sacu.*" *Neuphilologische Mitteilungen* 76 (1975):538–49. Wright believes that the poem's structure reinforces the theme that attaining sufficient spiritual knowledge to convert often entails considerable effort and pain.

Index